PUBLIC SPEAKING
and DISCUSSION
for
RELIGIOUS LEADERS

PUBLIC SPEAKING

PRENTICE-HALL, INC.

Harold A. Brack

ASSOCIATE PROFESSOR OF SPEECH
AND HOMILETICS; THEOLOGICAL SEMINARY
DREW UNIVERSITY

Kenneth G. Hance

PROFESSOR OF SPEECH
MICHIGAN STATE UNIVERSITY

and DISCUSSION
for
RELIGIOUS LEADERS

Englewood Cliffs, N.J.

PUBLIC SPEAKING AND DISCUSSION FOR RELIGIOUS LEADERS
Harold A. Brack and Kenneth G. Hance

© 1961 by
PRENTICE-HALL, INC.
Englewood Cliffs, N.J.

Library of Congress Catalog Card No.: 61-14151

Second printing .... *July, 1962*

PRINTED IN THE UNITED STATES OF AMERICA

73897—C

Preface

This book is designed for that great body of religious leaders—not only clergymen, directors of religious education, and other professional persons, but also laymen—who are at work in the service of the church. It is intended for the preacher, the president of a church organization, the chairman of a committee, or others who must assume responsibility in religious leadership. It is not oriented to any one church or denomination, nor to organizations of any specific size. Rather, it presents principles and methods that have universal application.

"Public speaking" refers to activities ranging from preaching in the pulpit to informal speaking at meetings of the church as well as to a variety of situations outside the church. "Discussion" or "conference" refers to committee meetings, study groups, classes in religious education, all-church meetings, and a host of other situations both inside and outside the church.

Among our objectives in writing this book are the following:

1. To provide a direct, practical analysis of public speaking and discussion situations and of problems encountered by religious leaders.
2. To help the reader develop a set of standards for preparation in public speaking and discussion that will save him time and improve the quality of his preparation.
3. To aid the reader in improving his work methods for preparation in public speaking and discussion.
4. To help the reader speak more effectively in public and participate more effectively in, and provide leadership for, discussion or conference activities.

We do not suggest that these principles and methods can be substituted for "something to say." Nor do we attempt to provide subjects for speeches or discussions. Rather, we give the person "who has something to say" and the group "with a subject to discuss" resources that should assist in meeting the demands of speaker-audience situations and of discussion or conference situations. At all times, we assume that the reader is, or will be, adequately informed about what he wishes to communicate or to discuss. At the same time, we assume that the understanding of a number of principles and methods pertaining to good oral communication can assist even the best informed person in more effective speaking or discussion.

This book can be effectively used in a variety of ways:

1. As a resource and reference book by those who wish to undertake independent study and practice.
2. As a resource or textbook by those who wish to participate in a workshop or training program for public speaking and/or discussion.
3. As a textbook in speech and preaching classes in seminaries and in church-related colleges that are training pre-seminary students.

HAROLD A. BRACK
KENNETH G. HANCE

Table
of
Contents

PART ONE

PUBLIC SPEAKING
and DISCUSSION
for
RELIGIOUS LEADERS

chapter 1

Getting
to
Work

Every speaker must analyze objectively his procedure for the preparation of a speech. For each phase of his preparation, he should have a definite goal in mind and a planned procedure for the attainment of that goal. This chapter considers the following topics: securing the subject, selecting a plan for the speech, and testing the preparation.

While reading this chapter, the speaker should keep his own method of preparation in mind, with the purpose of discovering how it can be improved. Disciplined procedures of preparation are the doorways to free, creative composition of the speech. Undisciplined preparational procedure leaves the speaker confronted with so many unresolved problems of preparation that he rarely has any real freedom to think creatively.

We recognize that the following procedures would have to be modified and expedited if one were asked to make an impromptu explanation at a committee meeting. However, if these methods are practiced whenever the situation permits, you will greatly facilitate your choice of subject and your organization of content during the few seconds which you have for preparation in an impromptu situation. The more mastery you have of a particular method of preparation, the easier it will be to modify and adapt the method to special occasions. Whenever possible, a speaker should request that he be informed about his task early enough to allow him to employ the following methods.

Securing the Subject

For most speakers, the real difficulty in making the final choice of a subject is the problem of making a decision. There are two reasons why most of us are reluctant to make a final decision about the subject for a sermon or a speech. First, once the subject is chosen, there is no longer any excuse for delaying the preparation of the speech. Secondly, we are always hoping that we shall discover another subject that we can develop with more ease. When we say, "I can't find a good subject," we usually mean, "I don't want to begin to work," or, "I don't want to work so hard." Many speakers squander one third to one half of their preparation time in searching for subjects. Such a large amount of time cannot be given to choosing a subject without seriously weakening other phases of the speech preparation. If you are now investing a large portion of your preparation time in the selection of a subject, you can improve your speaking by saving some of this time for more important preparation tasks.

The first improvement to be made in your method of selecting subjects is to *set a subject deadline*. This deadline should be an early one. If the speech is to be delivered one week from today, the subject should be chosen *today*. If the speech is to be presented one month from today, the subject should be chosen no later than one week from today. The early selection of a subject is of primary importance to a good method of preparation. In order to make this deadline effective, one should not ponder any actual development of the speech until the subject is chosen. If necessary, select the least undesirable of a group of undesirable subjects or choose by lot from a group of subjects of equal merit. But, whatever the method, press for a decision.

Once the subject has been chosen and recorded, *stick with the subject you have chosen.* The first time that you are unable to work through a segment of the idea, you will be tempted to change your subject. The second or third time you run into a blind alley in searching for information, you will say "I'd better get another topic." But every speaker must realize that there is intrinsic merit in the subject, and that in changing subjects he loses the work he has already done. The speaker should also realize that he could encounter similar and even more difficult problems with another topic. Moreover, he should understand that the more time he spends in going from one subject to another, the less time he will have for developing the subject that is his final choice. The early selection of a subject will give you two important advantages. First, you will be able to use the time normally wasted in pursuit of false subjects to study and analyze the one you have chosen. Secondly, you will do much to achieve a clarity of thinking about your subject because your mind will not be distracted by other possibilities.

After selecting the subject and determining to stay with this selection, you come to the third step, which is to *question yourself about the subject.* This self-questioning will help to discover what you already know about the subject. Taking pencil and paper, record your answers to the following questions:

1. What do I know about the history of this subject?
2. What have I read about this subject?
3. What is new about this subject?
4. What have I heard about this subject?
5. How does this subject affect me?
6. How does this subject affect the audience?
7. What is controversial about this subject?
8. What needs to be done about this subject?
9. What do political, social, educational, or religious groups say about this subject?

When these questions have been answered, *take the information you now have about the subject and place it in an outline.* After this first outline is made, you should be able to discover the information that is still needed to complete your speech. Your outline may reveal that you have no material for the introduction, inadequate statistics to support point two, and no illustration for point three.

Therefore, the next step is to *read and study to fill the vacant places in the outline*. If you set to work immediately to fill these gaps in the outline, you will gain confidence in your choice of subject. More important, you will avoid unnecessary, random reading. You will also avoid spending too much time with parts of the outline which could be satisfactorily developed from the knowledge you already have. Finally, the best way to confirm your choice of subject is to *develop a full outline of a speech on this subject*.

In summary, the subject for a speech can best be secured by:

1. Setting a subject deadline;
2. Sticking with the subject chosen;
3. Questioning yourself about the subject;
4. Placing the information you have about the subject in an outline;
5. Reading and studying to fill in the vacant parts of the outline;
6. Developing a full outline of a speech on this subject.

Where to Look

If the urging to make a prompt selection of your subject moves you to reply, "Well, that advice is more easily given than followed," you may find this discussion of further help, for we intend, in the following pages, to suggest areas of investigation that we feel will provide the speaker with good opportunities for discovering a satisfying subject. The purpose of pointing out these areas is to help you improve your ability to decide upon a subject promptly.

A Personal Inventory

First, we suggest that you take stock of your own interests, concerns, experience, and current program of study. A review of your interests could lead to the discovery that speaking on a particular topic would not only give you a worthy subject, but it would also provide you with the occasion for further investigation of, and thinking about, a matter in which you already have an enthusiastic interest. Likewise, a survey of your most vital concerns might suggest a subject which would challenge your hearers and which would give you an opportunity to support a "cause" in which you feel you have a stake. A perusal of your own experiences might lead to the discovery of a topic which would stimulate your audience and which you could present in a lively way because of your close acquaintance with the subject. Equally valuable would be an examination of your current reading and study projects. Such an examination might disclose significant subjects which you could develop with thoroughness and clarity because of the study which you are now making.

Examination of the Audience

Another rewarding area of exploration, when searching for a subject, is the group to whom you are speaking. Frequently a speaker is delighted to discover that one of the group's "purposes for being" makes a fitting subject for his address. Also, the history of this group may contain topical suggestions. Former leaders, past accomplishments, and contributions to the community all may precipitate the selection of a subject. Current work of this group may prove to be fertile ground. Services the group renders, products it produces, agencies it supports, and like matters, may stir up some similar interest or concern in the speaker and prompt the choice of a subject. Sometimes a consideration of the problems with which the group is now working proves to be potent stimulation. In addressing himself to a problem which is now before the group, the speaker frequently has a keener sense of his subject being relevant to this audience and this occasion.

Exploration of the Occasion

An inquiry into the nature of the occasion can produce valuable suggestions for a subject for your speech. The purpose of a particular meeting may be to commemorate a notable event or pay tribute to a founder. Records of observances of this occasion often indicate good topical possibilities. If certain ceremonies will be conducted or if the group will participate in a ritual, an examination of their contents may encourage you to choose an idea or theme from them. Even the day or time of year can make certain subjects more appropriate than others. Every speaker would do well to obtain a

calendar or calendars which list religious observances, national holi-
days, and anniversaries of important historical events to serve as
quick reminders of timely subjects.

Availability of Information

Another worthwhile approach for prompting the choice of a subject is a careful analysis of the sources of information available to
you. Such an analysis may provide good reasons for avoiding one
subject and equally good reasons for selecting another. A speaker
might well decide against speaking on recent developments in a
field if he did not have available the resources for discovering what
the recent developments have been; or a speaker could decide against
speaking on the history of a movement if he had no access to historical accounts, journalistic reports, persons who had participated
in the movement, and the like. On the other hand, a speaker might
consent to report on a conference which he had not attended if he
had available the approved minutes of the sessions, journalistic reports about the meetings, personal reports by participants, and
similar information. Such examples indicate that the sources of information available to you should be carefully considered when you
are selecting the subject for your speech.

In summary, we suggest that you begin your search for a subject
by taking a personal inventory, examining the audience, exploring
the occasion on which you will speak, and reviewing the sources of
information available to you.

Selecting a Plan

In order to outline a speech, a plan is needed to link the materials
of a speech together. The inability to select and follow a satisfactory
pattern is a devastating enemy of good preparation. Far too many
preachers and speakers have no evident plan or wander from one to
another, reorganizing the speech each time they consider a different
plan; and this temptation to juggle the items of the speech from
one plan to another has several bad effects. First, the development of
units of the speech is delayed because the size or importance of the
unit will depend upon the plan that is chosen. Secondly, organized

thought development is lost because continuous changes are made in the arrangement of the materials within the speech. As a result, when the speech is delivered, the speaker often has trouble recalling where an illustration belongs because he has rearranged its place each time he moved from plan to plan. Thirdly, transitional sentences are necessarily crude and vague, because they must be re-written with each choice of a new plan, and because the speaker does not have time to clarify and polish them. Finally, much time and effort are wasted in the pursuit of a perfect plan, while other tasks of preparation are poorly done because the speaker does not have *time* for them.

There is a method for selecting a plan of organization which will enable a speaker to make his choice accurately and quickly. The significant feature of this method is that the subject of the speech is a yardstick for selecting the plan for arranging the materials. This approach helps the speaker avoid the selection of a plan merely because he feels more proficient in developing and using it. That is, he will not try to make every speech a "problem-solution" speech or every speech a "climax" speech. Accuracy in the choice of plan is more likely to be achieved because the subject matter is used as a criterion for selecting the plan or organization. Time is saved because the speaker makes a systematic approach to the selection of a plan for organizing the speech.

In order to use this method, the speaker must first *become familiar with several plans of organization.* Study carefully the following ones.

1. *Time*—Arrange the content of the speech in chronological sequence. If you are speaking of the life of a saint, you might begin with his birth and list his experiences, in the order of their occurrence, up to his death. A report on the work at a youth camp could be organized about the history of the camp, proceeding from the purchase of the land to the development of a decentralized camping program.

2. *Space*—Arrange the content of the speech in a spatial sequence. If you are describing a proposed building plan for a church, you might begin in the basement, and move from left to right across it; then up to the first floor and move from left to right across it; and then to the second floor moving from left to right across it. Or, if

you are describing the home mission program of your church, you could start with the institutions of the East, go to the institutions of the Midwest, and finally consider the institutions in the West. In other words, you would organize your home missions speech around the geographical divisions of the country. A youth worker, explaining a folk dance, might diagram the movements from one place to another on the dance floor. Or the director of a religious census might explain the visitation phase of the census by systematically discussing the sections of the community for which the workers would be responsible.

3. *Problem-Solution*—This pattern proceeds from a description and analysis of a problem to a consideration of a solution. If you are speaking about the problem of segregation within the Christian Church, you could begin by describing the nature and extent of the existing segregation. Next, you could discuss efforts which have been made to solve this problem. Finally, you might advance, as your solution, a plan for teaching all members of your church the theological basis for a nonsegregated church.

A consideration of the problem of finding adequate space for housing growing church school classes might begin with a review of the current conditions of crowding and noise, move to an examination of the kind and amount of space needed, then advance to considering use of other areas of existing accommodations—the renting or building of additional facilities.

Young people desiring full attendance at a midwinter retreat could begin with discussing the difficulty of competing with other activities, then attempt to identify their real competition, and finally seek to discover some way to avoid conflicting with the more significant activities of their membership.

4. *Climactic*—Arrange the materials of the speech in the order of their significance, beginning with the least important and advancing to the most important. If you are describing the meeting of the World Council of Churches in Evanston, you could start with the people who attended, go on to the setting in which they met, describe the pageant in Soldier's Field, list the study groups which met, and finally report what had been stressed about the theme "Christ, The Hope of the World."

Diagrams (1) and (2) indicate two possible types of organization which may be employed when using the climax plan.

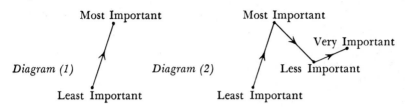

Most Important

Very Important

Diagram (1)   *Diagram (2)*   Less Important

Least Important   Least Important

Diagram (1) indicates a straight use of the climax pattern as described in the previous paragraph. Diagram (2) suggests an anticlimax arrangement by moving from the least important to the most important, then to a less important item and closing with a very important item. In the second pattern, the listener is approached with a climax sequence; but after the climax is reached, he is given a less important matter to consider, then is again impressed with a highly significant one. If the audience is in sympathy with you, the use of the second climactic pattern may seem to present an undesirable anticlimax. On the other hand, if your audience is inclined to resist or be critical, then a second climax may give you an added opportunity to make your point.

5. *Cause-Effect*—Begin with an action and carefully follow its repercussions until you have shown the effect which the action will cause. In using the cause-effect pattern, a preacher might begin with a definition of tithing. Then he might urge that every member of the congregation start to tithe. Next he could show how the church budget would be enlarged if each member of the congregation would tithe. Finally, he might show how an enlarged church budget would help the mission project which the church is supporting.

A speaker presenting a plan for establishing a Home for elderly people might begin by describing the facilities and program of such a Home. Then he could show how many elderly members of churches in that area could be cared for at less expense to their families. This cause-effect pattern could also be followed by a supervisor of church school teachers when explaining the value of visual aids for holding attention and increasing retention, by citing visual aids as the cause, and improved attention and retention as the effect.

On the other hand an effect-to-cause pattern might begin with the description of an effect of fewer members joining the church during the past year. Then the speaker might move from this effect to its cause by pointing out that fewer new persons had been visited and invited to join the church. Finally, he might indicate that fewer visits had been made and invitations extended because the commission on evangelism had been less active during the past year.

6. *Familiar to Unfamiliar*—In this case, we begin with the familiar and move to the less familiar or even the unfamiliar. An effort to explain the obligations of church membership to members of a fraternal order could begin with a discussion of the obligations of membership in a fraternal organization and then turn to membership obligations to the church; this is an example of moving from the familiar to the unfamiliar. Another illustration of this method would be a speech of explanation in which you begin with the order of worship which is used by your people and then move from it to an explanation of an order of worship which is used by another denomination.

7. *Simple to Complex*—When using this pattern, you move from the elementary to the complicated. A director of boys' work at a YMCA, when telling parents about the program for their youngsters, might begin with the "simple"—the time of the activity, the place, the number of boys participating, and the like. Then turning to the "complex," the director could speak of the value of boys' participating in such an activity. Or, if you were conducting a study of the book of Romans, you might discuss the writer of the epistle and the people to whom the epistle was written. Then you might turn to a consideration of what Paul wrote and of the doctrines contained in this epistle.

8. *Simple Enumeration*—If this pattern is used, the speaker lists his main points numerically. He may even say, "Now there are three things which I want to say in favor of this plan." If he were speaking about Christian symbolism, he might decide to discuss the cross, the IHS monogram, and the trefoil. In this case, he might say, "First, we will consider the cross; second, the IHS monogram; and third, the trefoil."

The director of religious education, speaking for a few minutes before one of the governing groups of the church, might decide to deal with the objectives, organization, and procedures of the church school. In this case she could say, "First, I will speak about the objectives; second, about the organization; and third, about the procedures."

Even though this plan is simple, it does provide the listener with a sense of order and progression in the speech.

Now you have eight plans (Time, Space, Problem-Solution, Climactic, Cause-Effect, Familiar to Unfamiliar, Simple to Complex, Simple Enumeration) which you can use to organize the ideas of your speech. We wish to stress that no one of these plans is best. The subject chosen, the purpose to be fulfilled, and other matters will determine which is the best one to employ.

Next, *gather a half dozen ideas which you intend to use in the speech.* As soon as you have done this, you are ready to select your pattern for arranging the content of your speech. Taking your five or six ideas, move quickly down the list of eight plans of organization. Pause at each plan and try to arrange your ideas for the speech in the order of that plan. *As you move down the list of plans, reject those which do not allow for an orderly arrangement of your ideas.*

If the president of a youth group were trying to encourage the group to attend a church camp, he might want a pattern for his speech that would allow him to conclude with a vigorous challenge. In addition, he might notice that his ideas about the camping experience varied in their order of importance. With these factors in mind, he could quickly rule out such patterns as time, space, or familiar to unfamiliar, and select, instead, the climax pattern.

To illustrate this method further, let us suppose that you are a preacher, you plan to preach on the subject of "forgiveness," and you have the following ideas in mind:

1. Men have always found it difficult to forgive sins—Jonah, Peter, and so forth.
2. We find it difficult to forgive.
3. Jesus taught us how to forgive.
4. We need God's forgiveness.
5. In order to be forgiven, we must forgive.

On the first trip down the eight plans of arrangement, you might reject the Time plan, the Space plan, the Cause-Effect plan, the Familiar to Unfamiliar plan, and the Simple to Complex plan. Then you would have the Problem-Solution plan, the Climactic plan, and the Simple Enumeration plan from which to choose. Reviewing the three remaining plans, you might decide to use the Problem-Solution plan. Thus, *from the plans left after the first elimination, you select a single pattern to be used as the over-all plan of organization for your speech.*

If, in the preceding example, you have chosen the Problem-Solution plan, you might use ideas (1) and (2) as a description of the problem and ideas (3), (4), and (5) as a solution to the problem. That is, you might say that historically men have found it difficult to forgive, and that we also find it difficult to forgive. But, Jesus Christ has taught us how to forgive and we are moved to forgive because we must forgive in order to receive the forgiveness of God.

You could allow ten minutes for the first checking through of the list of plans of organization and five minutes for the final selection of a single plan. *The important act is the selection, within a minimum period of time, of a single plan for organizing the content of the speech.*

In summary, the following four steps constitute an effective method for the prompt selection of an appropriate plan for organizing a speech:

1. Become familiar with several "plans of organization."
2. Gather a half dozen ideas which you plan to use in the speech.
3. As you move down your list of plans, reject those which do not allow an orderly arrangement of your ideas.
4. From the plans remaining after the first elimination, select a single plan to be used for the over-all organization of your speech.

Testing Your Preparation

Every speaker needs a system for evaluating the preparation of his speech, to be certain that it is adequately done. It is our belief that a good evaluation system should help the speaker discover flaws in his preparation which may have escaped his attention. Some of the imperfections in a speaker's preparation can be:

1. Poor logical progression,
2. Lack of proportion between units of the speech,

3. Lack of coherence,
4. Uncompleted thoughts or statements,
5. Omissions of data,
6. Monotony in choice of words. (Hints of this difficulty will appear even in a complete sentence outline.)

The early discovery of such flaws will enable the speaker to improve his speech so that he will present it more easily and so that the audience will receive it more readily. A speech with the flaws mentioned above would be difficult for the speaker to think through, and would be difficult for the listener to follow.

An effective method of testing one's preparation for speaking is a complete sentence outline with the following three special additions: writing out the first three sentences of the introduction and the last three sentences of the conclusion; placing transitional phrases in brackets between the units of the outline; and, if this is a speech of advocacy, using the conjunctions "for" and "and" at the end of the sentences. If the speech is cast in a complete sentence outline, the speaker will be forced to finish thoughts and to compose them in complete sentences. Writing out, in full, the first three sentences of the introduction and the last three sentences of the conclusion will provide the speaker with a definite beginning and a definite ending for his speech. Placing transitional phrases in brackets between units of the outline will assure the speaker that he has provided for clear progression from unit to unit in the speech. Finally, in a speech which makes use of argument, the use of the conjunctions will allow the speaker to check the logical progression of the speech.

Such a complete sentence outline might benefit a president of a men's group who was given an opportunity to address a class of preparatory church members. Let us suppose that the main points of his outline were as follows:

I. Our men's group helps us become more effective workers in the church.
   A. It helps us to become acquainted with other members.
   B. It helps us to discover worthwhile projects to undertake.
   C. It helps us to work together and make the best use of our combined talents and resources in serving the church.
   D. It helps us to show others that as men we are interested in supporting the church.

Notice that even with only the key sentences before us, we immediately become aware of the speaker's inclination to overwork the phrase "helps us" and that there is a danger of monotony in his choice of words.

This sort of outline might be an aid to the chairman of the finance committee who was presenting the church budget to the congregation. If the chairman attempted to outline his address in complete sentences, he might see something like this:

I. Our church budget is divided into three major units.
   A. The first section contains the expenses for operating our church.
      1. Salaries and wages total $8,600.
      2. Fuel for the year costs us $600.
      3. Stationery and office supplies amount to $200.
   B. The second section contains our various obligations for benevolent giving.
      1. Our obligations to foreign missions are $1,000.
      2. Our obligations to home missions come to $1,200.

This outline lacks clear transitions. Our chairman might quickly discover that a transition between the statement in *A* and *A.1* would lead the congregation more readily into a consideration of such items as salaries, stationery, and so forth. For example, "Let's take a look at the major items in this section of the budget."

The best way to understand the effectiveness of this testing method is to examine a complete sample of this type of outline.

Introduction

There is something admirable about an old soldier. His bravery and his wounds capture our imagination, and his age commands our respect. When an old warrior is abused, we become aroused. We would rather see an old warrior fade away than see him defeated.

I. Perhaps it is this admiration for an old warrior that causes us to respect Paul's words to Timothy (for)
   A. Paul has fought many hard missionary campaigns (and)
   B. He has survived shipwreck and persecution (and)
   C. Now he is in prison and soon to be put to death.

Discussion

[In this letter to Timothy]
I. Paul inspires us to become better evangelists of Jesus Christ (for)
  A. Paul's words are vigorous with triumph (for)
    [Paul tells us]
    1. "I have fought the good fight" (for)
      (a) I have not turned from the battle for the gentiles (and)
    2. "I have finished the race" (for)
      (a) I have completed the task which the Lord has set before
        me, even witnessing in Rome (and)
    3. "I have kept the faith" (for)
      (a) I have preached only the Lord Jesus Christ and him cru-
        cified (and)
    4. "The Lord will award me a crown of righteousness."
  B. Paul's words are vibrant with hope (for)
    1. He urges Timothy to continue to preach the gospel (for)
    [Paul writes to Timothy]
      (a) "Preach the word" (for)
        (1) There will be people who want to hear it (and)
      (b) "Do the work of an evangelist" (for)
        (1) There will be people seeking salvation (and)
      (c) "Fulfill your ministry" (for)
        (1) The Lord will give you the grace to do so.
  C. Paul's words are radiant with love (for)
    1. He declares that he loves the Lord's appearing (for)
      (a) He has loved His appearing ever since He first appeared
        to him on the Damascus Road (and)
    2. He also affirms that a crown of righteousness shall be awarded
      to all who have loved the Lord's appearing (for)
      (a) The love of the Lord's appearing is the real sign of a
        servant of Christ.

Conclusion

Certainly these words from an old soldier are a challenge to us who
battle for the faith. They call us to suffer in the service of Christ. In
His name let us be triumphant, full of hope, and radiant with a love
of our Lord's appearing.

The preceding outline of a meditation based on Second Timothy
illustrates the preparation of a complete sentence outline. Tran-

sitional phrases are indicated by brackets, and the conjunctions used for checking logical progression appear in parentheses at the end of sentences. Also, the first three sentences of the introduction and the last three sentences of the conclusion are written out word for word.

Reading through the outline you will discover that when *(for)* appears at the end of a sentence, it means that the next sentence is supposed to support this sentence. When *(and)* appears at the end of a sentence, it means that the following sentence is designed to support the same sentence that this sentence supports. That is, in the introduction, sentence *A* presumably supports sentence *I*. If at any point in the outline the sentences do not comply with these rules, the sentences are not in correct logical order. When an outline is logically adequate, the *(for)* or *(and)* can be inserted after each sentence, and the speech will read straight through without any conflicts. You will also notice that this outline provides a definite introduction and a definite conclusion. There is no need for confusion or rambling at these important moments in the delivery of the speech. Notice, too, that the phrases which appear in brackets in the discussion section of the outline link the preceding sentence closely to the following sentence. The failure to work out such phrases during the preparation of the speech often results in awkward moments when the speech is delivered, because the speaker has no planned way for moving from one point to another.

Now let us see if any of the flaws listed at the beginning of this section are apparent in our sample outline. First, is the logical progression good? Part "B" of the discussion provides an example of vague or even doubtful progression. See how the following extract from this unit of the outline reads.

> B. Paul's words are vibrant with hope (for)
>   1. He urges Timothy to continue to proclaim the gospel (for)
>   (c) Paul writes to Timothy "Fulfill your ministry."

The fact that Paul writes to Timothy "Fulfill your ministry" neither proves nor illustrates that "Paul urges Timothy to continue to proclaim the Gospel."

Second, is there a lack of proportion among units of the speech? An examination of the discussion section of the outline prompts us to answer "yes." In this part of the outline we can see that both *A* and *B* appear to be twice as large as *C*. (It should be remembered, however, that sometimes units may be deliberately shortened because of audience awareness or desire to place heavier emphasis on other units.)

Third, is there a lack of coherence? Between *I.A.4* and *I.B* there is no transitional phrase to link these two units of the outline. Thus, the coherence of this section of the outline needs strengthening.

Fourth, are there any uncompleted thoughts or statements? The thought indicated in *I.A.4* in the discussion section seems to be incomplete. All that we are given is the sentence "The Lord will award me a crown of righteousness." Something more is needed to designate what is "vigorous with triumph" in this sentence.

Fifth, are there any omissions of data? After a quick reading of the introduction we are able to answer "yes" to this question. The introduction could be improved by adding the names of Paul's missionary journeys and by giving examples of the persecution he suffered.

Sixth, is there a monotony in choice of words? Again the discussion section of the outline gives us reason to answer "yes" to this question. In *I.A* we notice the constant use of "I have."

These illustrations demonstrate the effectiveness of this kind of outline procedure for testing the adequacy of one's preparation for a speech. In summary, you can test the adequacy of your preparation by doing as follows:

1. Write out the first three sentences of the introduction and the last three sentences of the conclusion in full;
2. Outline the remainder of the speech in complete sentences;
3. Work out transitional phrases and place them in brackets between units of the outline;
4. Use the conjunctions "for" and "and" to check the logical progression of the outline;
5. Ask yourself the following questions after the completion of the outline,
   (a) Is there poor logical progression?
   (b) Is there a lack of proportion between the units of the speech?
   (c) Is there a lack of coherence in the outline?
   (d) Are there uncompleted thoughts or statements?

(e) Are there any omissions of data?

(f) Is there a monotony in the choice of words?

When you have revised the outline so that you can give a negative answer to each of the preceding questions, you will be reasonably sure that you have carefully prepared your speech.

The speaker may find it helpful, in his attempt to employ the suggestions of this chapter in his own preparation of speeches, to "log" the preparation of his speeches. The logging of the speech might be done in the following form:

Date	Time Spent	Work Done
March 8	15 minutes	Looked through my former speeches to the group and tried to decide on a topic.
March 10	½ hour	Talked with the Church School Superintendent and decided to speak on "Teaching The Child."

Such logging of your preparation will help you discover how much time you are spending on each phase of preparation, and it will help you detect procrastination and poor distribution of your preparation time.

By improving your ability to choose your subject, to select a plan of organization, and to test your preparation, you will improve the quality of the content of your speeches and you will give yourself a better opportunity to deliver them effectively.

chapter 2

On
the
Platform

The discussion of *delivery* in this chapter is focused on the prepared speech. We are assuming that the speaker knows in advance
that he is going to propose a motion, make an appeal, or present
a meditation. This does not mean that we are unsympathetic with
impromptu occasions when you may want to speak to a motion,
participate in class discussion, or even substitute for a speaker who
has failed to appear. As stated in the previous chapter, we believe
that the speaker who consistently practices good methods of preparation will develop his general competence so that he will be in a
better position to adapt to the impromptu situation. Under the
stimulus of the occasion he will be able to expedite his preparation
habits so as to deliver a clear, organized, and interesting speech
with directness, enthusiasm, and poise. We hope that the advice in
this chapter will bring you to a higher level of presentation of prepared speeches and that, in addition, it will help you become more
adept at impromptu speaking.

We wish to underscore the fact that in all cases we are assuming
that the motivation for expression comes from thinking about the

content of the speech (thinking the speech through) and from an eagerness to share these ideas with others. We subscribe whole-heartedly to the belief that gestures, for example, should be moti-vated by thinking about the content of the speech and by enthusi-asm for sharing this content.

However, it is also our belief that beginning speakers, in par-ticular, need specific suggestions for achieving the freedom to re-spond with voice and gestures to the content of the speech, and for achieving the abandon in use of voice and gestures that is required to share meaning with an assembled audience. The following de-livery suggestions are not intended as a substitute for thinking the speech through, but as a supplement to this process; and they are especially recommended for those who are just beginning this ad-venture in public speaking.

In Maxwell Anderson's *Joan of Lorraine* the director of the play addresses the following words to his cast: "What we're all waiting for and working toward is the miracle—the miracle that has to happen with every play that's going to go. Some day we'll start cold as usual, just reading lines, and then that holy fire'll begin to play around one actor—and then another—and then around a whole scene—and then the spirit'll descend on all of us at once—and we'll make a new world about the size of a star and set it down on a bare stage, sur-rounded by kitchen chairs and mockery and bungling mechanics and directors. And afterwards maybe we'll never hit anything as good as that again, but we'll get an echo of it, as much as we can recall—and we'll put that echo into costumes and sets and polish it up, and that's what the first night audience will be in on." [1]

Now the delivery of a speech or sermon must never be an echo. It must be the miracle happening. There must be free expression of inspired thought emphasized by unhesitating direct actions. Our eyes must be free to say all that is in our heart and mind; our voice must be free to proclaim, to rejoice, to challenge, and to inspire; our body must be free to move and gesture spontaneously. In short, we must be completely free to express all that we think and feel. The following pages present specific methods for achieving such freedom.

---

[1] Maxwell Anderson, *Joan of Lorraine* (Washington, D.C., Anderson House Publishers, 1947) pp. 5-6.

Freedom to express oneself fully in front of an audience has to be earned. Most speakers can begin by planning, and then forcing, eye contact, vocal changes, and bodily action. They must keep planning and forcing until they feel that they have developed some degree of skill in using these means of expression. As the speaker begins to develop confidence in his ability to express the thought of his speech through his eyes, voice, and bodily action, he finds that he has to plan and force less and less. After a while, he is aware that his bodily action, voice, and eye contact are now a free and natural response to the content of the speech. Free and natural responses to the ideas and concepts a speaker is presenting to his audience, is the goal toward which every speaker should strive.

It is not enough for a beginning speaker to try to be natural or conversational, because it is an unnatural thing for him to speak to audiences, large or small. What is natural behavior for a person who is speaking to twenty-five or a hundred people is not natural behavior for a person who is speaking to two other people. Nor are vocal projection and variety used in conversing with a person across the dinner table adequate for conversing with a large audience. Therefore, it is necessary for the beginning speaker to plan for, and make use of, eye contact, vocal projection, and bodily action until he appreciates the needs of the audience situation and becomes accustomed to meeting these needs.

Seeing Eye to Eye

If a speaker wants the freedom to look his audience in the eye and talk to them face to face, he must set out systematically to win this freedom. The first task is to *develop an ability to think while receiving visual stimulation.*

Speakers who look away from the audience, to the floor or the ceiling, when they want to think through a part of their speech, only add to the difficulty of speaking. For now, in addition to the problem of trying to move their thought along, they have the problem of re-establishing eye contact with the audience. The fact that a speaker is looking away from his audience, and thus has lost some control, is apt to make him force his thinking. Frequently, the frantic effort to hurry thinking along only makes the thought process more difficult.

If, on the other hand, the speaker is able to keep looking directly at his audience and thus maintain contact with them, he has a sense of control; and this feeling of control makes thinking easier. Also, the speaker's eyes, as well as his total facial expression, will suggest to the audience that he is thinking of the next unit in the speech, and that he will soon share his thoughts with them. Awareness that the audience is remaining attentive will add to the speaker's confidence and make thinking even more natural and effortless.

To develop the ability to think while receiving visual stimuli from his audience, the speaker should start with small, friendly audiences with whom he practices his speeches orally. The audience may be your family, a business associate, or some other good friend. Tell your practice audience that you are trying to learn to keep eye contact at those moments in your speaking when you are temporarily stalled. Ask them to raise their hands if you start to avoid their eyes at those awkward times. Whenever a hand goes up, *try to look directly at your hearer while continuing to think about how to move your speech along.* The first few practices are apt to be frustrating and to indicate little progress. Usually, however, after six to eight such practices you will be aware that you are beginning to conquer the problem, and your practice audience will report some degree of progress.

After you have learned to think while looking at people, tackle a real audience. Do not look over the heads of the audience; neither should you see a mass audience. Rather, *select individuals who are located in the center of audience groups and look directly at them.* Then move systematically from one audience group to another. In this way you will localize and personalize your eye contact. Everyone in the group will feel that you are looking directly at him.

While looking directly at individuals in the audience, let your eyes speak. Say with your eyes: I am excited about this, or this is important business. Remember you are looking at individuals in order that, through your eyes, you may communicate your ideas, or your feelings or attitude toward your ideas.

In addition to speaking with your eyes, also *observe the listening behavior of individuals in your audience.* Look for signs of understanding. Look for signs of interest or appreciation. Watch for indications of listening fatigue. That is, do not merely *watch* them watching you; observe them for the purpose of detecting their listening status.

After you have acquired some skill in maintaining eye contact, you may wish to *keep eye contact until there is some response from the more active listeners.* The response may be a more careful attention to what you are saying. Or the person may lean slightly forward or even nod in agreement. Be certain that you keep contact long enough to observe some response. As soon as a response is noticed, move on to a person in the center of another audience group.

In summary, if we follow these simple suggestions, we shall soon develop an ability to talk eye to eye with our audience. Remember:

1. Develop an ability to think while receiving visual stimuli.
   (a) Start with small, friendly audiences with whom you practice your speeches orally.
   (b) Try to look directly at the listener while continuing to think about how to move your speech along.
2. Select individuals who are located in the center of audience groups and look directly at them.
3. Let your eyes speak.
4. Observe the listening behavior of individuals in your audience.
5. Keep eye contact until there is some response from the more active listeners.

Vocal Projection

Once you have established eye contact with your audience, you will be expected to say something, and if what you say is to sound interesting, challenging, and vital, you will need some skill in using your voice. There are at least three requirements for a skillful use of the voice. These requirements are, (1) an adequate supply of breath, (2) a relaxed throat, and (3) control of the use of the breath supply.

The first step in developing skill in the use of your voice is to secure an adequate supply of breath. The strength, quality, and melody of the voice are all limited by the supply of breath which the speaker has available. A voice sustained by a small quantity of breath will sound small, thin, and flat.

You can achieve adequate breath support by the following practices.

1. Always start to speak with a good, full breath ready to be released for voice production. This means that you must carefully study the way in which you begin a speech, and try to have a full breath to use in starting. Eventually, this practice should be extended to the beginning of each unit within the speech. The habit of starting each unit with a full supply of breath will do much to strengthen and enrich your voice.

2. *Always take a full breath when inhaling during pauses and transitions in the speech.* Many speakers take only partial inhalations during these breathing opportunities. If speakers would expand all these partial inhalations to full ones, their supply of breath for speech purposes would be greatly increased. Once the speaker has developed the practice of starting with a full breath, he should next develop the habit of taking a full breath at each breathing opportunity during his speaking.

3. It may also be advisable to *engage in some breathing exercises to increase the amount of air you take in on a full inhalation.* The following exercise will be helpful for increasing the amount of air inhaled: on the count of *one,* rise on toes, raise arms over head and inhale (taking in as much air as you can); on the count of *two* resume normal stance, lower arms, and exhale. Repeat this exercise about twenty times in a single practice session. Practice at least three times a day.

The second step in developing skill in the use of your voice is to learn to relax your throat. If you fail to relax your throat, you will have a pinched, tight voice which is unpleasant to hear and uncomfortable to produce.

There are three ways in which we can detect a tense or tight throat. One, if the throat is rigid, the "Adam's apple" (thyroid cartilage) will have risen until it seems to be at the top of the throat. This can easily be observed in the male speaker because the "Adam's apple" is a more noticeable feature of the male throat. Second, when the throat is tensed, the quality of the voice will be changed to a tight or restricted sound. That is, the voice will sound tense. Third, the throat will feel strained and tight. In summary, we may say that a tight or tensed throat can be seen, heard, and felt.

There are several methods which can be used to relax the throat.

1. *Swallowing will relax the throat.* Stand in front of a mirror and start speaking with a tense throat so that the "Adam's apple" climbs up toward the top of the throat. Then swallow and watch how quickly the "Adam's apple" drops back to a relaxed, normal position.

2. *Sighing will relax the throat.* Again, watch as you start speaking with a tight throat so that the "Adam's apple" has risen toward the top of the throat. Then sigh, and notice how quickly the "Adam's apple" drops back to a normal, relaxed position.

Both of these methods can be used prior to, and during, the delivery of the speech. At a pause in the speech, first, swallow or sigh, next, take a full breath, and then begin to speak. This method can be practiced until your use of it is so skillful that it will not be detected by the audience.

3. *A relaxed posture and manner also help to induce a relaxed throat.* If the body is stiff and tense, and if the manner of delivery is nervous and fearful, the throat will respond sympathetically and tighten up. If, however, the posture is relaxed and the manner of delivery is natural, the throat will be relaxed and voice will flow freely through the throat and out of the mouth on the expiring column of air. This relaxed posture and manner can also be practiced prior to, and during, the delivery of the speech.

4. *Loose collars, ties, and jewelry help one to retain a relaxed throat.* It is important that the clothing worn about the throat be loose so that the sensation on the exterior skin surface of the throat is one of freedom. A shirt collar that is a mere half size smaller than you usually wear may give the sensation of restriction to the exterior skin surface of the throat. In no time at all this sensation may carry through to the interior of the throat and cause tenseness and restriction there. A "choke" necklace may also cause a sensation of restriction and tightness. You may help to relax your throat by loosening your collar or removing a tight necklace during the time before a speaking appearance, or between speaking appearances if they occur within a half hour of one another.

5. It should be mentioned that prior to, and between, speeches *some wide yawns will relax the throat.* You can feel the throat relax and observe the "Adam's apple" return to a relaxed position as you yawn.

6. *When there is a good breath supply to support the voice, the speaker feels no need to tense his throat in order to get a stronger voice.* An adequate supply of breath supporting the voice and carrying it out the throat is an important prerequisite to a relaxed throat. Many speakers tense their throats as an additional effort to get a stronger voice. If these speakers had an adequate voice to begin with, there would be no such tensing of the throat.

The third step in developing skill in the use of your voice is gaining control over the use of your breath supply. Increased breath supply can be more of a problem than a help if it rushes out unexpectedly and provides emphasis at the wrong point. Consequently, as soon as you increase your breath supply, you should begin controlling your use of it.

1. *Learn to release breath during exhalation at a regular, even rate.* The following is an exercise to help you obtain this kind of control. Select an easy pitch and sing "ha-a-a," striving to sustain the note at its full richness and strength. Each time you perform the exercise, sustain the note for a longer period of time than you did before.

2. *Learn to release breath in specific amounts for purposes of emphasis.* Using your strongest and clearest voice, do some cadence counting. Vary the place of emphasis so that you gain the ability to thrust out the voice on the number that you want to emphasize. The exercises might take the following form:

1 2 3 4, 1 2 3 4, 1 2 3 4, 1 2 3 4, 1 2 3 4
1 2 3 4, 1 2 3 4, 1 2 3 4, 1 2 3 4, 1 2 3 4
1 2 3 4, 1 2 3 4, 1 2 3 4, 1 2 3 4, 1 2 3 4
1 2 3 4, 1 2 3 4, 1 2 3 4, 1 2 3 4, 1 2 3 4

After doing this sort of cadence counting, read aloud from a book, concentrating on emphasizing particular words or phrases. Such reading should help secure a carry-over in breath control from counting to speaking. These two breath control skills should help you in the use of the new breath supply for more effective speaking.

These, then, are the steps to follow to increase your skill in the use of your voice.

1. *Secure an adequate breath supply by:*
    (a) always starting to speak with a good full breath,

   (b) always taking a full breath when inhaling during pauses and transitions in the speech,
   (c) engaging in some breathing exercises to increase the amount of air you take in during inhalation.
2. *Learn to relax your throat by:*
   (a) using the swallow,
   (b) using the sigh,
   (c) using a relaxed posture and manner,
   (d) wearing loose collars and jewelry,
   (e) using the yawn,
   (f) relying upon a full breath supply to produce the stronger voice.
3. *Gain control over the use of your breath supply by:*
   (a) learning to release breath during exhalation at a regular, even rate,
   (b) learning to release breath in specific amounts for purpose of emphasis.

Posture and Gestures

We now turn our attention to posture and arm-hand gestures. Since many beginning speakers are inclined to evaluate posture and gestures on the basis of personal prejudice or a comparison with their own speaking idol, it is important to set forth some criteria.

Criteria for Posture and Gestures

1. *Your posture and gestures should put you at ease.* If your posture or gestures are such that they make you feel tense, uncomfortable, or foolish, they will make your speaking more difficult. A rigid posture, or gestures that are studied imitations of other speakers will probably arouse such feelings.

2. *Your posture and gestures should be appropriate for the occasion.* If your posture or gestures clash with the concept the audience has of this occasion, your movements will make you appear out of harmony with the occasion. A speaker's bodily action should indicate a clear understanding of the occasion. If the audience feels

that this is an important, formal time, the speaker should avoid posture and gestures which suggest casualness or indifference.

3. *Your posture and gestures should communicate your ideas.* The motivation for the type of posture and gestures you are using should be the ideas which you wish to communicate, and the goal for the use of gestures and posture should be the communication of your ideas. If a speaker were to drape himself casually across the speaker's stand at the moment when he was declaring, "We've got to be alert to the dangers which threaten the American home," he would probably fail to communicate the feeling of the "alertness" of which he was speaking. If you make certain that your posture and gestures put you at ease, are appropriate to the occasion, and communicate your ideas, you can be relatively sure that your posture and gestures are contributing to your speaking effectiveness.

Now while these criteria may seem simple, they are not easily satisfied. Most of us tend to become self-conscious and overly critical of our posture and gestures the moment we find ourselves before an audience. Such feelings may make appropriate, natural, communicative posture and gestures an impossibility. The following suggestions for posture and gestures are given to help you gain some sense of confidence in your appearance before an audience, and in your use of posture and gestures for speaking. These are beginning suggestions, and you should work through them to the achievement of posture and gestures which are a spontaneous response to a keen desire to communicate the ideas that make up your speech.

Taking a Stance

Obtaining a relaxed posture depends on the ability to stand well and to move well on the platform. *First, your feet must be correctly placed.* To find this correct placement stand with your feet about eighteen inches apart with your left foot about six inches ahead of your right foot. (May be reversed if you are left handed.)

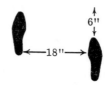

Adjust your stance slightly until you feel that your weight is evenly balanced and that the stance is comfortable and not forced. Then, to test the placement of your feet and the balance of this posture, make the following movements (*do not move your feet during any of these tests*):

1. Moving primarily at the hips, turn your body 90 degrees to the right so that from the hips up you are facing directly to the right.
2. Next, moving primarily at the hips, turn your body 180 degrees to the left so that you have passed the front position and are now (from the hips up) facing directly to the left.
3. Return to your original posture facing front. Now, moving primarily at the hips, bend forward. Then recover an erect position and bend backward. Again return to your original position.
4. Do a knee bend and recover your original posture.

If you have been able to make all of these movements without a major shift in weight or without a loss of balance, you have a firm, well balanced, basic stance. If not, you need to move your feet slightly farther apart or closer together, either from front to back or side to side, until you have obtained a stance which will survive these tests. Once you have found such a stance, you should use it as a base, or beginning, of all your bodily action. You should return to this basic stance when you have completed a unit of bodily action.

The use of this basic stance will soon give you a feeling of alertness and control. You will actually begin to feel comfortable while standing in front of a group of people who are staring at you and watching your every move. As you become more and more confident about your ability to stand well before an audience, you will begin to modify this stance or work out variations which give you more freedom. Such inclination to modify or improve this stance is a healthy sign of your maturation as a speaker.

Women should be particularly careful about maintaining a stance which keeps their weight evenly balanced. If a woman places all her weight on one leg, she will find herself looking awkward and unpoised. Since men generally are thought to be more awkward and clumsy in movement, the off-balance stance which causes a hip to jut out may occasionally appear natural for them. However, this off-

balance stance almost always detracts from the gracefulness of a
woman's posture when she appears on a public platform.

Getting Into Action

Once you have achieved a good basic stance, the next step is to
develop the ability to move freely on the platform. It is important
to practice movement so that your natural inhibitions about walking or gesturing in front of an audience in a formal situation do not
result in timid, rigid, or limited bodily action. Moving on the platform by walking from one point to another can aid the speaker in
three ways. First, such physical transitions can be used to suggest
transitions in the thought content of the speech or transitions in
the speaker's attitude toward his audience or his subject. Second,
walking by a speaker may help to capture the attention of the audience by presenting them with a new visual stimulus. Third, walking
on the platform may help the speaker to feel more at ease and serve
as a constructive release of nervous tension.

In walking, too, the speaker needs to develop a confidence in his
ability to walk well when speaking before an audience and an assurance that his walking is useful in communicating the ideas of his
speech. Once walking feels natural and purposeful, the speaker will
find that ideas in his speech provide instantaneous promptings to
walk toward or away from the audience or from place to place on
the platform.

Walking That Talks

Again the novice speaker will probably have to begin his speech-
walking by following certain rules and patterns. After the speaker
has followed these rules and patterns for a brief time, however, he
will have developed sufficient confidence in making such transitions
to walk in free response to his desire to communicate.

The following rules and plans will help you develop your ability
to walk while speaking in public. *Start with the foot that corresponds to the direction in which you want to move.* If you are moving right, start with your right foot. Failure to follow this rule will
result in moving one leg across the body. If you do start with the
right foot when moving left, you will appear awkward; and also,

you will put yourself off balance. At the moment when your right leg crosses in front of your left, your balance will be precarious. At this same moment you will look like a comic trying to get a laugh by appearing clumsy.

In addition to starting with the correct foot, it is also necessary to *keep your weight evenly distributed between your two legs.* If, as your right foot strikes the floor, you shift all your weight to the right and then, when you take the next step, you shift all your weight to the left foot, your walk will be marked by dipping shoulders and stiff legs. As you shift your weight, your leg will become stiff to support your weight and your shoulder will dip. By keeping your weight evenly distributed, you will avoid a wooden or stiff walk; and you will keep your shoulders level. Women, particularly, will want to avoid such heavy footed, lumbering walking on a public platform because it will make them appear exceptionally awkward.

When walking on the platform, you should *try to take steps of normal length with a normal speed.* Taking shorter steps at a slower pace may make you appear timid and uncertain. Moreover, if you walk at a normal speed and in a normal way, you will help yourself relax. If you walk carefully or with a severely limited stride, because you wish to stay close to the lectern or because you are afraid of misjudging the limits of the platform, you will emphasize the feeling that you are doing something strange and different. As a result of emphasizing that this is a strange and different activity, you will become tense and keyed-up. This tenseness, in turn, will make it difficult for you to move easily on the platform.

If you have never been able to initiate movement across the platform as you speak—if time and time again you have concluded a speech without ever having departed from the position you took when you started your introduction—or if, in fact, you simply cannot visualize where or how you would move on the platform, then you may be able to gain more freedom by planning your pattern of walking. *Move on the platform as there is movement in the thought content of the speech.* If there are four major transitions (movements in thought) in the speech, then there could be four major movements (walks) across the platform.

Thus far, movement on the platform has been recommended as a way of suggesting movement of thought in the speech. The speaker can also use movement to indicate the relationship that he desires

with his subject or his audience. By moving forward on the platform, the speaker can suggest that he desires a closer or more inti-
mate contact with the audience or with his idea. By moving to the
back of the platform, the speaker can suggest that he wants to withdraw from his audience or his subject for the moment. He may even
suggest that he wants to reflect for a moment before continuing with
the speech.

When moving to the back of the platform, do not just back up.
Walk to the back of the platform at an angle. If you are near the
right side of the platform, lead off with your left foot and angle
back to your left. Your move would look like this:

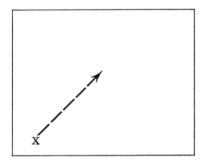

If you try to back up straight instead of at an angle, you will appear
to be moving in an awkward manner. This will be true because we
usually move cautiously when backing away, especially if we cannot see where we are going.

Now the speaker should realize that movement on the platform
not only suggests movement in the thought content of the speech
and infers his relationship to the thought content or to the audience, but it also implies the attitude with which the speaker moves
into the next idea. The speaker's movement may suggest that he is
moving into the expression of a new thought with hesitation or with
eagerness. His movement across the platform may imply that the
next idea strengthens his position or that this idea is really not too
important. The speed, confidence, and poise with which a speaker
moves suggest much to the audience concerning the speaker's feeling about the ideas he is expressing.

A speaker can develop an assurance about his speech-walking by
planning his movements across the platform, and by walking the

speech through and practicing these movements so that they will suggest movements in thought, his relation to subject and audience, and attitudes which he desires to communicate to his audience. Occasionally, speakers who must work on crowded platforms or in enclosed pulpits think that movement is denied them because of the limited space behind the lectern or pulpit. These speakers should carefully explore the full space available around the pulpit or lectern; then they should practice walking in this area until they can move naturally and meaningfully. Even the preacher who has a pulpit which completely encircles him may discover that by standing against the back right of the enclosure and walking diagonally across to the left front of the enclosure he may take two, or even three, steps. Just a single step backward might be enough to suggest that we are now going to view an idea or incident from a new perspective. A short while later, a good brisk step forward may be enough to indicate that we are moving on quickly to another section of the sermon.

However, it should be said that *movement must be adjusted to the area which is allowed to the speaker.* Do not despair of the speaking area if it is confining or if it is so large that it seems to swallow you up. The few feet behind your chair at a banquet table may offer surprising opportunities to suggest movement of thought, while the larger expanse of an auditorium stage can permit the kind of movement which gives real force and emphasis to your points. In order to adjust to the speaking area, it is well to practice the speech in an area which approximates the area of your predicted speaking situation. If possible, arrive early for your speaking engagement and walk through some of your speech in the place where you are to speak. There is no substitute for "getting the feel" of your actual speaking environment.

In order to walk well on the platform, one must:

1. Start with the foot that corresponds to the direction of one's movement,
2. Keep one's weight evenly distributed,
3. Take full steps,
4. Move as there is movement in the thought content of the speech,
5. Adjust to the speaking area.

The ability to walk naturally while speaking in public is a very significant aid to freedom of expression.

Saying It with Your Hands

Some people say that they do not know what to do with their hands in a social situation. The sudden awareness that several people are looking at you may result in the feeling that your hands are large, awkward, and out of place. Many people experience a similar feeling when they stand up to speak in public. This, too, is a social occasion; and several people are looking intently at you. If, as a speaker, you can cultivate the feeling that your hands look natural and that you can use them to share your ideas, you will have made an important contribution to your sense of speaking poise.

The first step is to *acquire a good "at rest" position for your hands*. Every speaker needs an appropriate position where his hands may be "at rest" between gestures. There are two such positions which a speaker can use. The first is to let your hands hang free at your sides. A good approach to this position is to stand at attention and then, leaving your shoulders back and your arms hanging straight down, relax slightly so that your posture is alert and erect, but not rigid.

It would be well to practice this position in front of a full-length mirror. While watching yourself in the mirror, let your hands hang free at your sides. Then move your arms and hands very slightly forward. Observe this position in the mirror. Next, move them slightly backward and observe this position. Now move your hands in tighter against your thighs. Then let them hang very lightly against your thighs. Try several places for your hands at your sides, observing each in the mirror, until you find the position which looks the most natural and poised.

When you find a position for your hands that seems natural to you, look at this position carefully so that you know just where your hands and arms are placed. After you are certain about this position, gesture with your hands, as though you were speaking, and then return them to this position. The purpose of this practice is to develop the ability to place your hands easily in this "at rest" position whenever you do not need them to express an idea. If you know that your hands are in a position which looks natural and appropriate, and if you know that you can return your hands to this position at will, you will feel much more confident about using them for speaking in public.

This first "at rest" position is the best because it gives you the most freedom to respond to an impulse to gesture while speaking. In this position there is nothing to slow down or inhibit the response of your hands. For example, you do not need to let go of the speaker's stand or remove your hand from a pocket before you can gesture. Moreover, in leaving this position to gesture, there is no feeling that your hands have moved from a place where they felt secure, such as a pocket or the speaker's stand, to the thin air where they do not feel secure. If a woman is wearing a full skirt, she may feel more at ease if she tucks her hands slightly into it. In this way, her hands can be hanging free at her sides and at the same time feel comfortable because they are partly concealed in the folds or the fullness of the skirt.

A second "at rest" position is to clasp one hand in the other behind your back. There are three favorable things which can be said about this position. One, placing the hands behind the back in this manner tends to pull the shoulders back and the chest up and out. Consequently, the speaker has a more erect posture. Two, this position allows the speaker to release some of his nervous energy by tugging the fingers of one hand with the other hand, or by clasping and unclasping his hands without the audience's being distracted by these signs of nervous tension. The opportunity to release tenseness in this way without showing tenseness to the audience may be helpful in adjusting to the platform situation. And, three, this position will allow the speaker a fairly large amount of freedom in responding to impulses for gesturing.

Women speakers may allow one hand to rest lightly in the other in front of them about waist high. This position may suggest weakness in a man, but it seems to be both a natural and a graceful posture for women. Moreover, if the hands are not clasped tightly or wrung, but allowed to rest together casually, this posture will suggest that a woman speaker is both poised and relaxed.

Now this is not meant to say that your hands should never be put in pockets or placed on a pulpit or speaker's stand. However, it should be said that the pocket or the pulpit is not a good basic position for the hands. When your hands are not being used to express a thought or to suggest a mood, they should be hanging free at your sides.

After you have found a good "at rest" position for your hands, the next step is to *become acquainted with various kinds of hand gestures.* You have probably used gestures often when speaking to a friend or to a small group of your neighbors; but when you attempt to use gestures in a public situation, they may seem strange and forced. It is possible for you to gain freedom in gesturing by studying and practicing some of the following basic gestures.

One frequently used gesture is the extended index finger. This gesture may be used to point to members of the audience or to geographical locations. Or the finger may be raised in warning or thrust forward as a means of emphasis. Another hand gesture is a palm upward and extended forward as though you are handing something to the audience. This gesture can be used to suggest that you are giving some information to the audience for their consideration. The clenched fist can be used to suggest the vigor with which you support an argument or the unity which a group needs. A hand, with the palm down, pushed down and away from the body may be used to indicate your rejection of a policy or plan.

These gestures, along with others which you may have observed speakers using, should be practiced until they feel natural and come easily. The importance of this kind of practice is that it "primes" gestures, or gets them started. Once a speaker has developed a few basic gestures which he can use effectively in public, he soon finds that additional ones are prompted quite spontaneously by his interest in his subject.

As a speaker, you should *work for gestures which are a full response to the idea or mood that you wish to convey.* In order to develop gestures which are full responses, the speaker must think of himself as responding, bodily, as a whole person, and responding in terms of thinking and feeling. In other words, all that you are should be responding to all that the idea or mood is. Walking at the same time that you are gesturing may help develop such total response in gesturing. You may also work into fuller gestures by unbending your elbows. Straighten your arms when gesturing, so that your upper and lower arm form an angle of 150 to 180 degrees, rather than an angle of 70 to 90 degrees. This straightening of your elbows will give your gestures a fuller range. Also, let your fingers relax a little. Do not keep your fingers rigid and frozen together like a wooden soldier—shake them out. Rigid hands result in restrained gestures.

We stated earlier that the goal for the use of gestures should be the communication of your ideas. Therefore, the speaker should *strive to communicate meaning through gestures.* Gestures will help suggest size, shape, direction, and location. They also indicate whether the speaker is serious, angry, casual, or enthusiastic. Gestures show us movements in thought and underline important statements in the speech. A speaker will be more eager to use gestures when he believes that they are helping him suggest ideas.

An excellent way to develop an awareness of communicating meaning through gestures is to visualize the presentation of the meaning of a part of a speech. The speaker should look through this part of his speech and ask himself questions like these:

1. What kind of attitude do I want to show in my facial expression?
2. What type of posture will help express my conviction here?
3. How can a gesture serve to emphasize this point or to indicate that relationship?

After trying to answer such questions, the speaker should deliver this part of his speech in front of a mirror, and watch carefully to see if his gestures are saying the same thing that his words are saying. Then the speaker should attempt to co-ordinate the meaning of his gestures with the meaning of his words. The best motivation for appropriate and meaningful gestures is the motivation that arises from the effort to communicate meaning through gestures.

To sum up, you can improve your ability to use your hands for gestures by:

1. Acquiring a good "at rest" position for your hands,
2. Becoming acquainted with various kinds of hand gestures,
3. Working for gestures which are a full response to the idea or mood that you wish to convey,
4. Striving to communicate meaning through your gestures.

Everyone who makes a public address needs to remember that the address is only half prepared when the outline and manuscript are completed. The oral delivery of this address may distort the ideas and distract the listener, or the oral delivery of the address may clarify the ideas and capture the attention of the listener. Speeches should be practiced orally several times so that the speaker can develop a state of readiness for effective delivery. Practice in surroundings similar to the actual speech situation and with a real audience of one or more persons will help ready the speaker for the actual delivery of his speech. Such practice will also give the speaker the opportunity to check the appropriateness of his posture and gestures as well as the strength of his voice.

Naturalness and freedom, essential for effective delivery, require a period of warm-up or tune-up in which voice and body are exercised. Also, they require an opportunity to become appreciative of the opportunities to clarify and emphasize content through the use of vocal variety and bodily action. Delivery practice should be started sufficiently early to allow spaced and thorough practice. These practices should not be hurried or crowded into inadequate time periods. If you do not now engage in several delivery practices before making a speech, you should ask yourself this question: "Am I weakening much of the hard work which I put into the composition of my speeches by presenting them in a dull or an uninteresting manner?" Perhaps you could do more to ready yourself for the effective delivery of your speeches.

chapter 3

Thinking
Aloud
in
Public

L et us suppose that you were to ask the question, "If I want to become a good public speaker, is there any one skill that I should particularly develop?" Without a moment's hesitation, the answer would be, "Yes! Learn to think aloud in public." When it comes to public speaking, the reader or the memorizer will not capture the attention of an audience as readily as the thinker. There is something thrilling about observing a mind hard at work in your very presence. A mind that challenges you to think with it, as it analyzes a situation or solves a problem, is extending an irresistible invitation. Moreover, the thinker is much more ready to solve problems that arise during the delivery of the speech than are either the reader or the memorizer.

Of course, even the speaker who is thinking aloud, rather than reading from a manuscript or repeating a speech word for word, will use some memorized information; and he might read some quotations or statistics. However, the memorized ideas and the in-

39

formation he reads aloud will be materials with which he thinks. He will still be, primarily, a man thinking on his feet, who, in the course of this thinking, may read an item and may call materials from his memory to round out his thought plan. Reading aloud and repeating word for word, done for the purpose of moving thought along, are more interesting than the same thing done with no awareness of moving the thought of the speech along.

Each time a speaker encounters an audience, he should lead them in a brand new adventure in thinking about the subject. All of his previous preparation, outlining his speech and practicing it, should be a preparation for this creative and co-operative journey in thought. But this prior preparation should not limit the speaker. Rather, the early preparation should give him such freedom, that, in the moment of communication, he is free to take alternate paths of thought and to use a variety of thinking methods to help this particular audience think with him. A properly prepared speaker does not have to read a manuscript laboriously, or fearfully repeat the speech from memory. An adequately prepared speaker can invite the audience to join him in some spontaneous thinking about the subject of his speech.

Not only is the thinker a more interesting speaker than a reader or a memorizer, but thinking a speech through is more enjoyable for the speaker than either reading or repeating word for word. Best of all, it is relatively easy to learn to think the speech through aloud.

Philosophy of Public Speaking

The following suggestions for thinking aloud when you speak are based on a philosophy of public speaking—a philosophy which holds that each public speech should be a unique, creative, artistic endeavor which never can be exactly anticipated or precisely duplicated. That is, the speaker should adjust his abilities, as he experiences them on the particular occasion, to these precise environmental circumstances, and to the mood and condition of the specific audience. To be the most meaningful, these adjustments must be made in a creative and artistic manner as the speaker is thinking

aloud with his audience. Thus, in spite of prior preparation, the
speech is never complete until the exact moment of communication
when the speaker's abilities are finally adapted to the speaking environment and to the mood and condition of his audience.

Public speaking, then, is an exciting and difficult art because of
this need to discover and produce, at every given moment in the
communicative act, the precise adjustment of speaker, environment,
and audience to permit the highest degree of communication. The
public speaker has a greater opportunity to practice this art than
does the author, the radio-TV performer, or the actor, because of
his immediate and direct person-to-person confrontation of the live,
responding audience.

This philosophy of public speaking demands that all preparation
strengthen the speaker and stimulate his creative and artistic abilities so that he is able and eager to adapt and adjust his thinking
aloud to the constant variation of his own ability as well as to the
constant variation of the mood of the audience and of the conditions
of their environment. Public speaking is a dynamic art which demands spontaneous, creative, "oral" thinking.

Suggestions for Thinking Aloud in Public

The first step in learning to think aloud in public is to *develop
an over-all thought plan for the speech.* You will remember eight
such plans were discussed in Chapter 1—Time, Space, Problem-
Solution, Climactic, Cause-Effect, Familiar to Unfamiliar, Simple to
Complex, and Simple Enumeration. The over-all plan for your
speech will need a place to begin and a place to end, and a method,
such as one of the eight just mentioned, to get from your beginning
to your conclusion. A written outline, such as the one specified at
the end of Chapter 1, will help you check the adequacy of your
over-all thought plan for the speech.

Once you have developed your thought plan, the next step is to
work out your transitional sentences. It is necessary to prepare them
carefully, because well developed transitions help the speaker think
his way through the speech. Usually the difficulties in thinking

occur when the speaker wants to move from one section of the speech to another. Difficulty arises at this point because it is no easy task to maintain the unity of the speech, indicate movement of thought, and introduce a new section of the speech all in a few words. This is why the speaker strengthens his ability to think his speech through when he prepares his transitional sentences in advance. These transitional sentences should be practiced aloud so that the speaker becomes familiar with their essential ingredients and with the arrangement of these ingredients.

After the speaker has developed his over-all thought plan and worked out the transitional sentences, he should *give the speech several trial runs.* In these oral practices, the speaker should work through the entire speech in each practice session. It is of the utmost importance that the speaker regard these practices as attempts to start thinking at one point and, following a particular plan, think his way through to a concluding point. The practices should not be regarded as memorizing sessions; these are practices in thinking, not in memorization.

During these trial runs of the speech, *the speaker should rephrase ideas when he cannot remember particular words or phrases.* This is not to say that the speaker should not attend to the choice and grouping of words. Neither is it to say that word choice is an unimportant phase of preparing to speak. Rather, this practice is intended to keep the process of choosing words, and of combining them in phrases and sentences, alive and active through the final moment of delivery. If the speaker concentrates on the accurate selection of words and the correct construction of sentences during the written preparation of his speech, he will improve his ability to rephrase portions of his speech during the actual presentation. You will find that rephrasing is a helpful method for keeping the thought moving when you cannot recall specific words or phrases, because it enables you to keep your attention fixed on developing the thought, rather than on the remembering of a word or phrase.

For example, let us suppose that a preacher wishes to make the point that we should not just mouth the words of the Apostles' Creed, but he cannot recall ". . . mouth the words of the Apostles' Creed"; so he restates, or says the same thing in another way, by saying, "When we say the Apostles' Creed we should not hurry through it without paying attention to its meaning."

In the preceding example, the thought is kept moving by re-stating or using other words to say the same thing. The ability to keep the thought moving without forcing yourself to recall exact words or precise phrasing will help you to think right through the difficult moments in the speech. This same ability also gives a speaker a sense of freedom, which may be precipitated by the ex-citement of his encounter with the actual audience, and which allows him to use alternate words and phrases. Again, let it be said that such a sense of freedom is equally dependent on thorough at-tention to word choice and phrasing during the outline and manu-script phases of speech preparation. The criteria which the speaker chooses for the selection of a word during the writing phase of preparation will be of great help to him if a choice must be made during the actual delivery of the speech.

As a speaker, you should also *decide to think with the materials that are available to you.* Speakers often make fetishes of illustra-tions, quotations, or examples, as well as of words or phrases. A speaker may stall and fumble in an effort to recall such an item and muddy or detour the movement of thought. Frequently, the thought can be advanced with sufficient clarity or force if these particular illustrations, quotations, or examples are omitted, or if others are substituted for them. You should be more concerned with develop-ing the total thought plan than with recalling a specific illustration or quotation. Attempting to delay in order to remember a particular content item may weaken the whole thought structure, as well as cost you the attention of the audience. Of course, the ability to omit or substitute content items, when necessary, depends on becoming thoroughly familiar with the thought structure while preparing your speech.

Just as it is true that you can keep the thinking process pro-gressing without using particular words or phrases, so it is true that you can keep it moving without using an exact number of examples or without using the precise illustration on which you had planned. The speech or sermon may be weaker at this point, but the total impact of your presentation can still be strong. An ability to adjust or alter your thinking response to the behavior of your memory is vital to effective thinking before an audience.

Limitations of Rephrasing, Substituting, and Omitting

These methods are valuable to the speaker only if he realizes their limitations and does not try to extend them beyond. The first limitation can be the frequency with which they are used in a single speech. Their use should be restricted to emergency situations, and the speaker should prepare thoroughly so that only a few such emergencies are likely to occur. Secondly, they should not be used in place of careful sentence construction or careful word choice. If a speaker habitually employs these methods in an attempt to short-cut adequate preparation, his speeches will soon lose their clarity and forcefulness. Finally, these methods should not be used as an escape from his responsibility to deal with a subject correctly and honestly. With such limitations in mind, a speaker can improve his ability to think aloud in public by rephrasing, substituting, or omitting, examples, quotations, or illustrations.

Audience and Occasion

Thinking with what is available to you also refers to the audience and to the occasion. If, for example, you ask the members of the congregation to raise their hands if they know of the work of the Goodwill Industries, expecting that only a few people will do so and instead over half the members raise their hands, do not think that your point is lost. Instead, adapt to the response the congregation has given you. Say that you are glad so many have heard of the Goodwill Industries because this means that you will be bringing news of a work which they already know and admire.

A speaker who was pleading for immediate financial aid for the improvement of the buildings of a church-supported orphanage expected that his announcement, that the state fire marshal had ordered the orphanage closed in ninety days unless the required standards were met, would make a forceful impression on the congregation. However, when he had completed this announcement, he could notice no observable change in the facial expression of the group. Consequently, he extended the point by showing that the closing of the orphanage would bring real hardship to nine-month old Carol and her father who was working and trying to maintain a home for his three school-aged children. As he cited the details of this specific case, the audience began to show signs of appreciating what it would mean to this family if the orphanage were closed. Then the speaker, wishing to use this audience response, suggested "Now multiply the hardship which this family will suffer by sixty, which is the number of children that our orphanage cares for, and you will have some understanding of the tragedy which will result if our orphanage has to be closed."

It is important that the speaker keep thinking of ways he can use any response or behavior of the audience to advance his idea, even if the response is an unpredicted one. If the speaker can avoid panicking when he receives a surprise response, and instead think more determinedly, he will discover that it is not necessary to abandon the thought pattern he has been developing; such unpredicted responses can often move him to a more emphatic and convincing kind of speaking.

The speaker must be equally resourceful in adjusting to the occasion. He must not allow the unexpected to interrupt and sidetrack his planned thought pattern for the subject. Let us suppose that you have been invited to speak at an annual countywide meeting of the WCTU on the topic, "Tainted Money." Let us also suppose that you prepare to speak to a large audience of middle-aged women, but on arrival at the church you find fewer than twenty-five primly dressed older women. When you see this small group of conservative looking women huddled over on one side of the church sanctuary, you become fearful that you do not have the sort of speech that will be appreciated on this particular occasion. The occasion seems more formal and more restrained than you had anticipated.

But once again, the speaker should use this occasion to reinforce his thinking. He could say that he was pleased to speak to such a group because he knew that they would give his words serious and careful attention. Then, in thinking his speech through, he could adjust and adapt the thought plan and content materials in terms of this audience. By adapting to the occasion, he could use the mood of the audience to support his own speech thinking. The speaker, then, should be ready to think with the best words and ideas which his mind gives him, with the responses which the audience makes, and with the mood or events which the occasion provides.

The two or three minutes the speaker has to himself while he is being introduced, or while a part of the worship service or a part of the program is being concluded, can be of real help in getting the thought plan of the speech effectively launched. You should *use the few minutes prior to your actual speaking as a thought warm-up for the speech*. During this warm-up period of thinking you should first review the introduction. Next you can review your thought plan for the total speech. Finally, as a thought stimulant, you should recall the original reason that prompted you to speak about these matters. Now, once more, quickly review your introduction and step up and start your speech.

This kind of thought warm-up is a real aid to thinking aloud. It replaces the usual mounting of nervous tension with constructive thinking practice. Moreover, it starts the speaker thinking before he must start speaking. This means that when he steps to the speaker's stand, his mind is primed and ready to go. Consequently, he begins his speech with greater assurance and more control. Such a start makes the subsequent thinking aloud easier and more enjoyable.

One further practice the speaker should follow is to *make his speaking goal the development of a complete unit of thought*. The goal should not be a twenty minute speech, or a speech without a single grammatical mistake; for if these goals are made primary or dominant, they will divert the speaker's attention from the thought plan, and interfere with his ability to think his way through the speech.

The speaker's primary and dominant goal should be to develop a complete unit of thought. While speaking, his attention should be directed to developing this unit of thought; and when he has completed it, he should conclude his speech. The fact that he is finishing two minutes early or three minutes late, or the fact that he has omitted parts of his planned speech should not be allowed to take his attention from the completion of the thought unit. When a speaker is able to make the developing of a complete unit of thought his dominant concern throughout the delivery of his speech, he will have the attitude most conducive to thinking aloud in public.

If you wish to practice the dynamic art of public speaking by thinking aloud in public, it is well to do the following:

1. Develop an over-all thought plan for the speech.
2. Work out your transition sentences.
3. Give the speech several trial runs.
4. Restate your ideas when you cannot think of particular words or phrases.
5. Be ready to think with what is available.
6. Use the few minutes prior to your actual speaking as a thought warm-up for the speech.
7. Make your speaking goal the development of a complete unit of thought.

One more word needs to be said about these seven suggestions for thinking aloud. You need to practice these suggestions many times while working in actual speech situations. Until you are able to use these suggestions with some skill, they may seem to be more troublesome than helpful. It is only when you are capable of using them skillfully that you will begin to appreciate their true value. Also, you should expect that if you attempt to change from a memorizing method of delivery to a thinking method of delivery, there may be some awkward and unpleasant moments. However, if you have the courage to suffer through such growing pains, you will gain a freedom and effectiveness in communication that will be more than ample reward for your effort.

Keeping the Idea Fresh

Another obstacle to thinking aloud in public is the loss of interest in one's subject. If the speaker allows the subject to become stale for him or if he becomes "tired" of it, his desire to think about it will wane; and this, in turn, will make him less able to think about it when he is delivering his speech. Losing interest in the subject or becoming "tired" of it can be a chronic affliction with some speakers. This affliction results in the audience's feeling that the speech is weak or uninteresting, and the speaker's awareness of this audience attitude further undermines his confidence and weakens his presentation.

There are several ways in which a speaker can keep his interest in his topic lively and growing. The first is to *stimulate his motiva-*

tion for speaking on this subject. Motivation for speaking on the topic may be stimulated by recalling and emphasizing those factors of the subject which first caught the speaker's attention, or by thinking about the good effects which can be produced by causing the audience to think about the subject.

Motivation to speak on the topic will be strengthened even more if you can picture particular persons who may be helped by the audience's response to your presentation. If a YMCA director is trying to raise funds for summer camp work, and he pictures to himself one of the boys who will be aided by a summer at camp, this boy may provide him with a definite and personal motivation for speaking. In an instance like this, it is well to fill in all the details by visiting the boy or by studying his case history so that you feel that you really know him and his needs.

A second way to keep alive your interest in a subject is to *continue to acquire more information about your subject right up to the time that you are going to speak.* The feeling that you are replacing generalities with specifics, that you are acquiring a better understanding of your subject matter, and that you are able to present more information, gives you a sense of growth and a grasp of your subject; and this makes your subject even more interesting to you. For this practice, it would be well to become familiar with the reference room of the nearest library and the special sources of information that may be found there. Also, you should do what you can to cultivate a curiosity about the subject with which you are going to deal, so that anything you read, anything you may hear on the radio or observe on television, or anything that occurs in conversation relating to your subject will immediately strike your attention.

In addition, it is wise to talk to someone who is informed about your subject—the more informed the better. Frequently, you will not only gather more information, but you will gain some of the other person's interest.

As one acquires more information, he is often moved to analyze his subject over and over again in an effort to make his information fit together and to see the picture as a whole. The desire to determine the meaning of new information and to see how this information relates to what you already know is an excellent stimulant to your interest in your subject.

A third means of sustaining interest in your subject is by *working on your speech with another person.* Discuss your speech with someone else and let him become a partner in its preparation. You might decide to talk your speech through with someone whose expert judgment and opinions you respect. On the other hand, you might choose a person who would be fairly typical of the audience to which you are going to speak, and check to see if this person understands what you are saying and if he has any suggestions for making your speech clearer and more interesting.

If your interest is really sagging, you might discuss your speech with a person whom you know will oppose your approach or your viewpoint. Often a hostile critic will arouse your determination to present as effective a speech as possible. In brief, he gives you an exciting cause for speaking, and this makes your subject more interesting to you.

Finally, you might want to discuss your speech with someone whom you regard as an excellent speaker and have him comment on the way you have put it together and on the materials you are using. It would be advantageous to allow this critic to hear your speech as well as to have him read your outline or your manuscript.

A fourth way to renew your interest in your subject is to go through your speech, paragraph by paragraph, and *try to make your statements sharp and penetrating.* Strive to make your statements so clear that they cannot be misunderstood by anyone in your audience. You may be surprised to see how alive and vigorous your speech becomes as you make it clearer and more incisive. Any speaker will become enthusiastic about lucid, cogent ideas expressed in plain, to-the-point statements, when they emerge from vague, repetitious, general phrases. To know that you will present your ideas in words that will be immediately and fully understood creates an eager anticipation for the time when the speech can actually be presented.

When a speaker faces the challenge of expressing himself in terms that are lucid and pointed, he becomes involved in an endeavor which allows him no idle or easy moments during which his interest may lag.

A fifth technique for keeping your interest in your subject is to *apportion your thinking about your subject and about what you have heard or read about it.* Pondering your subject at spaced intervals will reward you, every so often, with a sudden understanding of how one part relates to another, or with a new perception of what some phase should mean to you or to the members of your audience. By dividing your period of preparation, you allow for fresh starts and for the germination of ideas.

Your repeated personal effort to analyze the nature and meaning of your subjects will help you develop a facility for analysis and understanding which will, in turn, enable you to make a more thorough analysis and gain a more complete understanding of future subjects. The feeling that you, personally, are coming to grips with your subject and that you have developed personal convictions about it, will do much to make the subject interesting to you.

For example, if you were a member of a visitation team that was to call on prospective members, you might examine what the services of the church mean to you and your family, then decide how these services would be especially helpful to a new family moving into the community. You would be ready to do more than just list the services the church has to offer; you would be ready to speak with personal enthusiasm about what the church has meant to you and your family and what it can mean to families who are moving into the community.

A sixth means of maintaining your interest in your subject is to develop or explain it with references to the environment of the meeting, to the purpose of the meeting, to the tradition behind such meetings, and to other aspects of the speaking situation. *Such adaptation of the speech to the interests of this audience and to this occasion* assures the speaker that his speech is growing in its appeal to his audience. The speaker also feels that his address is becoming contemporary. This effort to localize and personalize his speech has real power to restore the speaker's interest.

If you were going to speak to a congregation about supporting a mission project and you wanted to include references to this local congregation in your speech, you might inquire if this church is supporting a missionary now, or if it has received any sort of recognition for its financial support of other missionary projects, or if there are any symbols in the church representing the world mission of the church. Answers to these questions could provide you with opportunities to adapt to this local congregation. Or, if the church had been originally founded through a missionary effort or if it has a local missionary society, you could refer to these facts in your speech.

Here, in brief summary, are our suggestions for keeping your ideas fresh and thereby maintaining your interest in the subject of your speech.

1. Stimulate your motivation for speaking on this subject.
2. Acquire more information about your subject.
3. Enlist someone else as a partner in your speech preparation.
4. Try to make your statements more sharp and penetrating.
5. Apportion your thinking on your subject and on what you have read and heard about it.
6. Further adapt your speech to the interests of the audience and to the occasion.

If by following such suggestions you succeed in maintaining a lively interest in your subject, you will find it much easier to think aloud in public. Your interest will help you focus your attention on your subject, and it will make you eager to share your thoughts with your audience.

Impromptu Speaking

The suggestions made in this chapter for "thinking the speech through" and for "keeping the idea fresh" have been made with the assumption that you had several days in which to prepare for your speaking assignment. However, we wish to point out that a number of these methods can be used even in an impromptu situation, where the speaker must deal with a matter that he had not anticipated, such as speaking on an item of new business, or responding to an unexpected request for information, or substituting for a speaker who has been unable to appear.

In attempting to think as you go along, you will find your task greatly facilitated by the selection of an over-all plan for the speech. If time permits, the formulation of the major transitions will also be an important aid to clear and direct development. Moreover, a readiness to phrase your ideas with the vocabulary which is at your immediate disposal, and to move the thought pattern along with the illustration and examples which are at your command, will be most helpful in the impromptu speaking situation. A quick mental review of your intended pattern of thought and key transitional sentences, just prior to lauching your impromptu speech, will serve to ready you for this speaking adventure.

Even on an impromptu occasion, a speaker can suffer a lag in interest or enthusiasm if there is a lapse in time between the warning that he is to speak and the actual time he does. When you sense that you are experiencing such a lag in interest or enthusiasm, you will find that you can arouse your interest by stimulating your motivation for speaking, sharpening your intended statements, and further adapting your speech to the interests of the audience and to the occasion.

In some situations, it may even be possible to employ the suggested methods of acquiring more information and enlisting another person as a partner in the preparation of the speech. The use of these latter methods will depend on the environment and on the degree to which this is an impromptu situation. The main point we wish to make is that the methods suggested earlier in this chapter should not be ignored just because you are faced with a sudden or unexpected speaking assignment.

chapter 4

Speaking
from
Notes

The successful practice of the art of public speaking depends on careful attention to each phase of speech preparation. One might say that an ounce of preparation is worth a pound of improvisation. In fact, the speaker's freedom and poise when confronting his audience are the direct result of his preparations to speak. Now, this means it is important that the speaker spend adequate time and effort in preparing to speak, and it is important that he concern himself with every step of speech preparation. Unfortunately, even experienced speakers frequently concentrate on only a few steps and neglect other equally important acts of speech preparation. Undoubtedly one of the most tragic kinds of defeat on the platform is the failure of a speaker who has industriously prepared to speak, as far as several factors are concerned, but who has neglected or slighted one phase of preparation. The realization that all your effort has been wasted because you carelessly neglected one step of preparation is a painful experience.

In this chapter we wish to deal with a step or phase of preparation which speakers frequently neglect. This neglect often seriously impairs speaker effectiveness and is responsible for a great deal of audience boredom. The construction and use of speaking notes is the phase of neglected preparation with which we shall be concerned.

Almost every speaker will have an occasion at one time or another to use notes for delivering a speech. The speaker may be forced to use notes because he has been given a short period of time in which to prepare and present an address; or he may find it necessary to rely on notes because he has some specific information which he wishes to communicate to his audience in accurate and precise detail; or he may use notes as a regular part of his delivery method. Whatever the reason, the important point is that he must prepare and use these notes with much care and skill.

Personal observation leads us to believe that a remarkable number of speeches and sermons have been partly or totally ruined by poor preparation of or poor use of speaker's notes. It is unbelievable that any speaker or preacher would spend several hours preparing a speech and then spoil it by careless preparation of his notes. Apparently, however, many speakers fail to recognize the damaging effect which poorly prepared notes have on the presentation of a speech.

While preparing their notes, speakers often write in such haste that when they use these notes, they are not able to read their own writing. As a result, the speaker may find it necessary to pause in awkward places while trying to decipher. Speakers often feel that it is important for the notes to be unnoticeable; thus, they squeeze and crowd them together, on a small piece of paper, until it is hard to separate one sentence from another. Again, when they go to use them while speaking, they have considerable difficulty in reading the notes at all.

Some speakers merely jot down several sentences without using any symbols or indentation to suggest the relation of one sentence to another. When these speakers deliver their speeches, they often lose their place in their notes because the sentences are not clearly identified, and they stumble around in delivery until they again find their place.

Other speakers who frequently lose their place in their notes are those who must have a handful of papers before they feel secure at the podium. Sooner or later, these speakers forget to turn or move a page of their notes, and then there is an awkward attempt to improvise while they hastily thumb through the pages trying to find their place.

Sometimes speakers even use notes originally prepared for a longer speech than they are to present on a particular occasion. The confusion resulting from trying to deliver a ten-minute speech from notes which were prepared for a twenty-minute speech is usually devastating to the presentation.

These are a few examples of speakers who need to give more careful attention to the preparation and use of their notes. The preparation of notes for speaking is not a task to be performed hastily and carelessly or as an afterthought. Notes that are well-prepared and well-used will add much to the effectiveness of a speaker's delivery.

Attitude Toward Notes

If your speaker's notes are to aid rather than impair your speaking, you must understand the role of notes in speaking. It is necessary to remember that these notes are to be used to help you think; they are not to serve as a substitute for thinking while you speak, but they are to serve as stimulants and aids to thinking. You will not think aloud for a while, then read for a while, then think aloud for a while, and so forth. The entire speech will be an experience in thinking aloud, and the references to your notes will aid this thought process. No one should carefully prepare speaking notes as a substitute for thinking when speaking. Every speaker should recognize that there is no substitute for thinking his speech through as he delivers it.

On the other hand, you should not feel that the use of notes is a sign of weakness. Most of the people who are listening to you would have to use notes to make the same sort of speech that you are making. It is not the presence of speaking notes to which audiences object, but it is the poor use of them which annoys an audience.

Therefore, the speaker should use his notes without apology; and he should use his notes skillfully. He should not try to hide his notes, nor should he try to sneak occasional glances at them. Instead, the speaker should use them deliberately and with an air of assurance. He should make it clear that these notes are helping him to think accurately, swiftly, and surely. In some cases, a speaker may even give added emphasis to what he is saying by pointing out that he is reading word for word from a statement by a particular person or group. When a speaker begins to use his speaking notes skillfully, as tools for constructing a unit of thought for his audience, you can be sure that he is developing a healthy attitude toward the proper use of them.

Preparation of Notes

Now that you understand how important it is to prepare good notes for speaking, let us consider some methods for preparing adequate ones. Every speaker should *set aside a specific period of time for the preparation of these speaking notes.* Too many speakers allot no time at all for this task. They assume that somehow they will find a few minutes here or there for preparing the notes from which they will speak. However, the time slips by; and suddenly, at the last minute, they find themselves hastily scribbling out phrases to refer to while speaking. Such last-minute preparation usually means that the speaker's notes are incomplete, unorganized, and illegible. The first step is to provide a specific time for preparing them; and the specific period of time should be ten or fifteen minutes more than the speaker thinks he will need. This will mean that even with making a last-minute change or two he will still be able to prepare a good set of notes.

Having set aside a specific period of time for preparing his notes, the speaker should next *choose proper materials for recording his notes.* The speaker should make certain that his notes are clear, distinct, and in sharp contrast to the page, and he should not be handicapped because he has used an inadequate instrument for recording. Consequently, when preparing his notes, he should avoid a hard lead pencil producing a very light line, a worn typewriter ribbon making indistinct impressions, or a pen with a faltering supply of ink. Obvious as this advice seems, it is, nonetheless, often ignored, and audiences suffer as a result.

The paper on which the notes are recorded should be heavy and stiff. If a thin, onion skin paper is used, the light will shine through from the back of the paper blurring what has been written, or the paper will tend to curl down over the speaker's hand and out of sight. On such paper, notes are apt to be less readable. The firmness and weight of heavy mimeograph paper is satisfactory for recording speaker's notes.

Not only should the paper be heavy and stiff, it should also be of adequate size so that you can write large and leave plenty of space between sentences. It would be better to record your notes on a large sheet (even 8½ by 11 inches) where you can read them easily, than to cram them on a few 3 by 5 inch note cards which you may have trouble reading.

The speaker should next decide to *use a particular system for recording the various kinds of information which will be included in his speaker's notes.* For example, all key sentences should be recorded in the same manner. Let us say that you underline in full each of these key sentences. Then, when you are speaking and you want to find a key sentence in your notes, you have only to look at those sections which are underlined in full. Or, you might decide that any quotations will be indented twenty spaces from the left hand side of the page and typed in capital letters. If you follow this system, you will only have to look at those specific parts of your notes whenever you want to use a quotation. The speaker will be able to use his notes with greater efficiency and advantage if he works out a definite system for recording material in them; and he will know precisely where to look when he needs to turn to his notes for help.

Next, the speaker should *be selective about the information which he includes in his speaker's notes.* If he crowds too much into his speaking notes, he will create serious delivery problems for himself. He will be tempted to read word for word rather than to use the notes to help him think; and he will have to scan a great deal of material in order to find his place in them. The speaker will be better off if he limits his speaking notes to items such as exact quotations, specific names or numbers, key sentences, transitional sentences, and items that he consistently forgets or omits in his delivery practices of the speech.

Furthermore, you will do well to avoid recording brief phrases, or sentences that are too vague or too general. Of course, people can speak from notes consisting of phrases and vague or general statements, but this will be true only so long as these phrases or statements immediately stimulate the proper sequence of associations in the speaker's mind. If you are experiencing difficulty in recalling the content of your speech, and the associations prompted by the phrases and sentences falter and then fail, these vague words will be of no further help to you. Since they are only phrases or vague or general statements, their only value is in triggering a series of associated ideas. If they fail in this function, they are able to give the speaker no further help. On the other hand, if a speaker would fill his notes with complete sentences which state in brief the points that are to follow or the area that is to be covered, these sentences can give the speaker guidance even though they do not start a rapid flow of related ideas.

For example, let us suppose that you plan to address a group who will canvass the members for pledges to the church budget, and that in your address you want to discuss pledge cards. In your speaking notes, if you intend to use phrases, you might jot down the phrase "Pledge Cards." Or, if you prefer to use sentences, you might write down "Pledge cards are important" or "People need pledge cards as a record." Now, if you follow the suggestion that you record your notes in the form of complete sentences which state the points that are to follow, you might write this sentence as a reminder: "The use of pledge cards will provide an important record, for the pledger and the canvasser, of the date and amount of the pledge." The sentence tells the speaker that he wants to stress that the cards provide a record of the date and amount of the pledge for both the canvasser and the person making the pledge. The phrase "Pledge Cards" would give the speaker none of this information. Likewise, the general statement "Pledge cards are important" fails to give the speaker this information. Even the statement "People need pledge cards as a record" is vague and fails to tell you which people or what kind of a record.

The few additional seconds it may take you to read the more complete sentence will be more than compensated for by the specific directions which you then have for proceeding with your speech. Such speaking notes ought to provide you with definite directions for proceeding with developing the thought pattern of your speech.

Sentences or ideas should not be divided with part of the sentence or idea on one page and the remainder on the next page. If you must turn the page in order to finish the sentence or idea, then find the place where the remainder of the sentence starts, you will have an awkward and perhaps even fearful experience. It is better to leave some blank space at the bottom of the page, and start the sentences or idea at the top of a new page where there is plenty of room to record the entire statement. Shifting from one page of speaker's notes to another is difficult enough, without trying to read through a broken sentence or idea. In order to deliver the sentence or idea smoothly when it is divided between pages, it is necessary to move from one page to the other with extraordinary speed and accuracy. No speaker should create this additional hazard for himself.

It is also necessary for the speaker to *number and arrange the pages of his notes in proper order.* The numbers should be bold and clear, and they should appear in the same place and in the same manner on each page. The failure to number the pages of your notes clearly and plainly, or the failure to check the order of your speaking notes before speaking, may mean that when you need to refer to them for a specific item, the page on which this item is located is not before you and cannot be quickly located. Consequently, there will be several moments of embarrassing hesitation while you try to find the specific sentence on the proper page.

The speaker's notes should also be adapted to the lectern or pulpit from which he will speak. Speaking notes should be recorded on sheets of paper which can be conveniently manipulated on a speaking stand of a size and shape similar to the stand which you will use. You should also allow for the area taken up by a microphone or by materials which are needed by the speaker who precedes or follows you. Again, if you are speaking at a banquet, there may be no convenient place to lay your notes; hence it might be well to record them on a 6 by 8 inch card which you could hold in your hand. However, if the speaker is continually adjusting or struggling with his notes because they were not properly prepared for the speaking situation, he may distract the audience's attention from his subject.

People who speak regularly in the same environment are apt to use the same kind of notes for every speaking occasion, including those outside of their regular speaking environment and regardless of the peculiarities of the new speaking situation. If a speaker persists in such a policy, he may find himself in a speaking situation where his notes are almost useless.

Let us suppose that a preacher always types his preaching notes on 6 by 8 inch pages and then places them in a loose-leaf notebook. Let us further suppose that these preaching notes have always seemed easy to work with when preaching in his church. One day, our hypothetical preacher is asked to present a meditation at the local radio station. When the day for the broadcast arrives, he appears at the radio station with his preaching notes carefully placed in his loose-leaf notebook. At the radio station he discovers that his notes are at an unfamiliar angle if the notebook lies on the table where the microphone is placed. Thus it is necessary for him to hold the notebook in his hand. Next, he discovers that when he turns the pages in his notebook, the director objects to the sound of rustling paper picked up by the microphone. Our preacher now decides to remove his notes from the notebook and hold them in his hand. Even this procedure is difficult, because it is not easy to turn each page in his hand without making paper noise over the mike. When our preacher finally delivers his sermon, he is tense and worried because his preaching notes have placed him at a real disadvantage. All of this trouble could have been avoided if he had adapted his notes to the broadcast situation; and adapting here would not have been difficult. He had only to type his notes on $8\frac{1}{2}$ by 11 inch sheets of heavy, soft paper, and double or triple space everything. He might even have typed everything in capital letters. Notes prepared in this manner would have been a help rather than a hindrance when he set out to broadcast.

Practicing with Notes

If a speaker has chosen to use notes for a particular speaking assignment, he should work with these notes during the practice delivery of his speech. It is important that he develop the feeling that it is the normal or ordinary thing to present the speech with notes. This feeling can be developed by attending to the use of his notes as well as to voice and gestures during the rehearsals of his speech.

First, *the speaker should develop the habit of looking up and making eye contact with his audience as he reads the last part of a phrase or sentence from his speaking notes.* You will notice that most speakers do exactly the opposite when reading from notes. That is, they look down at the sentence and get the first part of it in mind. Then they look up and speak this first part while attempting to look at the audience. As they near the end of the first part of the sentence, their eyes dart down to their notes and they finish delivering the sentence with their eyes glued to the page. This means that about 75 per cent of the time they are looking at their notes at the most important or most emphatic part of the sentence —the very time when they should be looking at their audience.

If the speaker will look down at the beginning of the sentence and then look up as the end of the sentence comes in view, he will be making eye contact with the audience at the most important time. You will discover that, once you habituate the pattern of looking up at the ends of sentences, it is actually easier to make eye contact as you conclude sentences, because you have the full one before you and you know which meaning should be stressed. It is also easier to look at the audience as you conclude a sentence, because there is then no hurry to get back to your notes. For one thing, you need to pause between sentences to suggest that you have finished one and are going to begin another. Second, it is easier to locate the beginning of a new sentence, with a period and a capital letter for clues, than it is to find your place in the middle of an old sentence. Under this system, you will look down to find your place in your notes at a time when you should pause anyway, and also at a time when you will be looking for the beginning of a new sentence. Moreover, your eye contact will be more meaningful because it will more frequently correspond to the points of emphasis or climax in the sentences you are delivering.

A speaker should practice the moving or turning of the pages of his speaking notes. The most obvious reason for such practice is that he needs to have the right page before him at the right time. One of the easiest things for a speaker to do is to talk his way off one page of notes and onto another without having turned or moved the page. When he looks to his notes, the wrong page is before him. If this happens to you when you are practicing your speech, you must determine when you should have turned the page in order to have the right one before you. After you have discovered when this page of your notes should be turned, then go through this section of your speech two or three times and practice turning this page at the correct time.

No speaker should think that the turning or moving of the pages of his speaking notes is a matter that will take care of itself; neither should he assume that this is a trivial or unimportant matter. If the wrong page of notes is before you, the frustrating search for your place will ruin a mood, destroy a climax, or wreck a train of thought. Three or four such interruptions can easily slow the momentum or prevent the climb of the speech. This means that the delivery of a speech can be seriously weakened and the effectiveness of your communication greatly impaired, because you have not practiced the effective use of your speaking notes.

Third, *the speaker should mark, in a special way, the parts of his notes that are hard to find while he is delivering his speech.* While practicing the delivery of your speech, if you find that there are some items in your notes that are consistently difficult to locate, it would be a good idea to mark these items in a special way. (This assumes that your difficulty is a result of the complex nature of this moment of delivery and not the result of a weakness in the notes themselves or of inadequate mental preparation. If your difficulty were due to a weakness in the notes themselves or to inadequate mental preparation, it would be preferable to strengthen your notes or your mental preparation.) We suggest that underlining such items in either red or blue pencil would be a good way to mark them. A contrasting color will help you locate them quickly.

A speaker must not ignore any item that consistently gives him trouble during the practice delivery of his speech. His ability to locate a particular item in his notes will not improve simply because he *wishes* it to do so. Neither will it be enough merely to mark these places. You should also practice using these marked sections of your notes while delivering your speech. If direct quotations are to be used, you should *present* these *quotations in full while practicing your speech.* These quotations should be included in your speaker's notes. Do not have them on separate sheets of paper or have each recorded in a different manner. Do not delay the securing of such quotations until the day on which you present your speech. If you intend to use quotations, you should locate them early enough so that they can be recorded in your speaker's notes and used in your first practice delivery of the speech.

If you wish to read directly from a book or periodical, this source should be carefully marked and used in each delivery practice. The problem is not only to have the book ready at the right time and open to the correct page, but also to find your place on the page quickly and accurately. While quoting directly from a book or periodical may add emphasis or prestige to what you are saying, it also complicates the delivery of your speech. You are apt to find that you do not have room for books and speaking notes and anything else that you may want to place on the speaker's stand. Also, you will find it somewhat more difficult to go from speaking notes, to a book, and then back to speaking notes, and so on. It is much easier to handle one kind of material than it is to handle several different kinds. Generally, a good rule to follow is: increase the number of delivery practices as you increase the different kinds of material you plan to use with your speaking notes.

Finally, *speakers should practice the use of their speaking notes on a speaker's stand or lectern similar in size and construction to the stand or lectern which they will use when actually delivering their speech.* Practicing with such a speaker's stand will help you work out the placement of your notes, the method of turning or moving your notes, and the viewing of your notes from various positions about the stand. If you practice in this way, when you use your notes in the actual speaking situation, you will be able to deliver your speech without any difficulties due to the handling of them. The ability to use your notes with certainty and skill will increase your speaking poise and directness. (If the speaker cannot ascertain the nature of the lectern he will use, he will not be able to follow this suggestion. However, he should be certain that his notes could be used on a variety of lecterns.)

Before summarizing these instructions for the use of speaker's notes, we should say a special word about the correct use of notes for preaching. Very often preaching includes strong elements of motivation and inspiration. The preacher will be freer to motivate and inspire if he is not fumbling around in his speaker's notes. Moreover, the congregation senses a stronger inspiration or motivation if the preacher is speaking directly to them. One is rarely inspired or motivated by a preacher who is speaking in a hesitating or uncertain manner and whose head is buried in his notes. If a preacher is using his notes incorrectly, he will likely destroy the suggestion that this is his personal faith or testimony. The sense of personal involvement and testimony by the preacher is more important to good preaching than it is to any other kind of public speaking. Personal involvement is vital to any kind of public speaking, but it is the *sine qua non* of good preaching. Preachers should realize that this not only means careful preparation of preaching notes; it also means several good delivery practices using them.

Now let us conclude by reviewing the suggestions which have been made for the preparation and use of speaking notes.

1. Use notes as an aid to thinking and not as a substitute for thinking.
2. Set aside a specific period of time for the preparation of these speaking notes.
3. Choose proper materials for recording your notes.
4. Use a particular system for recording the various kinds of information that will be included in your speaker's notes.
5. Do not divide sentences or ideas with part of the sentence or idea on one page and the remainder on the next page.
6. Be selective about the information you include in your speaking notes.
7. Adapt your notes to the lectern or pulpit from which you will speak.
8. Use these notes skillfully and without apology.
9. Develop the habit of looking up and making eye contact with your audience as you read the last part of phrases or sentences from speaking notes.
10. Mark the parts of your notes that are hard to find, while you are practicing the delivery of your speech.
11. Practice the moving or turning of the pages of your speaking notes.
12. Present quotations in full while practicing the delivery of your speech.
13. Practice the use of your speaking notes on a speaker's stand or lectern similar in size and construction to the stand or lectern which you will use when actually delivering the speech.

Speaking from a Manuscript

The problem of maintaining the quality of directness in speaking is accentuated when a speaker uses a full manuscript. Consequently, a manuscript which allows the speaker a maximum of freedom is highly desirable. The importance of a readable script, one that is properly spaced and clearly printed or written in large letters, can readily be seen by imagining yourself trying to speak from a manuscript which is prepared as this page is printed, and then turning to the reproduction of the manuscript used by Under Secretary of State Douglas Dillon when he addressed a commencement audience at Drew University. (See pages 66 and 67.) Note that the large type and ample spacing make the Dillon manuscript especially readable for one who is delivering a speech. The words that appear at the lower right-hand corner of the page are the first two words that appear at the top left of the next page, and they help the speaker continue a natural rate of delivery, even while turning a page of his manuscript. By making your manuscript as readable as possible, you improve your opportunity to speak in a natural and unrestrained manner.

Speaking without Notes or Manuscript

Finally, we urge all speakers to improve their ability to deliver their speeches without the aid of manuscript or notes. The freedom to meet your audience face to face and person to person, which is enjoyed when you are not bound to your manuscript or notes, presents such rich opportunities for communication that the achievement of it is worth a rigorous struggle. The best approach to obtaining such freedom is the practice of thinking the speech through by concentrating on becoming completely familiar with the development of thought; that is, the sequence of ideas. You can also improve your opportunity to think your speech through without the aid of manuscript or notes by constructing a speech with a definite and clear pattern of thought or idea development. The clearer and more definite

- 17 -

There should be no real conflict here. There is ample room for both cold self-interest and warm humanitarianism in our foreign policy, since it is designed to promote the safety and well-being of ourselves and of others at one and the same time. It is based on the

66

conviction that our future is inseparably

linked with the future of other peoples,

that we need them and that they need us.

We have been propelled into the

world through sheer necessity -- by war,

by the Communist threat to our free way

of life,

the pattern, the easier it will be for the speaker to follow it when thinking his speech through.

If you are now depending on a full manuscript for speaking, you may find the change to speaking without the aid of manuscript or notes easier if it is made gradually. Your first step might be to work from a complete sentence outline. Next, you might attempt speaking with a much briefer set of notes, and then finally without the aid of any notes. Also, you might begin these changes in short speaking situations that are simple in nature; then, after achieving success, attempt the changes in the more difficult situations.

Of course, it is true that the need for accuracy and thoroughness may merit the use of a manuscript. The desire to impart specific information or to achieve a certain finish and style might also make the use of a manuscript desirable; or the necessity of careful and precise statement might demand the use of a manuscript. While we recognize the values and often the necessity of the use of a manuscript, we also believe that there are many occasions when freedom from notes may increase the directness and persuasiveness of your delivery.

chapter 5

Clarifying
Your
Explanations

E very speaker soon discovers that an adequate presentation of his
subject frequently depends upon his ability to make an effective
explanation. For example, a church planning committee arguing in
favor of the erection of a new educational building may find that a
thorough explanation of the plans for the educational building is a
vital part of its argument. Or a speaker who is trying to persuade
people to contribute to the mission program of the church may discover that a careful explanation of the needs of the people who will
be ministered to is the most reliable way of motivating contributions. On other occasions, explanation may be the speaker's primary
task, as when a minister is explaining the basic beliefs of his denomination to a class preparing for church membership, or as when
a youth worker is explaining a folk game to a group of young
people.

The material in this chapter will help to make a purely informa-
tive speech more effective. In addition, it should be helpful in
making argumentative speeches more successful, for if people do
not understand your argument it will be less forceful. The importance of explanation for argumentative speaking is indicated in

the book *Argumentation and Debate* by McBurney, O'Neill, and Mills, where an entire chapter is devoted to the subject "Explanation as Argument." Moreover, a careful examination of the texts of speeches will show that explanation in one form or another is an integral part of almost any kind of public speaking. That is, almost every public speaking occasion will require the speaker to make use of the process of explanation. Indeed, one can hardly complete a simple conversation without indulging in some sort of explanation.

However, in spite of this frequent use of explanation, both in public speaking and in everyday conversation, it often remains a difficult and usually a poorly performed task. One reason is that we fail to understand how thorough an explanation is needed by our audience. When trying to direct a stranger to some particular location in our community, we often hastily refer to some landmark which is well known to us, but which is totally foreign to him. Similarly, speakers make poor explanations because they assume that the members of an audience are more familiar with a subject than they really are. Other speakers know their subject so well that they cannot visualize how complicated it will seem to novices.

Explanations are also inadequately prepared by speakers because they tire of the work of preparing them, often a tedious and laborious task. One must be precise in his choice of words, clear in his development of the explanation, and accurate in his descriptions. Such work is not as exciting as arousing the imagination or appealing to the emotions. Consequently, the speaker may neglect the preparation of the explanatory portions of his speech in favor of other parts which he enjoys more. Such neglect of the explanatory sections of the speech may occur even when these explanations are a part of arousing the imagination or of appealing to the emotions.

Since explanation is a task which is both necessary and neglected, most speakers will profit from improving their ability to prepare adequate ones. The following methods should help speakers develop this ability.

Definite Plan

The first and most important method to be used when preparing an explanation is the *placing of the various items of your explana-*

tion in a clear and definite plan of arrangement. Following a specific plan is important, because a successful explanation depends on the ease with which the listener can follow the steps in the explanation. If the listener can identify the plan of presentation which the speaker is using, and anticipate each step in the development of the plan, the listener should be able to follow the explanation quite readily. For example, if an usher were explaining the symbolism in the church chancel to some visitors, and he worked from left to right across the chancel in discussing the symbols, the visitors would be able to anticipate which symbol would be discussed next, and they would be able to follow the usher's explanation easily.

In the first chapter, eight plans for organizing the content of a speech were defined and illustrated. Five of these plans, *Familiar to Unfamiliar, Known to Unknown, Time, Space,* and *Cause-Effect,* are particularly useful for speeches of explanation. All the discussion in Chapter 1 pertaining to the development of these plans is especially relevant to explanatory speeches.

When preparing a speech of explanation, the speaker should follow his selected plan of arrangement explicitly and accurately. The stages in the plan should stand out like sign posts to guide the listeners through the explanation. If, when explaining, you use a specific plan of organization, you can avoid one of the most serious errors committed by speakers—the error of losing the listener during the presentation of the explanation.

To sum up, every speaker should organize his explanation in a clear, definite plan; and in presenting the explanation, he should follow this plan accurately and explicitly.

Careful Transitions

Second only to the use of a definite plan of presentation is *the construction of careful transitions for moving from section to section in the explanation.* If a speaker hopes to make a successful explanation, he must get the minds of the members of the audience to move with his mind so that they are all considering the same part of the explanation at the same time. If the minds of the audience are still considering step two of the explanation, while the speaker is presenting step three, the audience will miss part of the explanation. Carefully constructed transitions will help keep the minds of the audience moving with your mind, from step to step in the explanation. A GOOD TRANSITION SHOULD NOTIFY THE LISTENER THAT WE ARE MOVING ON, IDENTIFY THE UNIT TO WHICH WE ARE MOVING, AND TRY TO INTEREST THE HEARER IN THIS NEW UNIT.

Let us suppose that a Director of Religious Education is instructing some of her Sunday School teachers in the use of film strips. Let us further suppose that she has told them how to place the film strip in the projector and how to turn on the projector. Now she wishes to tell the teachers how to focus the projector. The transition from the explanation of how to turn on the projector to the explanation of how to focus the projector might be constructed as follows: "After we have turned on the projector, we must next turn our attention to the focusing process. At some time all of you have probably viewed a motion picture or a television picture which was difficult to watch because the focus was blurred or fuzzy. If we want these pictures to be easily viewed by the children in our classes, we must see that the projector is properly focused. Now if you will all look carefully at this lens, I shall explain how to adjust the focus of this projector."

Such careful preparation of transitions is vital to successful explanatory speaking, because the speaker must take the responsibility for directing the listener from unit to unit in his explanation. If the listener is left to follow the explanation as best he can, or as he is so inclined, there is little likelihood that he will fully understand the explanation which the speaker has presented.

Even if the speaker has carefully followed a particular plan of organization, he can lose his audience during a transition from one phase of the explanation to another. Therefore, the speaker should be certain that each transition notifies the listener to move on, identifies the unit to which the listener should move, and interests the listener in the new unit.

Defining Terms

A speaker may also weaken an explanation by using words which are unknown to the audience. If the listeners do not recognize the terms being used by the speaker, they will become confused during the explanation. Moreover, they are apt to be discouraged by these unknown words and not try to comprehend the explanation.

If a minister of music were explaining an order of worship to a youth choir and used the words Gloria Patri and Doxology without first defining them, he might confuse some of the youths who would not know what music these words were intended to identify. Or, if a pastor were trying to explain the composition of a prayer and used the words Adoration, Confession, and Petition, without defining them, there is every chance that he would discourage and even confuse his hearers. In all probability, these words would not have the same meaning for many of his listeners as they would have for him. Therefore, *a speaker should carefully define every important term which he intends to use in his explanation.*

When preparing an explanation, it is always safer to identify too many terms, rather than too few. An explanation is less apt to fail because the listeners have heard more terms defined than necessary, than it is because some terms which the hearers needed to have defined were not.

Moreover, words should not be defined in just a bookish or dictionary fashion. Words should be defined so that they can be quickly understood and easily used. Only the meaning of the word pertinent to the explanation should be considered. An enumeration of several possible meanings of a word might set up a distraction in the mind of the listener; and, as a result, it would actually compete with the explanation itself for the listener's attention. Instead of following the explanation, the listener might become involved in a personal evaluation of the various definitions.

The more familiar the speaker becomes with a subject, the more likely he is to fail to identify the words needed to be defined when explaining a subject to an audience. Speakers must remember that it is the understanding the audience has of the subject which should dictate the words to be defined. It is also important that when a speaker does define words, he use a vocabulary which will be understood by the people to whom he is speaking. Referring again to the pastor who wants to explain the composition of a prayer—if this pastor decided to define the word "petition," he might say something like this: "By petition I mean those supplications which we make to God in behalf of ourselves and others." It is quite possible that such a definition would leave the hearer no better informed than he was before. In this case the pastor might better say, "By petition I mean those requests which we make of God for His help."

In summary, when making an explanation, speakers should define all key words, which may not be understood by the audience; and these words should be defined in a way that is relevant to the explanation and in a manner that is clear and understandable.

Comparisons

Another important way of preparing a meaningful explanation is to *make use of comparisons*. If the matter you are trying to explain can be compared to something which your audience already knows and perhaps has experienced, your audience will be able to comprehend your explanation more readily. Such a comparison may help your audience visualize that which you are explaining, or the comparison may suggest a pattern which is to be followed.

If a director of religious education were explaining the arrangement of class periods in a Daily Vacation Bible School to a group of potential teachers, the director might compare the class schedule of the Bible School to the class schedule at the nearby grade school. She might begin her explanation by saying, "The schedule of the Vacation Bible School will be similar to the morning schedule of the grade school. The children will attend Bible School from nine o'clock in the morning to twelve noon. They will have two classes, recess, and then two more classes. The class sessions will be forty minutes in length, and the recess period will be twenty minutes. Since we shall be following very nearly the same system as the public schools, our students should adjust readily to our schedule."

By comparing the Vacation Bible School schedule to the class schedule of the public school, the director of religious education helps her prospective teachers visualize this schedule in terms of one they already know.

Or a director of the annual financial campaign to raise funds for the church budget might compare the financial campaign to a recent fund-raising campaign for the Community Chest. He might point out that just as a budget was prepared, the needs of the community publicized, and personal requests made for contributions to the Community Chest campaign, so in the church financial drive, these same steps would be followed; that is, a budget would be prepared, the needs of the church publicized, and a personal solicitation for pledges conducted.

Although comparisons are helpful in adding clarity to an explanation, they should not be used carelessly or indiscriminately. Only the part of the comparison precisely relevant to the point being explained should be discussed. Otherwise, the listeners may become more interested in the comparison than in the matter being explained; and it is important that the attention of the listener be focused on that which is being explained.

Speakers should avoid using so many comparisons that the hearers are burdened with the necessity of remembering a great number of them. Too many comparisons can add to the work of trying to understand an explanation rather than making the understanding of the explanation easier. It is also essential that the speaker analyze any comparison which is used, to be certain that the situations are really comparable. If the speaker says that the Beatitudes are like the Ten Commandments when, in fact, they are not like one another at all, the audience will be confused; and they will also think that the speaker does not really understand that which he is attempting to explain. (Of course, when a speaker confuses his hearers or places doubts in their minds about his own understanding of his subject, he places his explanation in real jeopardy.)

Contrasts

Another way of aiding the listener, in his comprehension of a speaker's explanation, is for the speaker to *explain the matter by contrasting it with what it is not.* This method, when used by Jesus, pointed out that fulfilling the command to love your neighbor was not passing a man by who had been beaten and robbed, nor was righteousness thanking God that we were not like other men.

A contemporary preacher might try to explain what loving your neighbor means by stating that it does not mean merely tolerating your neighbor. Love, he might say, does not recognize rights and privileges because of a grudging sense of duty. Love does not tolerate a neighbor, it actively "wills the good" for a neighbor.[1]

Or a layman pleading for the inclusion of an item in a church budget might say, "We cannot administer a church like a business which has the making of a profit as its primary objective. We must administer a church as we administer our home affairs, where the providing of a place where love and understanding may grow is our first aim."

Explaining through contrast has the advantage of adding something interesting or striking to your explanation, and, consequently, the advantage of calling the listener's attention back to your explanation. Moreover, explaining by contrast may help the listener understand the limitations that you want to stake out, or the lines that you want to draw. As a result, your listener may have a more definite or concrete understanding of that which you are trying to explain.

However, the speaker should be certain, when he uses this method, that he really has a true contrast. A preacher might say to his congregation that a worshipful participation in the Responsive Reading in the worship service is not simply reading in unison and accurately pronouncing the words. Such a statement would not be an accurate use of the method of contrast, because a congregation might be participating in the Responsive Reading in a worshipful way, and also be reading in unison and accurately pronouncing the words.

Or a Sunday School teacher who said to her class, "Now we don't want to be noisy like those Primary Children who don't show any respect for God's house," could also be using contrast incorrectly, because the noise might be a result of some activity designed to express reverence for God and the place where he is worshiped.

When a speaker inadvertently uses a false contrast in an attempt to strengthen an explanation, he will confuse or even irritate his audience, and consequently arouse some hostility toward his entire explanation.

One other danger to which the use of contrasts may lead, is spending most of your time explaining what something is not. The

---

[1] Soren Kierkegaard, *Purity of Heart* (New York: Harper & Brothers, 1948), p. 54.

preacher, mentioned earlier, might spend so much time pointing out that loving a neighbor is not tolerating a neighbor, being polite to a neighbor, and so forth, that he has too little time left to explain what loving a neighbor really is. In the parable of the Good Samaritan, you remember that Jesus spends the larger portion of the time explaining what the Samaritan does for the man who has been beaten and robbed.[2]

In summary, the speaker can make an explanation more interesting and definite by using the method of contrast, but the speaker should be certain that he is using a true contrast and that he does not rely on contrasts only.

Visual Aids

"Most people are visual minded; they more easily grasp and better remember what they see than what they hear." [3] The preceding statement suggests the great importance which visual aids have for the effective presentation of an explanation. Any method which enables the audience to grasp and remember more readily what is to be explained is very nearly indispensable.

By and large, speakers need to *develop a greater appreciation for the effectiveness of visual aids and a keener sensitivity of what sort of visual aids may be used.* In many churches, the Director of Religious Education will be the only person who has an adequate appreciation of visual aids; and unfortunately, even the Director of Religious Education may not be adept at using these aids in ordinary public speaking situations. The majority of speakers could markedly improve their efforts at explanation by making more use of visual aids.

One source of visual aids, frequently ignored by the preacher, is the religious symbols in his own church sanctuary. The number and quality of symbols vary greatly from church to church, but a careful examination of almost any place of worship will reveal some sym-

---

2 *The Holy Bible,* Revised Standard Version (New York: Thomas Nelson & Sons, 1952), Luke 10:29-37.

3 H. L. Hollingworth, *The Psychology of The Audience* (New York: American Book Company, 1935), p. 106.

bols which have a rich inheritance of religious meaning.[4] At an appropriate point in his sermon, a pastor can direct the attention of the congregation to one of these symbols in his church and use this symbol as a visual aid to help clarify an explanation. While preaching on the Holy Trinity, the pastor might direct the attention of the congregation to a trefoil or a triangle in the sanctuary, and use such a symbol as an aid to further his explanation of the three-in-oneness of the Trinity.

Sunday School teachers who teach children's classes employ a number of visual aids in their teaching, but teachers of adult classes frequently overlook the opportunity to use them. A map of the Mediterranean World would be most helpful, for example, in explaining the nature and extent of Paul's missionary journeys. Again, a "Chart of the English Bible," [5] prepared by the American Bible Society, would be helpful in explaining how our present version of the Bible has been developed. This chart would help the student learn each contribution to the Bible and its date, and also learn the relationship of one contribution to another.

Visual aids could be used with great benefit by laymen who have leadership responsibilities in the church. A chairman of a religious census committee might use an enlarged blackboard drawing of a visitation or census card to assist him in explaining how the card is to be used by the census takers. Also, the president of a church usher's club might use a diagram or floor plan of the church sanctuary to explain how the ushers are to perform their tasks of seating the congregation and collecting the morning offering. Or, a chairwoman of a church supper might use a diagram to explain how the tables will be arranged and how the workers will proceed down the aisles in the serving of the dinner.

The preceding illustrations list a few of the many types of visual aids which might be used and the variety of tasks of explanation in which visual aids might be employed. Every church worker should make it his business to become acquainted with the visual aids available to him, and he should cultivate a keen appreciation for their effective use.

---

[4] Thomas Albert Stafford, *Christian Symbolism* (Nashville, Tenn.: Abingdon Press, 1942), p. 24.

[5] "Chart of the English Bible," American Bible Society, New York 22, N. Y.

When using visual aids, every speaker should strive to observe the following rules. First, control the use of the visual aid. Do not allow it to distract your listeners either before or after it is used for your explanation. You should so control your presentation of the visual aid and the attention of the audience, that the audience is attending to the visual aid only while you are using it for your explanation. If you fail to exercise such control over the use of the visual aid and over the behavior of your audience, the visual aid may actually detract from the total effectiveness of your explanation.

Second, test the visual aid in the actual speaking situation, or in a situation similar to it, to make certain that the aid can be easily and clearly seen by all members of the audience. Frequently speakers fail to make such a test of their visual aids, and as a result, they offend and discourage their audiences. Their hearers are frustrated by being encouraged to observe and study a diagram or a picture which they cannot clearly or easily see. If you do not have the opportunity to test the viewability of your visual aids, try to check their adequacy with your audience as you present them.

Third, do not select or prepare visual aids which include items not relevant to, or not necessary for, your explanation. Do not show a group a complete building plan if you intend to explain only one section of the plan. Neither show an audience a map of an entire city if your explanation pertains to only one section of the city. A visual aid containing extraneous items brings competing visual stimuli to the attention of your audience, and may divert their attention from the subject which is being explained. The extra time required to select or prepare a visual aid, appropriate to the particular explanation, will be well spent, because such a visual aid will reinforce the explanation rather than steal attention from it.

Fourth, practice the delivery of your speech, using your visual aids so that you achieve some skill in a co-ordinated presentation of the visual aid and the oral explanation. Audiences are often confused and discouraged by visual aids which do not function, or which are misplaced, or which are presented in the wrong order. A clumsy, floundering presentation of visual aids may so interrupt and delay the explanation that the presentation of the visual aids hinders the audience from understanding the explanation.

Visual aids, then, enable the audience to grasp the explanation more readily and to remember the explanation better. Consequently, speakers should discover what visual aids are available, and cultivate an appreciation for opportunities to use them in presenting explanations. In using visual aids, speakers should observe the following rules:

1. Control the use of the visual aid.
2. Do not use visual aids which contain items not relevant to, or not necessary for your explanation.
3. Test the visual aid in the actual speaking situation.
4. Practice the delivery of your speech using your visual aids.

Rounding Out the Explanation

A general comment which can be made about the majority of explanations given by speakers is that these explanations are incomplete. More often than not, members of the audience would like to say to a speaker, "Won't you please finish this part of your explanation?" Unfortunately, few speakers have schooled themselves in hearing their explanations as others hear them. Consequently, audiences are often left puzzling over unfinished points in an explanation.

Whenever you are preparing an explanation, you should *go through your explanation at least once for the purpose of rounding out or completing each step.* Then, go through your explanation at least once more to see if it is complete as a whole. When trying to round out his explanation, the speaker should strive to replace vague words with concrete words, to complete the development of partially developed units, and to strengthen implied matter with explicit statement.

Let us assume that you have been given the responsibility of explaining to the junior choir their role in next Sunday's worship service, and that you have concluded your explanation with these words: "And after the benediction you will sing your threefold Amen." The part of your explanation hinging on the four words "And after the benediction" is vague and incomplete, and relies too heavily on what is implied. The word "after" is vague because the choir will not know just how long "after" the benediction, and they may be taken by surprise and not sing well. Moreover, the explanation is incomplete because it does not tell them where they shall be when they sing—in the choir loft or in the narthex. Also, it is implied that the pastor will pronounce the benediction but this is not stated specifically.

Now let us improve the explanation by rounding it out. "We shall remain in the choir loft through the concluding hymn and the benediction. Immediately following the benediction, which will be given by our pastor concluding with the words 'in the name of the Father, the Son, and the Holy Spirit,' we shall be given a chord by the organist. On the chord we shall all take a deep breath. Then at the organist's signal, we shall sing our threefold Amen."

For the most effective work in rounding out an explanation, the speaker should completely prepare his explanation, lay it aside for a day or two, and then come back to it with a fresh and more critical point of view. If the speaker tries to round out the explanation at the same session at which he has chosen a plan of organization, worked out transitions, developed some comparisons, and so forth, he will discover that familiarity will dull his awareness of the vague, the incomplete, and the implied. Even if his sensitivity about these matters is not dulled, he may feel tired of his task and have little enthusiasm for trying to correct them. Therefore, the speaker should complete the explanation at an early date so that it can be put aside for a short time while he regains some objectivity toward what he has prepared.

In summary then, every speaker should review his explanation for the purpose of rounding it out by replacing vague words with concrete ones, developing partially developed units, and strengthening implied matter with explicit statement. This rounding out of the explanation can best be done after it has been prepared and put aside for awhile, so that the speaker can review it in a fresh and objective manner.

Spaced Repetitions

"Repetition is most effective when the several presentations are separated by intervals of time." [6] This statement, from Jersild's study

---

[6] A. T. Jersild, "The Modes of Emphasis in Public Speaking," *Journal of Applied Psychology,* December 1928.

of "The Modes of Emphasis in Public Speaking," suggests that repetition is most effective when it appears at spaced intervals in the speech. Such information is useful to the speaker who is preparing an explanation, because there will be key points which he particularly wants his audience to remember. One of the most effective ways for fixing such key points in the minds of the audience is by *spacing three or four repetitions of these points at regular intervals in the speech.*

A president of the youth group of the church who is explaining the function of the youth group to the Official Board of the church might want to impress the board with three main points in his explanation:

1. The youth group aims to bring young people into active participation in the life of the church;
2. The youth group aims to help the young people mature spiritually;
3. The youth group aims to encourage young people to be loyal to Jesus Christ.

The youth group president might decide to impress these key points of his explanation upon the minds of the board by two spaced repetitions in his presentation. With this purpose in mind, he introduces his talk by saying, "Tonight I want to talk to you about the three aims of our youth group, namely, ..." Then, during the body of the speech, he uses each of these aims as a major division. Finally, he concludes with an appeal to the official board to support the youth program of the church, and closes with these words: "Remember, when you support our program, you are assisting us in bringing young people into the active life of the church, helping young people mature spiritually, and encouraging young people to be loyal to Jesus Christ." Such a presentation puts the aims of this youth group before the official board three times, and the repetitions add emphasis to the first statement of these aims.

Incidentally, this illustration also demonstrates how explanation can be used to advance an argument. Notice that the conclusion presents three good effects which are produced (caused) by the Board's support of a youth group in the church.

Summary

When a speaker presents an explanation, his immediate goal is to have the audience clearly and accurately understand what he is explaining. Consequently, the speaker needs to use a method of preparation which will provide him with a clear and understandable speech. The longer the speaker works at the business of explaining, the more certain he will become that good explanations are not the product of accident or chance; they are the result of a constant practicing and perfecting of effective methods. After a speaker has perfected good methods of preparing explanations, he will discover that this work has a salutary effect on the remainder of his speaking. This is true, because clarity and understandability are essential qualities of any kind of speaking, and focusing on these matters for the purpose of preparing explanations will sharpen one's appreciation for them in all speechmaking.

Speakers can clarify their explanations if they will diligently follow these suggestions:

1. Place the items of your explanation in a clear and definite plan of arrangement.
2. Construct careful transitions for moving from section to section in the explanation.
3. Carefully define every important term which you wish to use in your explanation.
4. Use comparisons which are relevant to your explanation.
5. Explain by contrasting the matter with what it is not.
6. Develop a greater appreciation for the effectiveness of visual aids and a keener sensitivity for the sort of visual aids which may be used.
7. Go through your explanation at least once for the purpose of rounding out or completing each step of the explanation.
8. Space three or four repetitions of your key points at regular intervals through your speech.

chapter 6

Making
Your
Speech
Interesting

One of the most dangerous enemies of good speaking is "listening fatigue." When the listener no longer pays attention to the speaker involuntarily because he is bored by the speaker's manner of delivery or because he is weary of the speaker's subject, listening fatigue is setting in. Listening fatigue is dangerous not only because it interferes with the receptivity of a particular listener, but also because it is contagious and can spread rapidly through the audience. Listening fatigue is a threat to the speaker, for when he notices signs of such fatigue, he is apt to lose confidence and deliver his speech less effectively. This means that one listener who is showing signs of listening fatigue can initiate two sets of circular responses which in turn can destroy the rapport between the speaker and his hearers.

Another dangerous enemy to good speaking is "speaking fatigue." Oftentimes, from halfway to two-thirds of the way through the speech we will notice that a speaker loses his drive or enthusiasm.

One significant cause of such loss is a weariness with the subject or a
tiring of the task of presenting the speech. Speaking fatigue can
also initiate a circular fatigue response. The speaker's loss of enthusiasm soon results in loss of listener enthusiasm, which in turn
can dampen the speaker's enthusiasm even more.

This means, then, that fatigue beginning with either the speaker
or the listener is a real threat to good speaking. Regardless of where
signs of fatigue first appear, they are so contagious that they can
quickly permeate the total speaking situation and produce harmful
effects in both the speaker and in the members of the audience.

An effective way to prevent listening and speaking fatigue is to
make the speech interesting. Unfortunately, many speakers do not
realize that by employing particular methods, speeches can be made
interesting. Such speakers think that the only way to produce an
interesting speech is to have the good fortune to stumble on to an
interesting subject or audience or situation. This viewpoint means
that if we have the bad fortune to be assigned an uninteresting subject, audience, or situation there is nothing to do but bore the audience for the allotted period of time.

However, this is not the case at all. In fact, a speech on almost any
subject can be made interesting by skillful use of the methods which

will be presented in the remainder of this chapter. The more likely it is that the audience will be fatigued, the more essential it is to employ these methods. If the audience is to assemble after having done a hard day's work, or if you are appearing on a program in which several speakers are preceding you, it is safe to assume that listening fatigue will be a present trouble, and it would benefit you greatly to use the following methods extensively throughout your speech.

These methods for making a speech interesting are derived from psychological studies pertaining to factors which gain or command attention. Before turning to these methods, we wish to direct your attention to the psychological principles on which they are based. Each of these methods utilizes one or more of the following principles.

1. An intense stimulus is more likely to attract attention than a mild stimulus.
2. A novel or new stimulus will command more attention than a familiar or old stimulus.[1]
3. A change (movement) in stimulus will secure attention more readily than a continuation of the same stimulus.[2]
4. A person's own interests predispose him toward one stimulus and away from another stimulus.[3]

You will have a greater appreciation for the value of these interest methods if, as you study them, you observe how they can be used to intensify a stimulus, to provide a novel or new stimulus, to provide a change in stimulus, or to strike the interests of the individual listeners. Narration, humor, or any of the other methods are not ends in themselves, but rather, ways of employing the psychological principles cited above to make stronger demands upon the attention of the audience and thereby produce a speech which has a high interest value.

----

[1] E. G. Boring, H. S. Langfeld, and H. P. Weld, *Foundations of Psychology* (New York: John Wiley & Sons, Inc., 1948), pp. 218-220.

[2] Harry A. Overstreet, *Influencing Human Behavior* (New York: The People's Institute Publishing Company, Inc., 1925), p. 12.

[3] Floyd L. Ruch, *Psychology and Life* (New York: Scott Foresman and Company, 1941), p. 164.

Narration

One way to make your speech interesting is to present your material in story form. The listener likes a story because of the movement of the plot, the appearance of the characters, the recognition of the setting, and the feeling of a mood. These, then, are *the key elements of narration—plot, characters, setting, and mood.* When narration is used in public speaking, these elements should be developed with precision, clarity, and co-ordination. They should blend together so easily that they contribute naturally to the total impression which the story makes on the mind of the listener.

It is important that the plot be developed swiftly and accurately. As long as the plot keeps moving, it will carry the attention of the listener with it. If, however, the speaker allows the plot to stand still while he develops character, setting, or mood, the interest of the listener is apt to lag. Therefore, information concerned with character, setting, or mood should be presented in such a way as to advance the plot. Speakers seriously endanger a story when they omit a crucial item in the development of the plot and then interrupt the story in order to insert it. Such an interruption spoils the mood of the story, lowers our respect for the speaker, and confuses the plot.

It is also important to realize that *the story must be presented for its own merit without labored effort to emphasize the point or to explain the relation of the story to the ideas in the speech.* While introducing the story or in "following through" after the story has been presented, such remarks may be in order. However, if these are made during the actual telling of the story, they will delay and distort it to the extent that the narrative will be robbed of its charm and forcefulness.

Emphasis of the point or the relation of the narrative to the thought pattern of the speech is done best when it appears as an integral part of the plot. If such explanation or emphasis is a natural part of the characters, plot, mood, and setting of the story, your point will be made in a most disarming and effective manner. In fact, if this can be done, the entire speech may be presented in the form of a story. An illustration of the use of narration for the entire speech is the children's sermon that follows.

Loving Our Neighbor

As the back door slammed, John called out, "Hey, Mom, how about some milk and cookies?"

"My goodness," said Mother, "is school over already? All right, John, I'll be right there."

As John sat down at the kitchen table, Mother came in and got the milk out of the refrigerator. "What did you do at school today, John?"

"Oh," said John, "we had fun this afternoon. We had a spelldown. Teacher made me and Susan captains. We chose up sides, and then we all stood up. Teacher gave us words to spell; and if we missed, we had to sit down. My side stood up the longest so we won."

"Well," said Mother, "that does sound like fun."

"Yeah, it was," said John, "except for one thing."

"Oh, what was that?"

"Well, you know that kid that lives down the street—Tim—the one that doesn't talk so good—the one they say stutters? Well, he wanted to be on my team, but I didn't pick him. I knew he wouldn't be any good in a spelldown."

"Why John, I don't think that was very nice."

"Aw, Mom, how could we win a spelldown with a kid on our side who can't even talk right?"

"Just the same, John, I don't think it was very nice. After all, Tim is your neighbor."

"Well, Mom, thanks for the cookies. I got to be going now."

"Now where are you going, John?"

"You know those big kids that live on the corner? Well, they're going to play ball over in the park, and I want to get in the game."

"All right, but you'll have to change your clothes first."

"Aw, Mom, do I have to?"

"Yes, you have to. If you played ball in those clothes, you wouldn't be able to wear them to school again."

"Okay," said John as he ran to his bedroom to change his clothes.

Mother had just put the cookies away when she heard the front door slam, and she knew that John was on his way to the park. It seemed that she had hardly had time to set the table when the front door slammed again and she called out, "Is that you, John?"

"Yeah."

"Did you forget something?"

"No."

"Is the ball game over already?"

"No."

"Well, what are you doing home so soon?"

"Oh, I just decided that I didn't want to play with those guys."

At that answer Mother came into the living room and said, "Now, John, what really happened?"

"Aw, you know that big kid that lives on the corner—that kid named Paul. Well he told the other guys that I can't hit very good so they wouldn't let me play."

"That's too bad," said Mother.

"Sure is, I could hit just as good as the rest of them if they'd only give me a chance . . . almost as good anyway."

"John," said Mother, "doesn't this remind you of something?"

"No. . . ."

"Something that happened this afternoon?"

"No, I can't think of anything."

"Well, doesn't this remind you of what happened at school when you didn't choose Tim to be on your team. Don't you suppose he felt just about like you do?"

"Aw, Mom, that was different. This is baseball!"

"Is it really so different, John? Don't you suppose Tim wanted to spell just as much as you want to play baseball?"

"Well . . . I suppose so."

"John, supper won't be ready for an hour yet. You're not going to sit around the house till then are you?"

"No . . . I guess not. . . . Say, maybe Tim would like to play catch. . . . Think I'll ask him."

"I think that would be very nice," said Mother. "Why don't you?"

The living room door slammed again, and soon Mother heard John shouting "Hey Tim, c'mon over. Let's play catch."

"Well," said Mother as she walked to the kitchen, "maybe my John has learned something about loving his neighbor today."

In this children's sermon the plot is dominant, and it unfolds quite rapidly. While the setting is suggested in the narrative, it is really incidental to the plot. Both the characters and the mood are suggested entirely through the dialogue. No undue emphasis is placed on the teaching point, and the point is a natural part of the story.

Narrative, then, is an important means of adding interest to a speech. When employing narration, the speaker should observe the following rules:

1. Check your story for adequate development of plot, characters, setting, and mood.
2. Develop the plot swiftly and accurately.
3. Present the story for its own merit, and do not interrupt it with efforts to relate it to your speech.
4. Make the point relating the narrative to the speech an integral part of the narrative.

You can cultivate an appreciation for the use of narration by reading the parables of Jesus. While these narratives are extremely brief, they are also of exceptionally high quality. If you will read and reread these parables until you have discovered and are familiar with every artistic touch, you will have unique examples to follow for your own use of narration. "Any careful appraisal of the parables of Jesus must recognize Him as an unrivalled teller of stories." [4]

Startling the Audience

Another method of making material interesting is the emphasizing of its startling aspects. *When using the startling, the speaker sharpens general statements until they cut like a two-edged sword.* If the speaker were to use the startling, he would not say that divorce is increasing at an alarming rate; he would say that during this past year one out of every three (hypothetical figure) marriages ended in the divorce courts. This suggestion indicates that *one way of sharpening a statement to make it startling is to cite particular numbers.* A second illustration of the use of this method is found in a recent statement of the problem of feeding the world's growing population. The problem was stated in these words, "an extra 100,000 people turn out for dinner every day."

Again, if a speaker were addressing a temperance meeting, instead of saying that alcoholism is now threatening the youth of our nation, he might quote from a retail liquor publication that advocates the production of a beer for babies in order that the taste for beer and the habit of drinking it might be developed at the earliest possible age.[5] *In this case the general statement would be given a cutting edge by citing a specific, extreme incident.*

A speaker may also employ the startling by taking a totally unexpected position. For example, a pacifist speaking to an American Legion Convention might say, "I advocate that we wage a ruthless war every three years and that we make this war as devastating and

---

4 George A. Buttrick, *The Parables of Jesus* (New York: Harper & Brothers, 1928), p. xvii.

5 "News and Quotes," *The Illinois Temperance League News,* May 1956.

deadly as we possibly can. The only way that the ability to retaliate can prevent a world war is to demonstrate this ability frequently and savagely so that the rest of the world will really be afraid to fight us." It may be assumed that the pacifist would go on to show that it would be impossible to follow such a plan, and therefore that it is really unwise to continue to build our retaliatory potential. However, if a pacifist actually started an address with such a proposal, it seems fair to say that he would startle his audience.

Thus, when the speaker wishes to make use of the startling to interest his audience, he should sharpen his statements by using precise figures, citing specific incidents, or taking an unpredicted position or point of view.

It is true that the startling cannot ordinarily be used in such large proportions as can narration. Whereas narration might be a part of the "main course," the startling is used more as "a seasoning" of the items that constitute the "main course."

Making Them Laugh

A third interest method which we shall consider is the use of humor. Humor is important as an interest method because it is almost irresistible. Let someone say, "I heard a really funny story the other day," and immediately we pay attention. We listen without even trying to listen. Even more important is the effect humor has on the audience. Laughter can actually send a tired audience home rested and refreshed. Humor is excellent treatment for a fatigued audience.

Fortunately it is not difficult to learn to use humor. The first steps are to increase your awareness of the humorous and your enjoyment of sharing the humorous with others. Many speakers who are just learning to use humor make the mistake of trying to borrow some other person's humor. They look in joke books or collect stories from their friends, and proceed to try to entertain their audience by telling jokes that others thought were funny. *The best way to put humor across is to share with the audience that which is really humorous to you.*

Although we may not be gifted at satire or play on words, most of us can retell, in an entertaining manner, a humorous life situation in which we have participated or which we have observed. *Taking a life experience, distorting or exaggerating it, and then showing us its funny side is a good way to begin using humor.*

For example, a man who had recently become a father could use the experience of waiting for his baby to arrive to provide humor for a speech. He might begin by saying that he entered the waiting room with the hope that his baby would arrive quickly, only to have one of the men tell him to relax because this was the third time that he had been to the hospital and his baby had not arrived yet. He had just received the idea that his baby might not arrive at all when a young mother walked in and started bragging about her twins. Now added to the suggestion that his baby might not come today was the terrifying idea that the baby might come twice in the form of twins, and he began to worry about where they would get two cribs, two baby buggies, and two of a hundred other things. While the young mother was showing pictures of her twins, two prospective grandparents walked in and began to tell the young fathers about all the work they could look forward to—changing diapers, fixing formulas, getting up in the night, buying all the extra food, clothing, and nursery equipment, and several other interesting tasks. With a bit of exaggeration and distortion, the speaker could give an audience several laughs at the expense of his terrified hours in the hospital waiting room when he was frightened to death by well-meaning companions. This is one of the innumerable life situations which could be used for humorous purposes.

However, the speech may not be of sufficient length to admit the development of life situation humor; in this case the telling of a joke, a play on words, or the use of understatement or overstatement may be more useful to the speaker.

The joke is usually characterized by the laugh line—by a single event or comment which casts the whole situation in a hilarious light. The whole joke must be told so as to create the mood for, and to build to, the laugh line. Then the laugh line must be presented cleanly and sharply. If the director of music were speaking to a church group and wanted to use humor for interest purposes, he might tell the following joke. "They laughed at me when I sat down to play the piano at the conference on church music. You see, they knew the bench wasn't there." Now this is only the skeleton of the joke. By making the situation seem more dignified and formal, the picture of someone attempting to sit down and falling flat before such a group might be made to seem even funnier. However, the line that makes the whole situation seem humorous—the laugh line —is the one that tells us that there was no piano bench on which to sit, and this is the line that must be immediately and clearly understood by the listeners.

A play on words is the using of a word that obviously means one thing to convey a second, unexpected meaning or a "double" meaning. This form of humor is particularly useful for making a speech interesting because it can be developed in a phrase or sentence. For example, a pastor speaking to the church treasurers about keeping church records might say, "Now you may find that keeping these records is like filling out your income tax forms. It's apt to be a bit taxing." Or a member of a committee on church property who was trying to persuade his committee to recommend that the church belfry be screened in, might say, "We don't want people to say that the Methodists have bats in their belfry."

In the first instance it is the single word "taxing" on which the play occurs, and in the second instance it is the phrase "bats in their belfry." When using this type of humor, it is essential that the audience be able to recognize instantly the "double meaning" or the play on words. If the phrase "bats in their belfry" is a colloquial expression, the speaker would want to make certain that his listeners commonly use this phrase to indicate that people are extremely confused in their thinking.

Understatement consists of reporting the situation as far less than it really is—of minimizing the situation to the point of the ridiculous. If the leader of the church ushers were discussing plans for seating the congregation on Easter Sunday morning, he might make use of understatement by saying, "We expect a slight increase in church attendance on Easter Sunday." Or if the chairwoman of a church dinner were suggesting wearing apparel, she might use understatement in describing the kind of shoes to wear by saying to the ladies, "I'd advise that you do not wear your highest heels." This sort of humor is said to be more typically British, but it is a welcome contrast to the American reliance on overstatement or exaggeration.

Overstatement means describing funny situations in such an exaggerated manner that they become comical. This type of humor is associated with the stories told by fishermen about "the one that got away" and by members of the various "Liars Clubs" throughout the United States. Mark Twain has provided us with many examples of humor through overstatement and exaggeration. One instance is this paragraph from *Roughing It.*

> On the inquest it was shown that Buck Fanshaw, in the delirium of a wasting typhoid fever, had taken arsenic, shot himself through the body, cut his throat, and jumped out of a four-storey window and broken his neck—and after due deliberation, the jury, sad and tearful, but with intelligence unblinded by its sorrow, brought a verdict of death 'by the visitation of God.' What could the world do without juries? [6]

Let us suppose that the church secretary were speaking to the members of the church staff and that she wanted to impress them with the necessity of giving her not only the title and number of the hymn which was to be used but also the number of the tune to which the hymn was to be sung. Let us also suppose that she planned to get the group interested in this portion of her talk by the use of humor. Choosing to use the method of overstatement, she prepared the following remarks:

> Now I would like to illustrate just how important it is to list in the order of worship the number of the tune as well as the number and the title of the hymn.
>
> I heard of a church where a guest preacher gave the secretary just the title of the processional hymn which was "All hail the power of Jesus' name." The hymnal for that particular church has this hymn printed three times to three different tunes. Now the congregation was accustomed to singing the first tune. However, the choir director preferred the third tune, and so he instructed the choir to sing the third tune. The substitute organist knew that they were not using the regular tune, but at the moment the processional was to start she could not remember whether it was the second or third tune. After a moment's hesitation she decided to play the second tune. Consequently when the service started, the congregation was singing the first tune, the organist was playing the second tune, and the choir was

---

[6] Harry R. Warfel, Ralph H. Gabriel, and Stanley T. Williams, eds., *The American Mind* (New York: American Book Co., 1947), pp. 1104, 1105.

singing the third tune. The choir detected the mistake first and started to sing the second tune. Shortly thereafter, the organist sensing that the congregation was not singing well, decided that she had been in error and started playing the third tune, and all the while the congregation was struggling bravely on with the first tune. At the end of the first verse the guest pastor arose and announced, "Let us all sing hymn numbered 164 please." This announcement only confused the situation more, because all three printings of the hymn are numbered 164.

With this announcement the substitute organist surrendered to the confusion and stopped playing. Fortunately the choir director had progressed to a point near the chancel and he called up to the organist to play the first tune. The service now continued smoothly but not before the organist, the choir director, and the guest pastor had all turned a bright crimson from their collars to their hair lines. I'm sure that none of you want to begin a worship service in such a hectic manner, so remember to give me the number of the tune as well as the title and number for the hymns that you wish to use.

Obviously the secretary would be overstating or exaggerating a particular situation to the point where it would seem humorous to her listeners.

If the speaker will flavor the content of his speech with some of the types of humor which we have reviewed, he will discover that his audience has been interested in what he has said because his speech possessed both disarming and refreshing qualities.

Perhaps you will be encouraged to make more use of humor by the knowledge that an experimental study (designed to measure objectively the effectiveness of humor in speeches where the speaker's purpose was essentially serious) indicated that humorous speeches were as effective as the nonhumorous speeches even though the subject was serious.[7]

Employing Human Interest Materials

Human interest material often catches our eye when it appears in a small box on the front page of the newspaper, as a closing item on

---

[7] P. E. Lull, "The Effectiveness of Humor In Persuasive Speech," *Speech Monographs*, Vol. VII, 1940, p. 40.

a radio or television newscast, or as a special feature story. *It consists of a report of a personal experience, of an event which is common to the life of all or most human beings—birth, growing-up, death, an affair of the heart, or a struggle to overcome illness.* The interest value lies in the recognition that here is a fellow human being experiencing that which we have experienced or will have to experience, and that we can empathize with his experience. If a layman were pleading for support for the orphanages, hospitals, schools, or homes for the aged supported by his church, he could readily interest his audience in the work of these institutions by relating the human interest stories that are a part of the history of every such institution.

In telling these human interest stories, it is important to emphasize the human part of the story, not the statistics, and to stress the part of the experience which is common to all men. If one were stressing the service that a hospital renders to a community, he might make the material more interesting by relating a human interest incident. For example, a young mother and father were awakened at 1:30 A.M. by their youngest son, who seemed to be talking in his sleep. After investigating his strange behavior, the parents were frightened and called their doctor. The doctor arrived shortly, and after a hurried diagnosis told them that their young son was delirious and that he appeared to have double pneumonia. The doctor ordered an ambulance and rushed the two year old to our hospital. In a short period of time, the emergency services of the hospital went into operation, and the lad was placed in an oxygen tent and observed carefully around the clock. The young parents, still not recovered from the shock of the sudden early morning discovery of their son's serious illness, were most grateful for the co-operative services of the hospital and their physician. Our story has a happy ending because in a little over a week a small boy was once again playing in the back yard. The ready availability of excellent hospital services had helped this family avert a near tragedy. This hospital stands ready day and night to help all of you meet similar emergencies.

Such a story illustrates the possibility of making the content of a speech more interesting by using human interest incidents which stress the human responses to an experience common to all of us.

Using Specific Details

Another way to make the content of a speech more interesting is to *replace vague or general words with specific details*. The use of specific details has the power of suggesting visual images, sounds, odors, and feelings which make listening more interesting.

If a scout master were reporting to the men's group on the work of the scout troop sponsored by their church, he could easily make his report more interesting by citing specific details. The interest value of specific details is best illustrated by comparing a portion of a speech using general statements with a portion of a speech citing specifics. Let us suppose that the scout master were going to include, as a part of his report, a statement about two members of his troop who had earned the God and Country Award. First let us see what this statement might look like if it were presented in general terms, and then how it might look if the specific details were added.

Report Using General Statement

I am happy to report that two members of our troop, working with the pastor of your church, have earned the highly coveted God and Country Award. They worked with the pastor on many significant religious assignments over a period of several months. These were the first such awards given in our area, and they have brought recognition to our troop.

Report Using Specific Details

I am happy to report that two high school sophomores from our troop—Duane Braden and Daryl Wilson—received the coveted God and Country Award on Sunday June 2nd in our church sanctuary. Each of these boys followed a program of work and study which included visits to a hospital and an orphanage sponsored by our church, improvement of the church landscaping, making calls on shut-ins, studies of church missions which were presented as reports to our youth group, and the planning and practice of a program of private devotions. Duane Braden served as church organist during this period, while Daryl Wilson sang in the youth choir. These religious activities were planned and directed by your pastor. Mr. Jameson, our district scout executive, has sent our troop a special letter of commendation because these are the first two God and Country Awards to be presented in this district.

You will notice that *the use of names, of particular activities, of a specific day and date,* and other definite details would make the second report more interesting because the men would receive a sharper and clearer picture of what had actually happened and of the particular recognition which these awards had brought to the troop.

Specific details must not impede the progress of the speech nor weigh it down. They should not be presented for their own sake. Rather, they should be used as replacements for vague words or general statements which do not suggest definite visual images or particular sounds, odors, or feelings. *Time Magazine* built its circulation by insisting on this kind of reporting, and featuring in its news specific details such as middle names, precise ages, color of hair, type of clothes, and place of birth. Correctly used specific details can help you develop the units of your address more accurately and rapidly, and at the same time make these units more interesting.

Presenting a Paradox

A paradox is a statement which seems self-contradictory. Jesus frequently used paradoxical statements in his teaching.

"Whoever loses his life for my sake shall find it." [8]

"Blessed are the meek for they shall inherit the earth." [9]

"Blessed are you when men shall persecute you and utter all kinds of evil against you falsely on my account." [10]

There is something contradictory about the loser's finding, about the meek inheriting the earth, and about the reviled and persecuted being blessed.[11] A seeming paradox has a unique power to prick our curiosity. A newspaper headline containing a paradoxical statement has stuck in my memory for many months. The headline appeared

[8] *The Holy Bible,* Revised Standard Version (New York: Thomas Nelson & Sons, 1952), Matthew 16:25.

[9] *Ibid.,* Matthew 5:5.

[10] *Ibid.,* Matthew 6:11.

[11] James H. Stalker, *The Life of Jesus Christ* (New York: Fleming H. Revell Company, 1909), p. 74.

in the *New York Times,* and read, "Profitable Loss Is Still Possible." [12] Since I think of profit as being on one side of the ledger and loss on the other, it seems paradoxical that a loss could be listed as a profit.

If one were addressing a group of older adults, he could gain their interest in a talk on retirement by beginning with the statement, "Life begins at retirement." Or if the church treasurer were addressing a Young Adult group on tithing, he could make his subject more interesting by speaking on the theme "Become Wealthy by Tithing," and then stress that one might be blessed with spiritual wealth if he reverently follows the practice of tithing.

The paradox can be used to sharpen an idea or to provide a new perspective. For example, when the Christian says that Jesus was both human and divine, he is stating a paradox which is not only interesting but which more clearly indicates the Christian understanding of the dual nature of Jesus.

There is a direct relationship between the obviousness of the contradiction in the paradox and its interest value. The more subtle or remote the contradiction, the more likely it is that the audience may not detect the paradox. Therefore, it is important to adapt any use of the paradox to the particular audience to which you plan to speak. Also, every effort should be made to state the paradox in plain and clear terms.

Finally, the paradox may be utilized in two ways. It may be used as a single statement, or it may be used as a method of organizing the content of the speech so that the whole address is built around it.

Introducing a Conflict

By its nature, conflict tends to be interesting. The struggle and the unknown outcome have a way of commanding our attention. Almost without intending to, we find ourselves favoring one side and opposing the other; and we may even become eager to enter the fray itself. There is a contagious excitement that emanates from a conflict. If a speaker wishes to enlist conflict to make his

---

12 *The New York Times,* December 9, 1956, sec. F, p. 7.

speech more interesting, *the audience should be quickly and straightforwardly informed about what is at issue and about the character of the fighters.*

Conflict can be introduced in many ways in the preparation of a speech. The speaker can describe a conflict that has taken place, or is taking place, and of which he and his audience are spectators. Or, the speaker may alert the audience to some conflict in which they are involved as citizens of their country or as members of the human race. Then too, the speaker himself may dispute some accepted theory or proposal. Still another way to introduce conflict is for the speaker to voice arguments that his audience would also like to raise against some policy of a local government or some other group or institution.

If conflict is used to make a speech more interesting, *the speaker must not deal with the conflict in an objective or detached way, but he must become involved in the conflict himself* and sense some of the struggle and excitement. If you want the conflict to interest your listeners, then you—the speaker—must get into the fight. Furthermore, it is important to remember that the purpose of utilizing these methods is to "embroil" the listeners in the conflict. Unless they become sufficiently involved to take sides and to be keenly curious about the outcome then the conflict will fail to command their attention.

Conflict can be used in a variety of situations. A Sunday School teacher, speaking to a class of young adults about "the authority of the Bible," could try to arouse their interest by describing the conflict which now exists between those who, coming from a fundamentalist background, take the Bible as "literally true" and those who approach the Bible from a critical and historical viewpoint and find another kind of authority in it.

Or a director of religious education, speaking to a high school young people's group about "God the creator," might try to arouse the interest of the young people by describing the conflict that raged over teaching evolution in the public schools and its climax in the Scopes trial in Tennessee.

Since conflict can be used in a variety of situations and since it seems to be inherently interesting, a speaker will do well to examine the content of his speech to see if it offers possibilities for the use of conflict as an interest method.

26561

Utilizing Interest Methods

In this chapter we have noted that listener fatigue is a deadly enemy of effective speaking and that it can be successfully combatted by making a speech more interesting. Then seven methods of making a speech interesting were considered: telling a story, startling the audience, making them laugh, employing human interest, using specific details, presenting a paradox, and introducing a conflict. These methods may be used separately or in combination. When telling a story (narration), one could include specific details, human interest materials, and conflict. While these methods can be used together, it should be understood that they are individual methods. When attempting to make a speech interesting, they should be considered separately as well as in combination.

When you wish to consider the use of these interest methods, you may find the following procedure helpful for incorporating them into your speech. First, make a rough outline of what you feel should be said in your speech—the information that should be given or the argument that should be advanced. Then, taking one interest method at a time, read through the outline, and wherever it seems that this method could be used, make a notation in the margin. Review the outline in this manner for each of the interest methods.

After you have reviewed your outline and noted where the interest methods might be used, study your outline and your notes. Where you have noted that two or three methods might be used for the same section of the speech, you will need to decide which method seems most appropriate, or how the methods might be combined. When you have completed your study of your outline and your notes on interest methods, prepare a new outline and develop the interest methods in the outline, remembering the suggestions which have been given in this chapter for the use of each of these methods.

You should also keep in mind the psychological principles that you are employing in these methods. It is important to realize that you are intensifying a stimulus, approaching your subject in a novel or new way, introducing change, or speaking to a person's interests, all for the purpose of commanding their attention. For example, the use of the startling or of specific details could intensify the stimulus; a paradox or humor might provide a novel or new approach; change would be a part of any use of narrative or conflict; and human interest material would be likely to strike the interests of the audience.

Of course it is also important that the speaker observe these rules for gaining and holding attention when using voice and bodily action to present his speech. His delivery ought to manifest intensity, change, poise, and, if possible, be adapted to the interests of the audience. Intensity would, at least, imply a well projected voice and a high degree of directness. Change suggests vocal variety as well as such things as variety in mood, gesture, and rate of delivery. Poise may be suggested by a firm command of the content of the speech and by an appearance of being at home before the group. Erect posture before military men, graceful movement before professional dancers, and good vocal quality before voice teachers are examples of adapting delivery to the interest of the audience.

The speaker who has advance notice that he is to speak will have a better opportunity to utilize these interest methods than the speaker who is suddenly called upon to speak in an impromptu manner. However, it is also true that a speaker who has become acquainted with such interest methods and developed some skill in using them will be more ready to produce impromptu remarks with a high degree of interest than the impromptu speaker who has no knowledge of, or skill in, the use of narration, humor, conflict, paradox, specific detail, human interest, or the startling. The knowledge that these are effective ways of making a speech interesting, and previous experience in using these interest methods will be advantageous to the speaker whenever he undertakes an important assignment.

You will improve your ability to make speeches interesting if you will develop the habit of examining interesting speeches for the methods of interest which the speaker uses and the way in which he uses these methods. Whenever you discover a new interest method, add it to the methods suggested in this chapter. Also include any suggestions or rules which you think you should follow in using this particular method. Then, the next time you want to make a speech interesting, consider this method along with the seven already suggested in this chapter, when reviewing your first outline of the speech. If you decide to use your new method, try to follow the rules or suggestions you have recorded.

In this manner, you will increase the number of interest methods that are available to you, and you will develop your skill in using them. You will also become more confident about speaking in public, because you will have proven to yourself that you have a reliable and practical plan which you can follow for making your speeches interesting. In addition, once you are certain that your speech is interesting, you will discover that you have more enthusiasm for speaking.

chapter 7

Humanizing
Your
Persuasion

*It is the business of the orator to persuade me to act
agreeably to the truth by engaging my affections on
its side . . . the orator must consider man as a crea-
ture moved by many different springs, and must act
upon them all. He must address himself to the passions; he must paint to the fancy, and touch the
heart. . . .*

—Hugh Blair

With great frequency, those who work in the church will be
faced with the necessity of engaging the affections of the congregation on the side of truth, justice, mercy, and compassion so that the
congregation will support the church as it works to fulfill its mission
in the world. The president of the men's group urging the members
to do volunteer work for a member who is bedfast or to assist a
widow in securing a just settlement for her husband's business—
the chairman of the missionary society seeking special contributions
for the erection of a school or dispensary—a preacher seeking
financial support from his congregation for the hospitals, orphanages, homes for the aged, and schools which his denomination sup-

ports—all these persons are faced with the task of rallying the congregation to the church's side as it engages in charitable works.

Before any worker in the church criticizes the members of the church for not rallying to support some worthy Christian endeavor, he ought first to ask himself, "Have I made an adequate effort to persuade them of the worthiness of this enterprise? Have I addressed their passions, painted to their fancy, and touched their hearts?" The members of the church deserve the same opportunity which you have had to become aware of the merit of this work. When you examine what has persuaded you to plead for participation in this undertaking, you will discover that something caught your fancy, stirred your passions, and touched your heart.

The church worker should learn and practice the art of persuasion so that he can appeal to the hearts and souls, as well as to the minds of the members of the Christian community when he is appealing to them to become more fully involved in the life and work of the church.

It may also be said that the church worker needs to learn and to practice the art of persuasion, because he will need to employ this art in order to communicate the *whole* gospel. The love, which the Christian faith holds that we should have for God and for man, is a whole love not only pertaining to how we think, but also how we feel; and therefore, our discussion of this love must be concerned with attitude and feeling, as well as with understanding. Consequently, it is imperative that we master the art of persuasion and employ it in the proclamation of the gospel and in extending the work of the Christian community.

Motivation

Persuasion is concerned with an appeal to the inner "drives," "motives," or "springs of action" which, when sufficiently aroused, may move a man to make the response that the persuader desires. The Christian who employs the art of persuasion must continually test the responses that he seeks to make certain that, as nearly as he can determine, they are in accord with the will of God. He must also constantly evaluate his appeals to be sure that he is arousing those "motives," "drives," or "springs of action" which can function most appropriately as motivation for Christian action—that is, the Christian persuader would prefer to appeal to the desire to perform an altruistic act than to the desire for personal pleasure.

Of course, in seeking to extend the work of the church, the Christian persuader will also want to appeal to those motives which have been given to us to help us become good stewards of the gift of life. He might appeal to church members to support their church financially or to attend worship services, because such facts were vital to their own self preservation. Or a church school superintendent might try to secure more participation in, and support for, the church school, by appealing to the motive to care for our young in both parents and grandparents. Another example of the use of such motives would be an effort to stir up our fear of injury from fire by a member of the official board who feels that the church needs to provide better fire exits for the sanctuary.

Motives

The beatitudes of our Lord suggest the kinds of motives which a Christian may, in all good conscience, seek to arouse in order to move an audience to respond. Reviewing the beatitudes as they are recorded in the gospel of Matthew:

Desire for Citizenship in the Kingdom of Heaven

This desire does not just represent fear of death nor a craving for a handsome reward in a future life; it also represents man's yearning to be inseparably linked to his surest and most enduring hope. Most of us have such a desire; and when it is appealed to, a yearning wells up within our souls and readies us for an action that will in some way satisfy this deep desire for citizenship in God's kingdom.

Desire to be Comforted

Since mourning is so closely associated with bereavement, we might think first of being comforted in connection with the loss of a loved one. However, there are other equally trying life situations in which we feel the need of genuine personal consolation. The sympathetic understanding of a friend at a time of personal trial meets an inner longing in a warm and assuring way. This desire for comfort is more than a wish to be coddled. It represents a craving for understanding and for help to meet a critical situation in the right or good way. If our desire to be comforted has been aroused, we are eager to follow some course which will help us satisfy this craving for comfort.

Desire to Inherit the Earth

This aspiration thrusts beyond mere ownership of, or authority over, and points to the desire for an inheritance through the ability to appreciate profoundly. This aspiration suggests that the artist who has been moved to set down the beauty of a landscape on a canvas more truly inherited that portion of the earth than did the landlord who owned it; or that the poet who expressed his love and admiration for his country in meter and rhyme more fully inherited that part of the earth than did the king who ruled it. Men aspire to an earthly inheritance that is more than the possession of title or of power. When this aspiration is aroused, we begin considering new approaches to the receiving of the fruits of God's universe; and we are most ready to act upon a promising suggestion for inheriting the earth in this way.

Desire for a Satisfying Life

We want so to live that we will find life satisfying in its deepest and most profound sense. If you can arouse in people the craving to feel that their life is, in the highest sense, satisfying, then you will have prompted a powerful motive. It is our common experience to pursue goals which leave us with an even keener hunger for satisfaction. No religious worker should overlook the possibility of appealing to the desire for completeness in life—the desire for a satisfying life.

Desire to be Treated Mercifully

We all know that if we were to be judged by others in terms of our moral perfection, we would be severely condemned. Since we are finite and subject to the weaknesses of the flesh, and since we are sinners with a strong inclination to do evil, we always find ourselves in need of asking to be judged with mercy. Consequently, we covet the company of those who will speak the truth to us in love. We want to be corrected with compassion. The cry for mercy is not a cry for luxurious pampering, but a cry to be dealt with in the spirit of Him who lovingly willed the good for each one of us. When a speaker excites our longing for mercy, he touches a keen desire which is capable of provoking vigorous response from us.

Desire to See God

This need to see God is at the heart of the longing which every man has for an ordered view of the world. So long as a man can see only chaos in his world, he has difficulty in becoming a part of his world. It is extremely hard to find one's place in chaos. However, once we have beheld the orderer, it is much easier to detect the order in our universe. For this reason, men long to behold—to see God. When a speaker arouses in his audience this longing to behold God, he has appealed to a desire for which men will make great sacrifices.

This brief resumé of the motives or desires suggested by the beatitudes indicates that one need not shrink from the use of persuasion because he does not wish to appeal to such motives as hunger, thirst, sex, or desire for social approval. When one studies the whole man, he soon discovers that there are "spiritual drives," such as the desire to worship, which match the familiar biological and social drives in their ability to move a man to action. The course to take is *not to avoid the use of persuasion, but to discover how persuasion can be used to the glory and service of God.*

Moreover, as indicated earlier, the "biological drives," such as hunger, thirst, and sex, and the "social drives," such as the desire to belong to the group and the desire for group approval, need not direct us to anti- or un-Christian behavior. Not only could one appeal to the "biological drives" to awaken a due sense of stewardship of life, but he might also appeal to "social drives" in an effort to develop a more adequate expression of love of neighbor. For instance, a layman coaching a church-sponsored athletic team might try to encourage the team members to work for the good of the team (the group) rather than for their own good by appealing to both the desires to belong to and to receive group approval.

A church worker could increase his appreciation for the use of such appeals and strengthen his skill in using them, if his understanding of such motives or drives could be increased. If he could come to see that the evil lay not in the motives themselves, but in an unhealthy perversion of such motives, he might desire to suggest ways in which people could respond to these motives that are both healthy and consistent with the goals of a Christian life.[1]

Persuasive Sequence

The remainder of this discussion of persuasion will follow a pattern which we suggest for the organization of a persuasive speech.

1. Arouse an appropriate motive, drive, or desire.
2. State the response that you desire from your audience.
3. Assure your audience that this desired response will satisfy the aroused motive, drive, or desire.
4. Again, arouse motive, drive, or desire and urge the audience to make the response desired by you.

This plan of organization has two particular merits. One, it can be readily followed by a listening audience. Two, it insures adequate coverage of the minimum requirements for an effective speech of persuasion. At this point a word should be said about the relation of these steps to the familiar breakdown of introduction, body, and conclusion and also about the relation of these steps to the speech-plans discussed in Chapter 1.

First, let us take up the matter of introduction, body, conclusion. It is possible that step one might serve as an extended introduction of the speech. However it is preferable to provide a brief introduction prior to the introduction of step one. Then steps one, two, and three of the persuasive sequence can serve as the "body," and step four as the conclusion. Second, this sequence is, in effect, another

---

[1] Carroll A. Wise, *Religion in Illness and Health* (New York: Harper & Brothers, 1942), pp. 70-73.

speech-plan like those discussed in Chapter 1. This is not the only plan that might be used in developing a speech of persuasion, since a problem-solution or cause-effect plan might also be employed. However, the merit of the persuasive sequence, which will now be described, is that it focuses our attention on the main requirements for a speech of persuasion, namely, arousing a motive, clearly stating the response desired, and assurance that this response is adequate to satisfy the aroused motive.

Arousing an Appropriate Motive, Drive, or Desire

A speaker can profitably devote one third of his speaking time to the development of this phase of the persuasive address. The aim of this step is actually to arouse a particular feeling. The speaker should lead the audience to such a lively sense of involvement in a particular situation, or to such an appreciation of a vivid scene or event, that they respond in a strongly emotional way. If the speaker has led the audience to an adequate involvement or appreciation, the audience should experience powerful yearnings or longings so that they are immediately aware of great needs and wants.

If a lay chairman were trying to persuade members of his committee on evangelism to call on prospective church members, he might dwell intently on the yearning that each person has—to spend his life in a venture that is worthy of his best. In this regard, he could point out our dislike for the plain, routine jobs or household chores that require no imagination or skill. He could also stress our reluctance to have our work lost—our desire to see something that will survive. Fathers like to have their sons carry on their business, and we like to see the traditions which we have supported in the city council or the school board carried on by those who follow us. The chairman might go on to say that we are especially pleased when some work we have done helps another person to find a new and better life. The discoverer of the Salk vaccine and the inventor of the plastic heart valve, he could continue, must have experienced this pleasure. Then the chairman could ask, wouldn't it be wonderful if we could find a work that would be worthy of our best efforts and which, at the same time, would help another person find a new and a better life? Such work, he could say, would challenge our imagination and skill; and it would be profoundly satisfying as we witnessed its good effect on another person.

This is a brief indication of how one might try to arouse a motive or desire to the point where a listener would become emotionally involved in a speech. Any such effort at motivation must be intensely personal. It must be precisely linked to the experiences, knowledge, and vocabulary of these particular listeners. This section of the persuasive speech must strike these people with a strong note of realism.

In your effort to personalize and localize, you will have more success if you aim your material at specific individuals in the audience, rather than at a mythical person who represents a composite of the characteristics of the various members of your audience. When selecting the content items for arousing a drive, think of specific persons in their particular environments, and then select materials which will speak to their precise condition and situation. If you try to select materials that will apply casually to every member of the audience, you will run the risk of choosing items that fit no one in the audience exactly, and therefore do not move the hearers to an emotional reaction.[2]

Notice that in the preceding example, the chairman analyzes his subject "calling on prospective members," and develops it, not from the viewpoint of the church or from the viewpoint of the prospective member, but from the viewpoint of the committee members. He tries to stir up a "felt need" in the members of his committee to make calls on prospective church members. Thus, in this persuasive sequence, you analyze and develop your subject from the perspective of the relationship of the individuals in your audience to the subject, with the intent of arousing in them a desire to become involved.

You should also make every effort to understand and appreciate the material which you are going to present in the motivation phase of your persuasive speech. At the moment of delivery, the speaker should give his material undivided attention and approach it in an appreciative and understanding manner, so that he is genuinely moved to react emotionally to it. Such a response must

2 H. L. Hollingworth, *The Psychology of the Audience* (New York: The American Book Company, 1935), p. 27.

not be faked or affected by the speaker. If the response is false, the audience will detect the faking; and the whole character of the presentation will be undercut. However, if you attend to your material carefully, in a fully appreciative and understanding manner, so that it moves you emotionally as you present it, you will give your audience important clues in voice and bodily action, so that they more fully appreciate and understand and, therefore, are more emotionally affected by it. If you are a careful, faithful, and devoted workman in the preparation and presentation of the motivation portion of your persuasive speech, you will assist your hearers to open their hearts to worthy tasks which you want to place before them.

While step one is called the motivation step, you should bear in mind that the remainder of the speech must be related to this aroused motive, and, as noted in step four, keep this motive active. In other words, while step one is specifically designed to arouse a particular motive, the remaining three steps should contain elements of motivation which will serve to keep this motive aroused.

Stating the Response which You Desire

At first glance this step might appear to be the easiest, but in reality it is the most difficult. In order to phrase this desired response clearly and accurately, the speaker must decide exactly what he wants these particular people to do in regard to the problem or situation which he is going to present.

When you attempt to go beyond vague suggestions to the requesting of a precise response, you will find that you have your work cut out for you. You will have to analyze the problem or need so that you are able to identify specific and helpful contributions. Then you will have to study your audience to determine what contributions they are able to make. After completing your analysis of the problem or need and your analysis of the audience, you must then select a specific response which you will urge this particular audience to make.

When attempting to select the precise response, it is well to keep in mind that you might seek responses at three levels. The first level can be designated as *acceptance*—acceptance of you as a speaker on this subject. That is, you aim to get this audience to listen to the

problem or need which you are going to present. It may be because
of a lack of understanding, coupled with existing prejudices and
attitudes, that this audience will receive your presentation with
great difficulty. Therefore, in this case, if they respond by giving
you an attentive hearing, you could say that you have secured a
significant response.

A second level of response can be described as *belief*. Now you
are asking for more than a courteous hearing. You are asking the
audience to make a decision. Perhaps you are not only asking them
to make a decision, but you are also asking them to supplement
that decision with faith. For example, a scout master might want
the members of the congregation to believe that the sponsoring of a
scout troop is consistent with the goals of a church that is seeking
to serve its Lord. At this particular meeting he does not want to ask
for funds or privileges, but he wants to persuade his hearers that
the sponsoring of a scout troop is an admirable way of pursuing the
mission of the church.

You might desire to secure a belief response as a preliminary step
to a request for action at a later date. Or you might wish to obtain
a belief response as a way of providing a supporting climate of approval for those who are already acting as you desire. In the case of
seeking a response of belief, it should also be said that such a
response may be all that is needed or all that can be hoped for at a
particular time from a specific audience. This could be true because the time has not yet arrived when action should be taken or
because the abilities of the audience are such that action cannot be
reasonably expected.

Action is the word which can be used to indicate a third level of
response. When we seek action from an audience, we assume that
we shall receive a fair hearing and that they do believe, or will come
to believe, in the approach that we are suggesting, and that they
are ready and able to act on their beliefs. An "action response"
might be sought by the chairman of the worship committee of the
women's organization of the church. She might want the women's
organization to conduct a 24-hour prayer vigil in the church as a
way of emphasizing the place of prayer in the worship life of the
church. In this case, she would be seeking more than an opportunity
to explain what a 24-hour prayer vigil is. She would also be seeking
more than a belief that such a prayer vigil would be a contribution

to the spiritual life of the church. Our chairman would be requesting her group to act by conducting such a prayer vigil in their
church.

One way, then, of wording a response in a clear and definite
manner is to determine the level at which you will seek a response.
You can also improve the wording of your desired response by
replacing words that are vague and general, with words that are
definite and specific. It will help to insure a fuller participation in
the response if you specify such items as time, place, and amount.
Returning for a moment to the response sought by our chairwoman,
we might say that a clear and definite wording of her desired
response would be, "I urge the women's society to conduct a 24-hour
prayer vigil in the sanctuary of this church from 1 P.M. on Monday,
January 6, to 1 P.M. on Tuesday, January 7."

In summary, let us say that in a "speech to persuade" the response which you desire should be framed from a knowledge of the
problem and of the ability of this audience to respond; and it should
be stated in a specific and unambiguous manner.

Of course, we have assumed in this discussion that every worker
in the church, while he is framing a response to elicit from an
audience, will be continuously evaluating this response in the light
of God's will, as he understands it in the face of this need or
problem. Presumably, the worker in the church will always desire
that the response which he seeks from an audience will be a way of
loving God, or a way of loving our fellow men, or both a way of
loving God and our fellow men. While it is true that a non-Chris-
tian might seek responses that are in conflict with the Christian life,
certainly every Christian will want to test each response that he
intends to secure from an audience, to make certain that it is an
expression of the Christian life and, preferably, the Christian life
at its best.

Assurance of Satisfaction

Fully one-third of your speaking time ought to be devoted to
*assuring the audience that the response which you desire will satisfy
the motive or drive which you have aroused in them.* The mastery
of this step is crucial, because this step recognizes that persuasion is
far more than a sneak attack on a person who is emotionally hyp-

notized. As a matter of fact, a speaker, who stirs up an audience emotionally and then does nothing more than push them into a desired response, should expect nothing more than a minimum of response. For you see, if a speaker succeeds in arousing a motive or drive within the members of the audience, he has, at the same time, aroused in them the criteria by which they will judge the response that he urges. The listeners will immediately ask themselves if the response that the speaker is urging will actually satisfy the longing or craving which they now feel. Within the scope of this large question they will be asking: "Is the response big enough?" "Is it practical?" "Are there any better responses?" and so forth. Moreover, the speaker should again remind himself that listeners behave as whole persons and that they will test the response he is suggesting, not only with their emotions but with their ability to reason. Consequently, at this point in the persuasive speech, the speaker must become more reasonable and convincing.

This kind of audience evaluation of persuasive speeches can be particularly expected from American audiences, because Americans have developed a good deal of sales resistance. Having been victimized by high pressure salesmen and misleading advertising, Americans frequently begin to balk at the precise moment when the response is suggested.

The basic question which the persuader must answer for his listeners in this assurance step is "Will my individual response make any significant change in the situation which has caused me to experience this craving or longing?" That is, you must show your hearers that their personal responses will be of such relevance and value that they will significantly affect the circumstances which have caused the problem or produced the need. Only if a listener feels this, will he experience adequate emotional satisfaction in responding as you direct.

If a layman were asking each of his fellow churchmen to contribute five dollars to a program of religious broadcasting as a means of reaching unchurched people, he would have to demonstrate that five-dollar contributions would provide sufficient funds; and that there was a group in the church who were capable of producing the kind of a program that could effectively appeal to unchurched people; and that broadcasting time could be secured. If the layman could not convince his fellow churchmen about these matters, they might well refuse to contribute their five dollars, not because they were unmoved by the need for religious broadcasting to the unchurched, but because they did not believe that the program which their speaker suggested would, in fact, meet this need.

The organization named CARE, which has supported a program of feeding and clothing the world's needy, has been particularly effective in this assurance step. They have told their contributors exactly what food a certain number of dollars would buy and how many days this food would feed an individual, and they have even provided for signed receipts which would be evidence that the CARE package had actually been received.

The discussion of *evidence* and *reasoning* in the following chapter will be helpful in strengthening this assurance step. In addition, you should remember that your assurances about the value of the response which you suggest should be explicit and personal. Moreover, this assurance step should be so convincing that you are reassured of the practicality and the adequacy of this response at the very time when you are assuring your audience about it. Then, not only will you be explicitly stating the significance of this response, but your mood and attitude will assure the audience of the value of the response which you are urging them to make.

Finally, you should keep in mind that the more successful you are in arousing motives or drives, the more demanding your audience will be of assurances that the response you suggest will satisfy their aroused desires. You cannot, therefore, compensate for a weak assurance step by strengthening your effort to arouse motives or drives; because strengthening the arousal of motives and drives will only further alert the hearer to the impracticality or the inadequacy of the responses which you are proposing.

There is, however, a special way of strengthening this section of the persuasive speech which is particularly useful for the church worker. If you are suggesting a response that you believe to be in accord with the will and purposes of God, you will also feel that God will bless such a response and cause it to prosper. Now, while such a statement of faith should not be used as an escape from making a substantial effort to assure the audience of the merit of the response, certainly every assurance step should include a statement that God is with us in our endeavor and should indicate the ways in which we believe that He will help us. In this regard, historical examples of the way God has blessed similar efforts will do much to assure the audience of the likelihood of God's help in this venture.

The persuasive speaker, then, must not only arouse appropriate drives or motives and state the response he desires in clear and definite terms, but also he must assure his hearer that this response will enable the listener to satisfy those aroused drives or motives.

Arouse the Motive and Urge the Response

This second effort to arouse the motive or drive should be brief and deft. An illustration painted with a few quick strokes or a short, sharp description of an experience might serve you well at this point. The aim is once more to excite or enliven the aroused motive so that it may move the hearer to respond in the manner which you will again suggest.

Concluding with a second statement of the response which you desire takes advantage of *repetition* and *recency* as a means of fixing this response in the listener's mind so that he may act upon it. The conclusion of a speech of persuasion is most important because you do not want to lose the response of the audience by dampening their aroused emotions, suggesting doubts about the value of the response, or confusing your hearers as to the nature of the response. When the audience has been assured of the worth of the response and is ready to act, then you should conclude with clarity and dispatch.

It should be added that in making your final effort to stir up a desire in the hearers, you should have some new way of accomplishing this task and not merely repeat what you have said earlier. You ought, also, to use illustrations, examples, or descriptions which are at least as powerful as those used in your first effort to arouse your hearers. That is to say, this fourth step of the persuasive speech should not be repetition, nor should it be anticlimactic.

In order for your delivery of this phase of a persuasive speech to be as effective as possible, it will be important for you to expect that these members of your audience will respond as you suggest. This is the time to have faith in your audience and to expect that the Holy Spirit will work among them in support of your efforts. Remembering that you are a workman with God in this task of persuasion will help you to conclude your persuasive speech in a mood of expectation that your audience will respond.

One additional way to avoid any negative suggestion in your delivery is to have this fourth step well prepared so that you are confident you have a lucid and moving conclusion for your speech which will aid your hearers in deciding to respond as you suggest. If you are confident of the quality of the conclusion of your speech, you are more apt to present it with great expectations.

Over-all Approach

Now, as you have probably surmised, these four steps in the persuasive speech must be carefully integrated. The whole speech must have a basic unity. The motive aroused, the response suggested, and the assurance given must all appear to belong together. This means that, in the construction of the speech, you must carefully relate motive, response, and assurance. It also means that the transitions linking these four steps must be carefully prepared so that they make the relationship explicit and unmistakable. In addition, as you present the speech, you must keep your attention fixed on the development of these relationships so that they are exceptionally clear to you as you are talking about them.

Finally, let us say that the decision to learn and practice the art of persuasive speaking will, in all likelihood, be prompted by your Christian love for your fellow churchmen. That is, you will so desire to help them respond as you know they really want to respond, that you will undertake the difficult task of showing them that they are concerned in a vital way about this matter, that here is a response that they can make, and that this response will have real value.

When you undertake this task, it is indeed a work of love, because persuasive speaking is no shortcut to good reasoning. Neither is persuasive speaking any way of tricking your audience into a desired behavior. Rather, it is an approach that fully informs and alerts your hearers to the meaning and the value of such a behavior and relates it to their personal lives. Consequently, persuasive speaking demands full understanding of personal needs and problems, an adequate knowledge of abilities of the members of your audience, and a keen appreciation of the way in which the problem and the audience are related. The delivery of the persuasive speech also requires complete dedication of the speaker to his task. Any hint of the speaker's lack of concern for the need or problem or any suggestion of a lack of good will toward the audience will lessen sharply the amount of audience response.

Developing Your Talent for Persuasive Speaking

Although persuasion is exacting and demanding for the speaker, it is well worth pursuing, because it represents a great service to the cause for which you are pleading, and because it also represents a great service to the people to whom the cause will be presented.

No one of us should excuse himself from the effort of persuasive speaking with the assertion that he has no talent for it. The talent for persuasive speaking is not something that a person either has or does not have. On the contrary, the talent for persuasive speaking is developed by those persons who faithfully and energetically practice methods like those which are presented in this chapter, and who, through constant practice and evaluation, become more and more skillful in the use of these methods. If you will so endeavor to master these methods, one day your fellow churchmen may say of you: "Here is one who loves us enough to help us place our affections on the side of truth by addressing himself to our passions, painting to our fancy and touching our heart."

chapter 8

Strengthening
Your
Argument

The finding of suitable arguments to prove a given point and the skillful arrangement of them may be considered as the immediate and proper province of rhetoric.[1]

"Come let us reason together" are words that suggest the mood which we frequently want to encourage among fellow church members as they deliberate on church policies. Whether we are considering action on a social issue, a method of raising funds, the opening of church facilities to a community group, or other important matters, we want most to hear a fair and accurate presentation of the significant points. In fact, it is only when the group has had a complete and clear presentation of the arguments on both sides of the question that it is in a position to make an informed and wise decision.

When the presentation of a point concerning a proposed policy is supported by strong reasoning and pertinent evidence, and grows

1 Richard Whately, *Elements of Rhetoric* (Boston: James Munroe and Company, 1844), p. 28.

120

out of a sound analysis of the problem, we feel that we have really heard a telling argument. We are even more likely to be favorably disposed toward the argument if it has been equally well developed in all three areas—analysis, evidence, and reasoning. This is to say that an argument becomes convincing when it is well proven— when by logical demonstration it establishes the truth, justice, or wisdom of a proposition.[2]

However, we do well to remember that it is not our task to build an incontestable logical structure. If a proposition is debatable, it is not likely that we shall be able to present incontrovertible proof in support of our contentions. Our aim should be to demonstrate a reasonable degree of *probability* in support of our stand.

In addition to attempting to prove your point—to establish a reasonable degree of probability in favor of your position—you should also take both sides of the question into account. If the listeners feel that they have heard the major arguments on both sides of a question, they are more apt to feel that those who seek their co-operation or their vote have given them a due chance to fulfill their responsibilities as policy makers. If only one side of a question has been presented (particularly if the presentation has been weak), the group may be reluctant to respond favorably, even if they agree with the speaker, because they know that they are acting without a full and proper consideration of the question. When a speaker presents a carefully constructed argument which takes into account the major arguments of the opposition, he increases the respect of the audience for his grasp of the question at the same time that he compliments the audience by showing them that he believes that they deserve a full and careful evaluation of the issues.

Most speakers fail to present a careful and complete argument for the side of the question which they represent, even though they realize that their cause would be more likely to be advanced if they did. They fail to present a good argument because they do not know how to prepare a thorough and substantial one. It will be the aim of this chapter to show you how you can prepare stronger and more comprehensive arguments.

---

2 J. H. McBurney, J. M. O'Neill, and G. E. Mills, *Argumentation and Debate* (New York: The Macmillan Company, 1951), p. 9.

Types of Propositions

In argumentation, a proposition is a judgment expressed in a declarative sentence which the listener is asked to accept.[3] There are several types of propositions which can serve as the basis for argument. There is the proposition of *policy,* which proposes a change in policy or a new policy and calls for some specific action. There is the proposition of *fact,* which concerns itself with the existence or occurrence of things and asks "Is it so?" For example, "Do the total pledges exceed the church budget?" is a question of fact. The third type of proposition is one of *value,* which deals with merit or worth. "A city wide evangelistic crusade would benefit the churches of this community" is an example.

Stating Your Proposition

The first step in developing a strong argument is to state your proposition clearly. Your hearers must be certain about what you are advocating or proposing—attacking or defending. Avoid the use of vague or ambiguous words. Moreover, be certain that the words you use are not only definite and precise, but also known and understood by the audience to whom they are addressed.

Second, let your proposition deal with only one policy change, or only one evaluation of merit or worth, or only one question of fact. If you include more than one policy change in the same proposition, you make it more difficult for your listeners to keep in mind which portions of your argument support which change of policy. Essentially the same problem develops if you attempt to include more than one evaluation of goodness or badness or more than one question of fact in a proposition. The listener could easily become confused about which portion of your argument relates to which question of value or to which question of fact. In order to give the audience the best opportunity to understand accurately and to consider fairly your proposal, you should limit your proposition to

---

3 *Ibid.,* p. 18.

the consideration of one policy change, or one value judgment, or one question of fact.

Thirdly, you will most likely meet the mind of your audience (when dealing with a proposition of policy) if you state your proposal so that those arguing in favor of the proposition will have the burden of showing that there is a need for this change, and that such a modification in policy would be practical and desirable. Since there is a tendency to favor the existing policy, the audience will expect anyone who advocates a policy change to undertake the task of proving that the existing policy should be altered. It would be inadvisable to take the position that it is the person who is defending the continuation of the present policy who must prove that it should be continued, and that you have only to point to the weakness in the present policy to secure the adoption of the new one. You would lose the support of your hearers because they disagreed with your approach to this discussion of the policy change.

In other words, the proposition should be stated so that the affirmative has the "burden of proof" and the negative has the advantage of the "presumption." Archbishop Whately clarified both of these terms when he wrote, "Presumption in favor of any supposition means . . . such a pre-occupation of the ground, as implies that it must stand good till some sufficient reason is adduced against it; in short, that the Burden of Proof lies on him who would dispute it." [4]

Let us see how these rules can help us frame a proposition concerning a change in policy regarding the number of worship services to be conducted on Sunday mornings. We shall assume that at present there is only one morning service, which begins at 11 o'clock. The change which we want to propose is that this church offer two worship services, one at 9:30 A.M. and another at 11:00 A.M. After much discussion in our church's worship commission, we approve the following motion to be presented to the proper church board: "We move that our church have two Sunday morning worship services, one beginning at 9:30 A.M. and one beginning at 11:00 A.M."

First, let us ask if our motion (proposition) is vague or ambigu-

---

4 Whately, *op. cit.*, p. 74.

ous. The motion seems to be vague because we do not specify the date when the two services should begin or how frequently they should be conducted. Perhaps the solution would be to reword the motion to read, "We move that, as of next Sunday, our church have two worship services each Sunday morning; one beginning at 9:30 A.M. and the other beginning at 11:00 A.M."

Next, since this is a proposition of policy, we must ask: does our motion suggest more than one change in policy? In this regard, we have a good motion. The only intended change is in the number of worship services to be provided on Sunday morning. No other policy change is explicitly stated or purposely implied.

Finally, we want to inquire if our motion assumes that those who are proposing it will need to show why it should be adopted; rather than assuming that the existing policy of one service on Sunday should be discontinued unless someone can demonstrate that it should be retained. Again, we seem to have a satisfactory motion, because it is those who seek the change who must secure the adoption of the motion in order to produce a change. If the motion is lost, the existing policy is retained. Consequently, the burden of demonstrating why the policy they are advocating is the best is clearly on the shoulders of those seeking the change in policy.

While we have illustrated the principles for stating a proposition of policy, they are of equal importance when framing propositions of fact and value. All propositions should be plainly and accurately stated, deal with one central idea, and put the burden of proof on the affirmative.

Defining the Terms

Now that we have a satisfactory proposition as a basis for argument, our next task is to define the terms in the proposition. Looking again at our motion, as we modified it when we sought to make it more specific, we find only one phrase that needs defining: "worship service." In explaining our proposal, we would want to indicate whether we mean a preaching service when we say "worship service"; and whether we mean a full worship service, including special music and all parts of the worship service ordinarily included in the 11:00 A.M. service. The importance of defining even such a well-known phrase would become clear if objections were raised because the 9:30 service would crowd in on the 11:00 service, or because it would be difficult for everyone involved in the full worship service to be present from 9:30 A.M. until after 12:00 noon.

Much time can be saved in the arguing of any proposition if you define the terms that might be misunderstood. There is no use in wasting time or confusing your hearers by dealing with false objections just because the proposition was not clearly or accurately understood by your audience or your opponents.

Discovering the Issues

Once you have clearly stated your proposition and defined its terms, you will undertake the third step of building a strong argument: investigating the problem and locating the key issues. In advocating or attacking any proposition, you should build your argument about the main issues. In a proposition of *policy,* such as the one we have been considering, there are four major areas in which we can look for issues. These areas can be stated as questions:

1. Is there a need for a change?
2. Has a practical way for achieving the change been proposed?
3. Would the change really be beneficial?
4. Would the change be more beneficial than other possible changes?

When investigating these areas, we must look for any questions which we would have to answer in the affirmative in order to prove that the new policy should be adopted, or in the negative to show that the policy should not be adopted.

Looking at our motion for two worship services on Sunday morning, let us see what issues we can discover in the areas of *need, practicality,* and *desirability.* When we ask "Is there a need for a second worship service?" we want to know how many people actually want to worship in our church on Sunday mornings.

Second, we shall want to be shown that these people cannot now be accommodated at one service. Third, we may wish to have it demonstrated that there is a need for the second service to be provided at 9:30. If those who are supporting the motion fail to show us that there are more people who want to worship at our church than can be conveniently accommodated at 11:00 A.M. on Sunday morning, or if they fail to show us that, for reasons of family schedules, there is a need to place the second service at 9:30 A.M., we may feel that there is no adequate need for an additional worship service at 9:30 A.M. on Sunday.

Next, we must look for the issues in the area of *practicality*. For example, the board would want to know if an adequate staff could be assembled to conduct a worship service at 9:30, and if a reasonable number of worshippers would be able to come to church at that time. The board would want to be certain that the sanctuary could be cleared after the 9:30 service and properly prepared for the 11:00 A.M. worship service in the brief interval between the two. If those who urged the passing of the motion did not assure the board that (1) an adequate staff could be assembled, (2) that a reasonable number of parishioners could attend, or (3) that there would be adequate time after the first service to make ready for the second, it is doubtful that the board would feel that the proposal for a second worship service at 9:30 was a practical one.

Now, let us search out the issues in the area of *benefits* or *desirability*. In order to round out your argument, it is important to consider the issues raised by the need for a change which you have presented. Here you will want to demonstrate that this proposal will be beneficial because it will enable more people to worship in the church each Sunday morning. A second issue might center on what effect this change would have on the quality of the worship services provided. A third issue might develop around the extent to which this proposal assisted the church to fulfill its purpose. If you were unable to demonstrate that this change would be beneficial, the board members might vote down your motion because of your failure to convince them.

Finally, let us consider the issues that evolve out of the question of whether this is the best possible change. Undoubtedly the board would want to know how the cost of this change would compare with the cost of other possible changes. The speed with which this change could be made, as compared with other changes, might also be an important consideration. Advantages of this change, compared with the advantages of other possible changes, would constitute another significant issue. Likewise, the disadvantages of this change, compared with the disadvantages of other changes, would be an important matter for deliberation. Thus, one might claim that the proposal for two worship services is the better one, because it could be accomplished with less cost and more speed than the other proposals, and because it would have more advantages and fewer disadvantages than the others.

So far in our discussion of finding the issues, we have thought about only those issues which would be important in presenting an argument on a proposition of policy. Let us now consider the issues for a proposition of fact, which does not concern itself with whether a change should be made, but deals with the existence of things or the occurrence of things. For example, if someone asked if the church had fire insurance coverage on a new organ, we would be dealing with a proposition of fact. Stated as a proposition it might read, "Our present fire insurance policy provides coverage for the new organ." The issues involved in this proposition of fact would be:

1. Do we have a fire insurance policy?
2. Is it in force?
3. Does it contain a provision which covers the new organ?

Notice that the above issues do not focus on the need for insurance, the practicality of insurance, or the benefits of insurance. Rather, they concern themselves with the existence of a policy and the existence of a section in that policy which provides coverage for a new organ.

A proposition of fact which is concerned with the occurrence of things might be, "Many young people dedicate their lives to full-time Christian service while attending our church youth camp." Anyone supporting this proposition would have to show that many of the young people attending the church youth camp had made decisions to enter full time Christian service. He would also have to indicate that these decisions were made at the youth camp.

Again, notice that the issues do not deal with *need, practicality,* or *benefits*. The issues are concerned with whether certain young people made particular decisions in a specific situation.

Next, let us consider the issues for a proposition of value which deals, not with policy or fact, but with value or worth. "Floral bouquets would add to the beauty of the chancel of our church" is a proposition of value. The issues in this proposition would center on what constitutes beauty in a church chancel, and whether floral bouquets can make a contribution to such beauty. Notice that the issues here are not concerned with *need, practicality,* or *benefits*, nor do they focus on the existence of things or the occurrence of things.

In summary, let us remember that the rules for constructing propositions apply with equal force to all three types of propositions, but that the kinds of issues discovered under each type of proposition will be distinctly different, due to the unique character of each of the three types of propositions—policy, fact, and value.

Relationship of Propositions, Issues, Evidence, and Reasoning

Now, having stated our proposition, having defined its terms, and having discovered the issues, we are ready to begin constructing our argument. In order to construct an argument, we must turn our attention to the "stuff" of which arguments are made, and to the "methods" or "ways" by which arguments are put together. The stuff of which arguments are made is called *evidence,* and the methods or ways by which arguments are put together is called *reasoning.*

Before proceeding to a discussion of evidence and reasoning, it will be helpful to see the relationship among the proposition, the issues, the evidence, and the reasoning. We who wish to construct an argument may compare our task to that of a contractor who is going to construct a wooden building. The proposition tells us the kind and size of argument (policy, fact, value) we are going to construct, just as the contract will tell the contractor the kind and size of building which he is to erect. The issues will tell us where to raise the structure of our argument, as the blueprint will show

the contractor where to build his walls. The evidence is the material
of which we construct our argument, just like the boards are the
material with which the builder erects his walls. The reasoning is
the means by which we hold the evidence in place, just as the frame
is used to guide and hold the boards in place.

In brief review, we can say that without evidence, we would have
nothing with which to build an argument; without reasoning, we
would have no way to guide or hold the argument together; without issues, no indication of where to construct the argument; and
without a proposition, no clear indication of the kind and size of
argument to construct.

With this understanding of the relationship of proposition,
issues, evidence, and reasoning, let us turn our attention to the
types of evidence and their value.

Evaluating the Evidence

Usually we think of two kinds of evidence, namely, fact and
opinion. Like a proposition of fact, evidence pertaining to fact
deals with the existence and occurrence of things. Such evidence is
not concerned with the future. If a worship committee were advocating the purchase of a new pulpit Bible, they might present the
following factual evidence.

1. There are torn pages in the present pulpit Bible, such as
   pages 24, 103, and 507.
2. The binding is broken on the present pulpit Bible.
3. The print in the present pulpit Bible is of an older style than
   is now used.
4. The pages of the present pulpit Bible are faded, and there is
   not a sharp contrast between the print and the page.
5. The present pulpit Bible is a King James version.

The second type of evidence, pertaining to opinion, may deal
with prediction or with an interpretation of facts. That is, a person
gives us his understanding, or judgment, of what certain facts
mean. Our worship committee would probably present some opinion evidence. Perhaps they would have the pastor voice his view

that a new Bible, in which the pages were not torn or faded and in which a modern style of type was used, would be easier to read. The committee might also ask the superintendent of the church school to state his opinion that a Revised Standard Version of the Bible would contain fewer archaic words, and therefore be better understood by the youth of the church. Notice that both the pastor and the church school superintendent presented conclusions that were expressions of opinion, and not of fact.

Now, whereas almost any member of the church could have reliably ascertained and reported the facts submitted as evidence, ordinarily we would want someone of special ability or experience to provide an opinion about the readableness or understandableness of the present pulpit Bible. This suggests that each of these types of evidence will have to meet certain tests in order for it to be considered as reliable or useful.

One can check the strength of his facts by asking these questions about them: Are they correct? Are they definite and clear? Are they consistent with each other, within themselves, with other known facts, and with reason? Are the sources of the facts clearly identified?

If we were to apply these tests to the facts presented by the worship committee in regard to the pulpit Bible, we would discover certain weaknesses in that presentation. Assuming that the facts are correct, we must still say that they are not definite and clear in regard to the number of torn pages, the extent of the fading, or the degree of difference in the type. The facts are consistent within themselves and with each other, but no attempt is made to identify their source; in other words their observer is not identified.

Opinion evidence should also be tested before we employ it in building an argument. The following are some of the questions we should ask about opinions which we plan to use as evidence: Were the opinions actually expressed? Were the opinions clearly and definitely stated? Are these opinions consistent with facts, reason, other opinions expressed by this expert, opinions expressed by other experts, and within themselves?

It is difficult to apply these tests to the testimony in which we suggested the worship committee might have the pastor and the church school superintendent present. Nevertheless, we could say that these opinions would actually be expressed, that they would probably be clearly and definitely stated, and that they would be consistent with facts, reason, and within themselves. However, since these are the only statements of opinion which we have from the pastor and the superintendent, we could not say whether they were consistent with other opinions expressed by them. Also, unless we sought other expert opinion, we could not compare the two opinions with the opinions of other experts to see if they were consistent.

For both fact and opinion evidence, it is important that the person who testifies be a qualified, reliable, and competent observer or interpreter, and that he be known to have been in a proper environment and condition to make accurate observations and reasonable interpretations. This means that before evidence is used to build an argument, both the evidence and its source should be carefully evaluated.

Types of Reasoning

After we have secured our evidence, the next step is to use this evidence in a process of reasoning to build an argument. There are four basic kinds of reasoning which we can employ in constructing our arguments. We shall identify these ways of reasoning as example, analogy, cause-effect, and sign.

Reasoning by example consists of citing several similar instances or examples, and drawing a general conclusion from them. For instance, the church school superintendent might have said that the Revised Standard Version of the Bible is used in the worship services of the church school, that the Revised Standard Version of the Bible is used by the students in the Senior High church school class for Bible study, and that a copy of the Revised Standard Version of the Bible is given to each young person who completes the church membership course and takes the vows of church membership. Then the superintendent might conclude that these examples indicate that the Revised Standard Version of the Bible is the version which this church is using to teach its young people.

In evaluating any such effort to reason by example, there are several important questions which we should ask. First, have enough examples been cited to justify such a conclusion? That is, could we say, on the basis of only three examples, that the Revised Standard Version of the Bible is the version which this church uses to teach its young people? A second question which should be asked is "Are these examples typical?" It might be that the super-intendent had selected just those cases where the Revised Version is used, and has selected only those examples which would support his conclusion. Finally, we would want to ask if there are any negative cases or examples. Do we know of any teachers in our church school who use another version or translation of the Bible? While the discovery of a negative instance does not mean that the conclusion should be discarded, provided that the negative instance can be explained, a negative example is cause for a careful study of the general conclusion.

Reasoning by analogy consists of comparing two objects or cases with the intent of showing that, because they are alike in several important respects, they are alike in the matter about which we are concerned. While reasoning by example draws a conclusion from one or more cases, reasoning by analogy arrives at a conclusion about one case by comparing it with another.[5]

In requesting the purchase of a new pulpit Bible, the worship committee could have used analogy as a way of presenting their argument. They might have reported that the First Church of their denomination in a nearby community had found that their worn and faded pulpit Bible needed to be replaced. They, too, had to decide about the version to be purchased and about how to properly withdraw a memorial Bible from use in the chancel. A new Revised Standard Version was purchased and dedicated as a memorial, and reports were received from those who read aloud from the new Bible in worship services that it is easier to read aloud from this new Bible. They also said that the high school young people were commenting more favorably on the reading of the scripture in the worship services.

Therefore, the worship committee might say that if we purchase a Revised Standard Version pulpit Bible, we may expect that our worship leaders will also find it easier to read aloud from this new

---

[5] McBurney, O'Neill, and Mills, *op. cit.*, p. 106.

Bible and that reading from the new Bible will have more impact on our young people.

There are two key questions which ought to guide us in examining such reasoning by analogy. First, we should ask if these two situations are really alike or similar in their conditions, prior to the proposed action. It might be that before the church in the other community purchased a Revised Standard Version of the Bible, the church embarked on an educational campaign to acquaint everyone with the merits of the Revised Standard Version. Someone might point to this fact and say that because we have not had such a campaign, we cannot expect that a new version would be so well received in our church.

A second key question to ask about reasoning by analogy is, "Is the same sort of action being proposed as was taken in the first situation?" Perhaps we are proposing to buy the same size pulpit Bible as we now have, whereas the other church bought a pulpit Bible that was larger than their former Bible, and that it was the larger print rather than a new Bible that made it easier to read. Then, they might say that we should not expect that the new Bible will be easier to read unless we are ready, not only to buy a *new* Bible, but a *larger* one.

Another important method of reasoning is concerned with causal relations. This method moves either from the cause to the effect or from the effect to the cause. An example of arguing from cause to effect would be the declaration that the operation of a bus for transporting children to and from church school would produce a twenty per cent increase in church school attendance. In this case, it is said that the operation of a bus (cause) will effect a twenty per cent increase in church school attendance. Now, in this same case (after the bus had been put into service), one could reason from effect to cause. One could start with the effect, twenty per cent increase in church school attendance, and work back to the cause by saying that the new attenders are coming because they now have transportation in the form of a bus which the church is operating.

Once again, this reasoning can be tested by asking appropriate questions: For example, "Is this cause big enough to produce this effect?" That is, does this bus transport a sufficient number of students to account for a twenty per cent increase in attendance? Another significant question is, "Are there any other causes contributing to this effect?" Someone might want to suggest that the attendance crusade in the Sunday School is partly responsible for the increased attendance. A third question would be, "Has any relationship been shown between the cause and the effect?" Has it been demonstrated that those students who come by bus are new attenders or more regular in their attendance, and that their attendance is due to the transportation which the bus provides? A final question is, "Would this cause produce any other effect?" Some might express the fear that parents will attend church less frequently or that the operation of the bus will place an undue strain on the church budget. These four questions are equally pertinent, whether one is reasoning from cause to effect or from effect to cause. It is wise to be especially persistent about the matter of causal relationship.

In addition to asking these four questions, one should also be certain that the cause or the effect (depending on whether we begin with the cause or the effect) is identified and known. Do not develop a structure of argument from an assumed cause or an assumed effect. In the preceding illustration, we would want to be certain that the bus was in regular operation or that there actually was a twenty per cent increase in attendance.

A fourth way of reasoning is to draw conclusions from signs. A sign is a thing which is thought to indicate the presence or absence of another thing. A sign may be an attribute of a substance, as whiteness is an attribute of snow. If one saw that the ground was white, he might say that this is a sign that the ground is covered with snow. Jesus refers to this kind of reasoning in the gospel of Matthew when he says, "Ye hypocrites, ye can discern the face of the sky; but ye cannot discern the signs of the times." This way of reasoning differs from example, in that the signs are not "like instances." It differs from cause-effect reasoning, in that it is not concerned with a causal relationship. That is, there is no concern for what causes an effect. Finally, this way of reasoning differs from analogy, because it does not draw its conclusion on the basis of the way one event compares with another. As the word "sign" suggests, we draw a conclusion from signs—appearances—that are not examples, analogies, or in a causal relationship. For example, we might say that the following items are signs that the present pulpit Bible has been used for many years.

1. The pages are faded.
2. The pages are torn.
3. The print is of an older style.
4. It is a King James version.

The following questions are two main tests of reasoning by sign: "Are those certain signs?" and "Is the relationship reciprocal?" Applying this to our reasoning about the age of the pulpit Bible, we would ask, "Are fading and torn pages certain signs of many years of use?" We would have to answer that they are not certain signs. Fading might be produced by peculiar conditions of climate or environment, and tearing might indicate only careless use. That is, one could not say for certain that *every time* he finds a book with pages that are faded and torn, he has found an old book.

The matter of the older style of print suggests the importance of asking if the relationship is reciprocal—that is, can it be turned around. One might say that any Bible which is printed with a style of type that was created ten years ago could be no more than ten years old; and this would be a *certain sign,* since a book could not possibly have been printed in that style of print earlier than ten years ago, because that style of print did not exist prior to that date. However, (reciprocal) we cannot say that every Bible printed in a style of type created earlier than ten years ago was printed more than ten years ago. It might have been printed only five years ago by a publisher who chose to use an older style of type. This means, then, that the modern style of type might be a certain sign that a Bible was no more than ten years old, but it is not a certain sign that a Bible, printed in an older style of type, is more than ten years old. The sign relationship is not reciprocal.

The signs cited earlier—fading, torn pages, older style print, and King James version—indicate that the Bible may have been used for many years. However, they are not certain signs regarding the number of years that the Bible has been used, and this matter would have to be verified by other evidence or reasoning.

Review of the Steps in the Building of an Argument

In order to review the steps of building an argument, let us suppose that we were the worship committee, and that we wanted to

prepare an argument for the purchase of a new pulpit Bible. We
would proceed to prepare our argument in the following way.

First we would develop a clear and definite statement of our
proposition: "This church should purchase a new Revised Standard Version Pulpit Bible."

Second, we would define the terms. In this instance we might
want to define the term "Pulpit Bible."

Third, we would try to discover the issues. Since this is a question of policy, it will help us to look for issues in the area of *need,
practicality,* and *benefits.* After a careful study and analysis, we
decide that in the area of *need,* we shall show that there is a need
to replace the Bible because it is not the version which our young
people are trained to read and understand. In the area of practicality, we shall deal with the issues of acceptability of the Revised
Standard Version to older members, the retiring of the present
Bible which is a memorial, and the question of financing the purchase of the new Bible. Finally, in the area of *benefits,* we shall
deal with the readability of the Bible which we propose to purchase, and with the appreciation the young people will have for
reading from this new version. As you can see, at this point we
already have a rough outline of the major sections of our argument.

I. This church should purchase a new Revised Standard Version
   Pulpit Bible, because
   A. We need a new Pulpit Bible, because
      1. The present Pulpit Bible is badly worn, and
      2. The present Bible is a version that is not easily read or
         understood by our young people.
   B. The purchase of a new Pulpit Bible would be practical, because
      1. We plan to persuade the older members of its worth, and
      2. The present memorial will be continued in the purchase
         and presentation of the new Bible, and
      3. There are two Church School classes that wish to underwrite
         the purchase of the new Bible.
   C. The purchase of a new Pulpit Bible would be beneficial, because
      1. Those leading the worship services would find it easier to
         read from the new Bible, and
      2. Our young people would have additional understanding of,
         and appreciation for, the reading from the new Pulpit Bible.

The fourth step is to gather evidence which can be employed to
support each of the points in the above outline. Under point *A.1,*

"The present Bible is badly worn," we would list the reports that it is torn and faded and that the binding is broken. After assembling our evidence under the various points, we would apply the tests of evidence in order to select the strongest evidence for building our argument.

Fifth, we would examine the evidence under each point, to determine what type of reasoning should be used to organize and interpret this evidence. Under point *A.1,* we might use examples of torn pages 24, 103, and 507 to support the general statement that the Pulpit Bible has torn pages. Then we might use the general statement that the Bible has torn pages as a sign to show that the Bible is worn. In section *A.1,* then, we could decide to use the reasoning methods of example and sign to interpret our evidence.

Sixth, we would set out to construct a complete sentence outline of our case. First the proposition would be stated. Then the terms would be defined. After we have defined the terms, the outline would be developed following the issues relevant to this question. For a proposition of policy, the major steps in the outline would be: Need, Practicality, and Desirability. Under each of these major steps would appear the various questions which must be answered to establish or prove the issues. The organization of the evidence chosen to provide the answer to each of these major questions will be determined by the structure of the method of reasoning which we have decided to use.

All of the advice about the outlining, which is given in Chapter 5 dealing with explanatory speaking, should be followed when preparing your argument. One sure way to strengthen your argument is to make it clear and understandable. Audiences are much more likely to be convinced by that which they understand. If audiences are clearly able to understand your argument, you must give them a good outline to serve as a guide to the structure of your argument.

If you wish to argue against a proposition, instead of for it, your procedure will be much the same. You will seek to discover the issues. Then you will find the evidence and reasoning which will enable you and the audience to say "no" to the issue questions. That is, you will build your argument so that it shows that there is no need for a change, there is no practical way to effect this change, and there are no benefits which will result from this change, or that this change will not be as beneficial as another change which could be made. Except for this basic difference, you will select the types of reasoning to organize and interpret your evidence in the same manner as described for the person who is arguing in favor of the proposition.

As these steps of preparation indicate, good thinking is prompted by careful analysis of propositions, by the use of tested evidence, and by responsible reasoning. You can best strengthen your ability to present arguments by mastering the basic skills of building a speech of argumentation as they have been described in this chapter.

The ability to state a proposition clearly, analyze it accurately, and marshal reasoning and evidence in the support of your arguments will be of help to you when you want to suggest changes in policy, advocate the worth of a proposal, or support a factual judgment. Your able use of argumentation will greatly facilitate the functioning of any policy-making group of which you are a part.

chapter 9

Speaking
for
Special
Occasions

T he numerous activities of a local church offer a variety of occasions for speeches.[1] Several of these occasions are so distinct that
they require a particular kind of speech preparation and presentation. If a speaker fails to recognize the unique nature of these
speaking occasions, he may founder miserably when attempting to
fulfill such a speaking assignment. Indeed, many people mistakenly
assume that occasional speeches or speeches for special occasions
require little preparation and can be adequately presented in a
casual, impromptu manner. This attitude is so far from a correct
appraisal of occasional speaking, that we can say without reserva-
tion, it is a sure recipe for failure.

---

[1] H. A. Brack, "Why Pre-Ministerial Students Need Forensic Training," *The
Gavel* (January 1957), pp. 41, 42, 52, 54.

Characteristics of Occasional Speeches

A speaker must develop an appreciation for several important characteristics of the occasional speaking situation. To begin with, you should discover what the relationship of the occasion is to the life of the institution or organization that has provided the opportunity for making the speech. You may obtain a better understanding of the speaking situation by viewing it in the light of the purpose and history of the organization which is serving as its sponsor. It will also be helpful to know the significance of this occasion in the current program of the organization or institution.

Second, you will do well to inquire into the history of the particular occasion. Who has participated in this event in the past? What actions have been taken? What was the nature of the program in other years? Acquaintance with the history of an occasion provides a speaker with many suggestions for establishing common ground with his hearers.

Third, it is advisable to ask what this event means to the people who are participating in it. The speaker must not only be sensitive to the institutional and historical importance of the occasion, but also be aware of the meaning it holds for the people who are now sharing in it. You can find real help for both the selection and the development of your subject by knowing the meaning the occasion has for your immediate hearers.

A fourth important factor in the preparation and presentation of your speech is its place in the program for the occasion, for whether you are at the beginning, in the middle, or at the end might easily determine the length and the spirit of your remarks. It would be helpful to see a plan of the program and to know its time breakdown. It would also be helpful to know if you are regarded as a preliminary performer, as a courtesy speaker, or as the main speaker. Briefly, we may say that it is important to discover your place in terms of format and time, as well as in terms of prestige and function.

Fifth, you will find it imperative to determine what purpose you are to fulfill in the program. Be careful that you do not assume that you know what your purpose is. Do not let the person who has asked you to speak assume that you know what your purpose is. Similarly, do not be reticent about interrogating the program chairman thoroughly until you have a precise understanding of the purpose of your speech. It would be unfortunate if you were expected to speak some words of tribute for deeds accomplished, and instead you spent your time speaking of the work that lies ahead. People who are planning programs are so familiar with them that they assume that other participants are also well informed, and they often do not provide the speaker with an adequate briefing unless they are persistently prodded for such information.

Sixth, some knowledge of the mood of your audience on this occasion is vital to a successful fulfillment of your speaking engagement. If people were meeting with feelings of sorrow and respect, then frivolity would alienate them. On the other hand, the awareness that a dinner meeting will be conducted in a mood of relaxed gaiety might be the incentive you need to make a really entertaining speech. Working with the mood of the audience is like riding a jet stream, whereas working against the mood of the audience is like bucking a headwind. If a speaker desires to have rapport with his audience during these speeches for special occasions, he had better attempt to predict with great care and shrewdness their dominant mood.

Finally, a speaker ought to make every effort to discover what is appropriate in terms of conduct and speech. If this is the sort of occasion where everyone puts forth his best manners and his most refined ideas, the speaker will want to behave accordingly. Presiding officers and attending dignitaries should be addressed by their proper titles and according to prevailing protocol. Established customs and practices should be understood and followed. No speaker should run the risk of arousing audience hostility, because he has been careless about the feeling of an audience concerning what is appropriate for the occasion.

These seven characteristics will not only enable the speaker to fulfill his assignment for occasional speaking more adequately, but also they will be the means by which the speaker recognizes that he has a special kind of speech to deliver and that it will require a special preparation.

Types of Speeches

Let us now discuss in some detail several types of speeches that are frequently given for specific occasions in the life of the church. These speeches, as well as the frequency with which they are given, may vary in nature from church to church. Therefore, the suggestions given here for their preparation and delivery are offered not as final or complete advice about any specific speech, but as a guide to help you formulate what needs to be done in the case of the particular speech for which you are preparing.

Speech of Welcome

Present trends toward church co-operation and ecumenicity result in a large number of joint endeavors. Consequently, groups in the church are often hosts to other church groups from their community. On such occasions program committees frequently request that a representative of the local church "say a few words of welcome." One of the more important features of a speech of welcome is the proper identification of the person or group being welcomed. The failure to state correctly the name of the person or group is so destructive to the feeling of being welcomed that every precaution should be taken to prevent such an error. Secure the name in writing with a marking of the pronunciation which the person or group prefers. Then fix this name firmly in your memory so that you can recall it in an instant and pronounce it correctly.

An equally important matter in the speech of welcome is that the welcome be sincere. An audience has an uncanny way of detecting insincerity, and it is of little avail to pretend or fake sincerity. The best policy for the speaker is to acquaint himself with the purpose for bringing the person or group to the church, and with the character of the person or group. The intent of such investigation should be to discover genuine reasons for being happy to welcome the person or group to the church.

Third, we would suggest that it strengthens the note of welcome to mention specific achievements of the person or group. Such mention of specific achievements gives those being welcomed a feeling of being known and approved.

Next, it will strengthen the welcome to indicate that this church has a history of interest and work in behalf of this person or group. The awareness of a history of interest in our welfare makes any stranger feel that he has, indeed, not only been known and approved, but also fully accepted. In fact, he may quickly envision your church as an old friend whom he has longed to know better.

Fifth, if a group is being welcomed, it is advisable to state the facilities and services which are being placed at their disposal. This indication of definite accommodations reinforces your words of welcome with signs of concrete acts of welcome. Such information serves as a kind of proof that their coming has been anticipated and that provisions have been made for their comfort.

Finally, in a speech of welcome, choose words that are specific and concrete. Moreover, it is wise to be concise. A wordy speech of welcome, full of vague generalities, sounds like a speech that is made to any person or any group that you happen to be welcoming, and it has a kind of hollow and empty sound. This hollowness or emptiness can be avoided only by filling your speech with specific, concrete, and concise references to the person or group whom you are greeting.

Speech of Introduction

The times when new officers, new members, guest speakers, visiting dignitaries, former members or officials, and substitute teachers have to be introduced to church groups are legion. Even in churches of moderate size, at least one speech of introduction is given every week. These speeches of introduction are worthy of attention, not only because they are given so frequently, but also because they can become either a spring board or a stumbling block for the person who is being introduced. When making a speech of introduction, our aims should be to build a bridge to the audience over which the speaker may walk, and to avoid raising any barrier between the audience and the speaker. In our discussion we shall assume that the person being introduced intends to respond to the introduction by addressing the group to whom he is introduced.

Here too, the matter of first importance is that we be exact in stating the speaker's name, topic, and accomplishments. Failure to introduce the speaker accurately is apt to make him uneasy, and it is likely to raise doubts in the mind of the audience. If the speaker feels that it is necessary to correct our mistakes, the effect of the introduction of his own remarks will be seriously impaired. Therefore, we should attempt to secure accurate information in writing from a reliable source about the speaker's name, topic, and achievements. We should then take care to become familiar with this information and to practice presenting it accurately.

Second, give the speaker reasonable praise or "build up." When you introduce a speaker, you should take advantage of this opportunity to build the speaker's prestige with the audience. An able presentation of those facts about a speaker's life and work which demonstrate that he is eminently worth listening to, will help the audience decide to give this speaker a good hearing. However, it is important to bear in mind the word "reasonable." A well-meaning person can try too hard to impress the audience with the merits of a speaker. Once a well-meaning Methodist preacher at a Union Service of several Protestant congregations concluded a long and excessively complimentary introduction of Bishop Oxnam with "Now I present MR. PROTESTANT." The Bishop, himself embarrassed by this overly zealous effort of personal tribute, said, "Sometimes love and respect make a friend too extravagant in his praise." You ought to say a good word for the person whom you are introducing, but avoid showering him with bouquets of superlatives.

Third, when introducing a speaker, create an air of expectation. This can be done, in part, by building the speaker's prestige; it can be done more effectively by exciting us about the speaker's subject. There are several ways by which you can stir up subject interest. If the audience is strikingly reminded about the relevance of this subject to the solving of a persistent daily problem, they will become more interested. A sharp reminder that this speaker is going to deal with a subject that is at the center of current controversy will alert the audience. A vivid suggestion that the speaker is going to present some information about which there is a great deal of contemporary curiosity will whet the intellectual appetite of the audience. In the use of these or other methods to create an air of expectation, the introducer should always remember that he is trying to help the audience prepare to give the speaker a good hearing. Going to extremes with any of the above methods might, of course, embarrass rather than help the speaker.

Fourth, you will want to suggest to the audience that you have respect and admiration for the person whom you are introducing, by delivering your speech of introduction proficiently and with enthusiasm. A lack of readiness to deliver the introduction or a sort of casual, even careless, delivery will suggest a lack of expectation or appreciation on your part. Do not kill, by a halting and feeble delivery, what interest the audience does have. You ought, at least, to present the audience to the speaker in the same state of interest in which you found them when you began the speech of introduction.

In addition to the four previous suggestions, there are two cautions which every person making a speech of introduction should observe. The first is to omit anything that does not help introduce the speaker. The speech of introduction ought not to be prolonged by even one extraneous item. One of the worst offenses is to weary the audience with much speaking before the person who is being introduced has had a chance to speak. The second caution is to avoid any hint of negative suggestion. Do not apologize because the speaker has been ill, has a cold. or has just arrived and is still out of breath. Do not apologize because this is a different speaker from the one originally announced, or because the topic is different from the one which you had assumed. In short, do not suggest any reason to the audience for being disappointed in the speaker.

When making a speech of introduction, remember that you are a member of the speaking team. If you do not do a good job of "running interference," the speaker will not be able to advance. If you stumble in front of the speaker or if you fail to "block out" opponents like ignorance or apathy, you must accept responsibility for the speaker's failure to achieve rapport with his audience.

Speech of Presentation

In the life of almost every church there are several annual occasions for the presentation of awards or gifts. These are important moments in the lives of the individuals who are receiving the awards or gifts. For them, their families, and their friends, a shoddy speech of presentation will be an offense. Consequently, it is necessary to prepare a speech of presentation carefully and to deliver it with due solicitude and enthusiasm.

First, be certain that you have the correct name of the recipient and that you can pronounce it accurately. Muffing the name of the recipient is apt to be viewed as careless indifference, totally inappropriate to the occasion.

Second, take pains to identify properly the group that is giving the gift or award. Since you have agreed to be their spokesman on this occasion, they will expect you to represent them well. In fact, if a group has invested a great deal of effort and money in order to provide a gift or award, they are apt to feel that you rob them of due recognition when you do not correctly identify them.

Third, discuss the reason for this gift or award. At this point it is worthwhile to be analytical and specific. "This gift is presented in recognition of the many years of fine service" is not a good way to discuss the reason or reasons for giving a gift. When one hears such a line in a speech of presentation, it suggests a standard patter which you might have used on other such occasions. You can personalize the above phrase by stating the actual period of time and the particular kind of service performed. Moreover, if the service was cheerfully, reliably, and sacrificially given, these characteristics deserve to be mentioned. When there is a presentation of an award for a particular kind of achievement, this achievement ought to be described in definite terms, so that those who are present may better appreciate the kind of work which had to be completed by the recipient in order to earn the award.

Fourth, you should explain the significance of the gift or award being presented. If a medal, or pin, or badge is being given, there may be symbols and words which can be interpreted. If this is a gift, it may have been selected because it symbolizes the work that has been done, or because it will fulfill a wish or desire expressed by the person receiving it. Such explanation will make the recipient and the audience aware of the appropriateness of the gift and add to the feeling that the presentation is being carried out in a fitting and proper manner.

Fifth, the characteristics which strengthen the speech of presentation are originality and genuine sincerity. Originality suggests that an effort has been made to tailor the speech to this particular occasion and that the speaker has a personal interest in it. The mood or spirit of genuine sincerity suggests a personal appreciation for the recipient and his work or service. These two characteristics can best be achieved by making a determined effort to become familiar with the work and the life of the recipient. Speakers rarely succeed in communicating a sense of personal interest unless they have taken a personal interest in the recipient.

Only a brief word of warning need be said about the use of language. If a speaker drifts to flowery expressions and overstatement, he is apt to be thought insincere and ignorant of the recipient's life or work. Lack of information or lack of sincerity cannot be masked by extravagant, ornamented overstatement. Unusual or excessive flourishes in delivery might also have the same unhappy effect. A speech of presentation, then, must be carefully prepared and well delivered.

Speech of Tribute or Memorial

There is a kinship between this type of address and the speech of presentation. However, there are also distinct differences. This address is usually of greater length and is prepared and presented with a greater degree of formality. Also, it has a dual purpose of honoring the person who is being memorialized, or to whom tribute is being paid, and of moving the members of the audience to gratitude, respect, and emulation. The language of this type of speech may properly be dignified and "eloquent." Often when tribute is to be paid and a gift presented, these acts are separated, and both a speech of presentation and a speech of tribute are made. Founders Day, Homecoming, and Memorial Day are a few of the many occasions when speeches of tribute or memorial are made.

An appropriate way to begin a speech of tribute or memorial is to recognize the occasion and its value. For example, "Today we are gathered from all parts of this country and from three neighboring states to pay tribute to a teacher in our Church School. It is altogether fitting and right so to honor those who make such significant contributions to the religious education of our children."

Launch your speech of tribute by explicitly stating the occasion for our gathering and the worthiness of the purpose which we are striving to fulfill.

Continue the speech of tribute or memorial with an appreciative citing of the deeds and actions which have won our admiration and our gratitude. These items ought to be arranged in an order that will move toward a climax of sacrifice, or faithfulness, or of some sort of behavior that will elicit responses of gratitude, respect, and emulation from the audience. It is also advisable to clothe your outline of the person's deeds with some human interest items so that the personality of the honoree becomes vivid and real in the minds of your hearers.

Next, your address should emphasize the obligation we have to the person being honored. One method of making this point is to trace the way in which the deeds and actions of the honoree have produced beneficial effects for our own lives. In order for this phase of the speech to be convincing, it will be necessary to do more than assert that the person being honored is our benefactor. You will have to present an accurate and sufficiently detailed description to establish a convincing relationship between our current benefits and the previous behavior of the subject of your speech.

In addition, this section of the speech can be strengthened by quickening appreciation of these benefits through citing interesting, contemporary, local examples of them. If this section of the speech of tribute or memorial is not done well, the speaker will fail to generate in himself and in the audience, the mood appropriate for the occasion.

There is a fourth step which is particularly important if this is a memorial speech. It consists of moving out from the tributes which have been paid and the personal example which has been praised to an advocating of a new behavior for the group—"It is rather for us to be here dedicated to the great task remaining before us." That is, let the memorial move the audience to undertake a mission. This fourth step is essential to completing the purpose of such an occasion; for the purpose of paying tribute or conducting memorial services is not only to honor the subject of the tribute or memorial, but also to provide inspiration and guidance for those who are gathered to pay tribute or to memorialize.

Delivery of this type of address deserves dynamic dignity. The delivery should suggest due respect for the honoree and genuine concern for those who are assembled to do honor.

Address at a Recognition of Educational Achievement

The educational program within the local church is being extended to every age group and also to week days as well as Sundays. This means that there is an increased need for speakers at occasions which recognize the educational achievement of those participating in the educational program of the church. Whether the speaker is making a commencement address or whether he is speaking for three minutes, he must appreciate the uniqueness of the occasion which demands special attention.

You may well begin such a speech by indicating your personal appreciation of this occasion. Try to state clearly and succinctly what such achievement means in the life and work of the church, and why you are glad for such accomplishments.

Second, attempt to identify yourself with the air of nostalgia which is peculiar to the occasion. You will discover that this is one of those interludes in life when most of those present are happy to see an experience completed and yet reluctant to see it come to an end. If a speaker can capture this mood in words, express it well, and then lead out to a consideration of his theme, he will have seized a rich opportunity for achieving rapport with his audience.

Third, you should utilize quotations from the Bible, from great books, and from great persons. Since one of the common assumptions about formal education is that it attempts to make us familiar with our heritage, such quotations have particular prestige on these occasions. You will find the audience receptive to your efforts to share with them quotations which represent a fine distillation of wisdom.

Fourth, in choosing a theme or subject for your address, you will do well to choose a theme on which you can express yourself with some feeling or conviction. Since, in one sense, this occasion of recognition is viewed as a climax of the educational experience, those participating in the program will expect (or at least hope) that your remarks will lift the occasion to a climactic moment in their educational experience. In order to lead any audience into such an inspiring moment, a speaker needs the directness and spontaneity in delivery which come when he is speaking on a theme about which he has keen feelings and compelling convictions.

In conclusion, let us say that an address on an occasion of recognition of educational achievement ought to show a personal appreciation of the occasion, identify with the air of nostalgia, employ excellent quotations, deal with a theme about which the speaker has keen feelings and compelling convictions, and make use of narrative, human interest material, and specific details.

After-Dinner Speech

With the current effort to emphasize the aspect of "fellowship" in the church, church dinners are employed less and less to raise money and more and more as an opportunity for fellowship. Often the program at these fellowship dinners includes an after-dinner speaker. Moreover, there are the traditional father-son and mother-daughter banquets, as well as annual dinner meetings of various church organizations, which also provide opportunities for after-dinner speaking. These church opportunities, as well as the numerous community after-dinner speaking situations, indicate the importance of becoming informed about this type of public address.

Usually audiences will expect that the after-dinner speech will be well seasoned with humor—they will be looking for the "light touch." The use of humor on such an occasion can be justified, not only on the basis of tradition, but also on the basis of the need to make the speech interesting and refreshing. Moreover, humor is consistent with the mood of cordiality and friendliness which is created by the act of dining together. The chairman or toastmaster frequently adds to the expectation of humor by introducing the speaker with humorous remarks.

The first step in preparing the after-dinner speech is to develop the right attitude toward its presentation. An essential ingredient of the speech with a light touch is that the speaker have a good time while delivering it. In order to have fun in the delivery of this speech, you must secure genuinely humorous material, organize it clearly, and so thoroughly prepare for the delivery that you are confident of your material and of your ability to present it. You will find helpful suggestions for discovering humorous material in

Chapter 7 on making the speech interesting. The section of that chapter dealing with humor points up the merit of humorous life situations, the play on words, understatement, and overstatement.

Second, remember that in the presentation of the humorous story, the two important elements are *timing* and *certainty of the punch line.* If the timing is wrong, the mood which is part of the humor of the situation will be lost, and the item will not appear as funny as it really is or it may not seem humorous at all. If the punch line is missed, there is no humor because the turn of events necessary to indicate the true humor of the situation never occurs. Thus, in preparing to deliver the humorous speech, we should pay special attention to the timing of the humor and to the correct statement of the punch line.

Third, the after-dinner speech should be designed to give the impression of clear and brisk movement toward a goal or a conclusion. Vagueness, subtle distinctions, rambling development, or confusing transitions serve as invitations to the audience to indulge their drowsiness or their inclination to attend to the noises in the kitchen or the activities of the waitresses or other diners. Work for a clear outline in which each point advances the thought of the speech. Compose your transitions with words that indicate movement—"Another example of the absent-mindedness of students is . . ."; "A third type of listener that distracts a speaker . . ."; "They gave me my next scare the following evening." Use summaries to indicate that we have already covered a good deal of ground: "Now that we know that students are absent-minded about taking examinations, about fulfilling assignments, and about personal articles which they bring to the classroom. . . ." Let the clarity of outline, movement in the transitions, and review of completed tasks in the summaries suggest to your audience that this speech is marching along.

Fourth, the after-dinner speaker will want to deliver his speech in a way that makes a firm demand for the attention of the audience. Usually this means that the delivery must be vigorous and forceful and yet seem relaxed and easygoing, for the latter mood is associated with a humorous or a light touch. Consequently, the speaker should plan to project his voice strongly, and to use vocal variety and gestures to help hold the attention of the audience.

When fulfilling an after-dinner speaking assignment, remember to secure genuinely humorous material, organize it clearly, and prepare thoroughly. As you present humorous stories, pay particular attention to timing and be certain of the punch line. Move your speech along clearly and briskly. Let your delivery make a firm demand for the attention of your audience.

Summary

We have now considered six types of "occasional speeches" which are frequently given in the church. Since speaking in the church involves many additional speaking occasions which are sufficiently distinct and unique to demand special preparation, we urge you to continue your study of these speaking occasions and the types of speeches demanded by them. Pay particular attention to:

1. The relation of this speaking event to the life of the institution.
2. The history of the speaking occasion.
3. The meaning of the event to the participants.
4. The place of the address in the program.
5. The purpose of the address.
6. The prevailing mood of the occasion.
7. The kind of behavior which is appropriate to this occasion.
8. The customs which are observed for this occasion.

In addition, consider what the above information means to you in terms of selecting a purpose for your speech, choosing apt words, selecting content materials, the length of your speech, your attitude as the speaker, and the degree of formality to be maintained in the composition and delivery of the speech.

chapter 10

Discussion and Conference: An Introduction

As we approach this subject of Discussion and Conference, let us look at some experiences of persons at work in the church and in related settings. It may be helpful if we observe, in particular, the relevance of these situations to the life and work of the church, the purposes of these situations, the forms in which they appear, and the obligations and opportunities which are inherent in them.

Situation No. 1. It is a few minutes before noon on a Sunday morning. The preacher is bringing the sermon to a close. For some twenty minutes he has been projecting, to the best of his ability, his *convictions* regarding a theme (perhaps his *solution* to a *problem*), using all available resources of rhetorical or homilectical theory associated with conviction and the desire to convince others. To the extent that he uses these methods to the full, he is likely to be successful in achieving his goal—and at the same time, to be regarded as a good *preacher*.

At 12:15 P.M., however, this same man finds himself as a leader
of a meeting of the church Personnel Committee, of which he is the
chairman. Here he is in another position of *leadership*—and he is
using the instruments and processes of oral communication; but
here the similarity ends. Obviously there is a difference between the
two situations in terms of *size* and *form*. However, as we shall soon
see, there are even more important factors of difference; and a
number of the attributes which would make this man a good
preacher would not necessarily make him a good *discussion leader*
—in fact, would actually prevent him from being such a leader.

If at 12:15 P.M. he were to find himself as a *participant* in a meeting of the Pastoral Relations Committee or of the Board of Elders,
essentially the same circumstances would prevail. To put it simply,
*the skills of good preaching are not necessarily those of good discus-
sion (or conference) leadership or participation.*

Situation No. 2. A layman may be a "good speaker," may be an
effective salesman, executive, or leader in his field; he may even be
a good parliamentarian, toastmaster, or presiding officer; yet he will
not necessarily be a good leader of, or participant in, many of the
meetings, discussions, or conferences in which he will participate
as an active member of the church. In fact, some of these experiences and capabilities may actually be harmful unless modified
by other principles and practices.

Situation No. 3. The Executive Committee of the Church School
is meeting under the leadership of the superintendent as chairman.
Even though the problem is clear and the members of the committee are well informed concerning it, little constructive progress
is being made. There is little logical progression of thought; some
of the members are not participating as effectively as they might;
and the leader frequently monopolizes the discussion. It is only with
much effort and after considerable lost motion that some decisions
are made.

Situation No. 4. During the same week, a special committee on
Office Space for the church, with a layman as the chairman, and the
board of Women's Society, with one of the leading laywomen as its
chairman, experience similar difficulties as they attempt to think
through their respective problems. In essence, they have difficulties

in "getting somewhere" and in using effectively the human resources represented by the participants.

Situation No. 5. At a meeting of the Official Board, one of the groups in the church is using the *panel discussion* method as a means of presenting its program to the Board. (It might as well be using the *symposium* method as far as we are concerned at this point.) Several complications in the form of inadequate leadership, faulty organization, and unsatisfactory adaptation to the audience develop—with the result that the purpose is not achieved and, perhaps, that some persons begin to disparage discussion methods.

Why have we described these situations? Not to indict the pastor or the lay persons as "poor churchmen," but to point to three significant phenomena: (1) both pastors and laymen are constantly involved in what we are calling "discussion or conference sessions" as they go about the work of the church; (2) no matter how dedicated these persons may be, difficulties arise pertaining to the *process* of discussion (preparation, analysis of the subject, leadership, participation, and so forth) which cause trouble—and which can be avoided if attention is paid to the principles and methods which we shall consider in this and subsequent chapters; (3) no matter how skilled or competent preachers and laymen may be in the several aspects of their professions—and no matter how skilled in those aspects of oral communication discussed in Part I of this book—they are not, thereby, necessarily competent in discussion or conference situations.

In this chapter we shall attempt to do five things: (1) briefly review some of the discussion or conference situations confronting both professional and nonprofessional church workers (not only those situations in which a group seeks to find solutions to problems, but those in which it studies a subject by means other than a single speech or a lecture); (2) note the nature and purposes of discussion or conference, particularly with reference to the public speaking situations described in Part One of this book; (3) observe some relationships between discussion or conference, on the one hand, and such current concepts as "Group Dynamics" and "Brainstorming," on the other—concepts which are frequently thought of as synonymous with discussion or conference; (4) comment upon some important values which stem from the proper use of discussion or conference in church work; and (5) note at what points, and in what respects, discussion or conference situations "break down."

Some Discussion or Conference Situations Related to the Church

Needless to say, we could approach this subject in a variety of ways. For instance, we could explore the *uses* of the discussion or conference method made by the pastor and those made by the layman. Also, we could think of the forms, purposes, and uses of discussion or conference. Finally, we could think in terms of the occasions in which the clergy and the laity meet to "talk things over" under less formal circumstances than those covered in Part I —occasions in the church itself and in related organizations and situations. Perhaps the last of these approaches will best serve our needs at this moment—emphasizing the situations and minimizing many somewhat unnecessary details. Perhaps, too, an outline of the several situations, of the roles of the pastor, and of the roles of laymen, such as the following may be most helpful.

SITUATIONS	ROLE OF PASTOR	ROLE OF LAYMAN
General Church Organizations		
Official Board or equivalent	Chairman Participant Resource Person	Chairman Participant
Church organization meetings (Men's Club, etc.)	Coach of Officers Participant Resource Person	Leader Participant
Planning sessions, committees, etc.	Leader Participant Coach of leaders Resource Person	Leader Participant
Staff meetings (clergy)	Leader Participant	
All-Church Meetings		
Family-Night programs	Leader Participant Coach of laymen Resource Person	Leader Participant

SITUATIONS	ROLE OF PASTOR	ROLE OF LAYMAN
Study-meetings (Bible, Issues of Life, etc.)	Leader Participant Coach of laymen Resource Person	Leader Participant Resource Person
The Church School		
Commission on Education	Participant Coach of laymen Resource Person	Leader Participant
Staff meetings	Participant Coach of laymen Resource Person	Leader Participant
Teacher-training meetings	Leader Participant Coach of laymen Resource Person	Leader Participant
Teaching of classes	Leader Participant Coach of laymen	Leader Participant Coach of other laymen
The Youth Fellowship		
Leadership groups (officers, etc.)	Coach of laymen Participant Resource Person	Leader Participant Resource Person
Programs	Coach of laymen Participant Resource Person	Leader Participant Resource Person
Institutes	Coach of laymen Participant Resource Person	Leader Participant Resource Person
Counseling		
Family or individual meetings	Leader Participant	Participant Leader
Court conferences	Participant	Participant
"Larger Church" Meetings		
City, County, etc. councils	Leader Participant Resource Person	Leader Participant
Inter-church conferences, committees, etc.	Leader Participant Resource Person	Leader Participant

SITUATIONS	ROLE OF PASTOR	ROLE OF LAYMAN
Community Organizations		
PTA, Rotary Club, etc.	Participant	Leader
	Leader (?)	Participant
Teachers' Institutes, etc.	Participant	Leader
	Leader (?)	Participant

Even a cursory glance at this outline will indicate the fact that any person who is active in the work of the church is confronted almost constantly with what we are calling discussion or conference situations. Nor is it enough to say that he is confronted with them (literally, can hardly "avoid" them); it is perhaps even more important to say that these situations are virtually waiting for him to use most efficiently. It is clear, also, that these situations vary to some extent in purpose and form; and it is equally clear that both clergymen and laymen have a variety of roles in connection with these several types of discussion groups.

Perhaps we should underscore two of the most important roles that can be played by the pastor in these situations—that of coach and that of critic. As a coach, he can work with the lay persons as they prepare for the meeting, serving as their guide in the realm of methodology. As a critic, he can be present as a sympathetic but critical observer, not actually participating but carefully noting the work of the leader and the participants, and later making helpful suggestions to the lay person or persons responsible for the meeting.

The Nature and Purpose of Discussion or Conference

From the several situations presented thus far in this chapter, some idea of what we mean by "discussion or conference" can be derived. It would appear, for instance, that it pertains to small groups (in most circumstances), with the attempt to solve problems or to answer questions, with something other than formal speech-making, with something like committee activity, or with the discussion of problems or other subjects by a few persons for the benefit of others. In fact, it may be defined or described as *the thinking through of, or the talking about, problems or topics by a relatively small number of persons—usually in an informal situation—for purposes of finding solutions or of learning something about the subjects.*

Perhaps the following key terms or concepts should be kept in mind: (1) *Purpose*—to solve problems or to learn about a subject; (2) *Form and Size*—in most instances, quite informal and small, the committee or board meeting being the most typical situation; although, on occasion, it may be somewhat more formal and somewhat larger. (These matters of *purpose* and of *form and size* will be discussed in some detail in subsequent chapters.)

Perhaps, also, some distinctions between discussion or conference and the traditional forms of public speaking which were considered in Part I may serve to clarify matters at this point. Let us think in terms of: (1) number of participants; (2) purpose; and (3) format.

Number of Participants. Normally in "public speaking" there is only one speaker, who is speaking to (or with) an audience, whose participation is largely that of listening. On the other hand, discussion or conference implies two or more participants in an active role—with the interaction between (among) these participants constituting the essence of the process.

Purpose. Quite clearly, the two primary purposes of public speaking are to present information and to influence attitudes and/or behavior concerning subjects which the speaker is presenting *to* his listeners. On the other hand, discussion or conference has, as its two principal purposes, the presenting of information and the solving of problems (personal problems—as in counseling—and group, institutional, and related problems). In the latter case (the solving of problems), the *starting point* is a felt need or a problem, and the *outcome* is the formulation of a solution to the problem.

Format. Essentially, by definition, public speaking embodies a formal speaker-audience situation, with modifications in the direction of informality being largely those of *degree* rather than those of *kind* (the speaker stands near to the audience; the speaker is seated while speaking; the audience is seated informally; the audience asks questions at any time during the speech; and so forth). However, discussion or conference is normally informal, with the participants seated around, or at, a table, and with each person a potential contributor to the discussion at any moment (the "round-

table," the committee meeting, and so forth). While it is true that
in such discussion situations as the "panel discussion" or the "symposium" there is an audience, these situations are essentially only
adaptations of the discussion process to the needs of a group too
large to use the round-table format.

Some Relationships of Discussion and Conference to Group Dynamics and Brainstorming

In response to the often-asked question regarding the relationship between discussion or conference, on the one hand, and group
dynamics, on the other, it may be said that while embracing many
of the elements of group dynamics, discussion is much broader.

To the extent that both are concerned with the nature of persons
in groups, and with their methods and processes of interaction—
and means of facilitating the interaction—they are essentially the
same thing. On the other hand, when discussion or conference is
concerned with the nature of problems for discussion, with patterns
of thought and organization, with the reasoning process, with
methods of preparation, and with forms of discussion—to mention
only certain factors—it is, of course, much more inclusive than group
dynamics.

While we are in sympathy with much of the doctrine of group
dynamics, we wish to go farther and explore the several factors
mentioned above. In short, we wish to consider, insofar as possible,
all of the facets of "logical" and "substantive" as well as "psychological" interaction.

As for the relationship of discussion or conference to "brainstorming," the latter represents, in essence, *one* of the steps in the problem-solving pattern or procedure—the step which we shall sub-
sequently refer to as the "suggestion of solutions or possible courses
of action." To the extent that this is an important step in the
process of analyzing problems and of seeking solutions (and indeed
it is), brainstorming is most useful. In fact, we shall cite and explain
many of its principles later in this book. However, to the extent
that much more is needed in the attempt to solve problems—and
much more *is* needed—this book will go far beyond the limits of
brainstorming as commonly defined.

Some Values of Discussion or Conference in Church Work

As suggested earlier, there are many uses of discussion or conference in church work. Applications are found, for instance, in boards, committees, commissions, workshops, and other all-church groups which devote their sessions to the analysis and solutions of problems. Furthermore, this is the process used by boards and committees of individual organizations within the church, such as the women's society, the men's club, and so forth. Nor is this all. Within the context of *problem solving*, it is used in church-family conferences, in counseling, and in connection with canvasses and visitations carried on in the interests of the church. Within the context of *learning about subjects*, it is used, as we have noted, in workshops, in church school classes, in programs of church organizations, and so forth,—usually in what we shall call "panel discussions" and "symposiums."

With respect to values accruing from this procedure, discussion or conference may be said to make several important contributions to the life and work of the church. The following are suggestive of the possibilities:

1. It is a means of developing a helpful climate for church life and administration—the climate in which "sharing," "team spirit," "give-and-take," and "two-way communication" are major factors. In fact, here is one of the greatest values of the discussion method. It is an important factor in individual and group therapy in that it places a high premium upon co-operation, open-mindedness, and objectivity. It is a means by which a person or a group can discover whether it possesses attributes which make for satisfying human relationships.

2. It is a means of advancing the basic purposes and tenets of the church—respect for persons and ideas, respect for the basic methods of democracy, and the like.

3. It is a valuable means of using or "tapping" laymen and their many resources.

4. It is a means of supplementing solitary thought in the solution of problems (supplementing, for instance, the thought of the pastor or the thought of only one layman in a given instance).

5. It is an important means of developing group understanding concerning problems facing the church.

6. It is a valuable means of making committees, commissions, and boards functional, and active organizations more than a mere aggregation of persons who attend meetings but who rarely participate effectively in the on-going work of the group.

7. As a teaching or instructional method, it is a useful variation from the more traditional means (speaker or teacher alone), and it is also a proven method of actually transmitting more information, and more fully retained information, than is the more traditional method.

Once again, we wish to emphasize two points concerning the place and the values of the discussion method in the church. First, many of these situations are already in existence, whether the pastor or the layman so wills or directs; committees exist, for example, as do commissions, boards, and similar groups, and any person who is active in the church confronts them almost daily. Second, it is probable that some of these discussion situations are not realizing their full potential in terms of content or of human values; and it is also probable that more of these discussion situations might well be introduced into the life and work of the typical church.

"Breakdowns" in Discussion or Conference Situations

While it is true that all human institutions and activities have their problems and points of breakdown, the majority of such troubles with the discussion or conference method can well be avoided, or minimized, by a careful analysis of their nature and their causes. For this reason, we are devoting a portion of this Introduction to an inventory of some of the more common problems encountered by committees, board, panels, and similar groups. Perhaps a review of the five situations presented earlier in this chapter would indicate some of these trouble spots. Perhaps, too, a mental inventory of the difficulties experienced by some committees would reveal still others—possibly an inept chairman, an over-zealous participant, a sense of "getting nowhere," a feeling that the subject under discussion is not being fully organized, and so forth.

For purposes of orderly, even if somewhat brief, analysis, it may be helpful to think of these difficulties with discussion or conference situations in terms of the four major factors which constantly operate: (1) the *content;* (2) the *leadership;* (3) the *participation;* and (4) the *physical situation.* Let us consider these factors in order.

The content. In terms of this factor, discussion groups usually have such difficulties as the following: (a) lack of commonly understood purpose; (b) a poor beginning; (c) little sense of direction; (d) lack of depth or definiteness in the handling of the material; (e) lack of clearness in the discussion; (f) excessive or uncritical agreement upon issues; (g) lack of a clear outcome or conclusion. (As we shall note in subsequent pages, these difficulties are not inherent, even though they do appear with alarming frequency.)

The leadership. The leadership, or chairmanship, may often be at fault for a number of reasons (some of these seemingly inconsistent), depending perhaps upon the personality of the leader, his experience in the position of a leader, or his conception of the role of the leader in a discussion. Such situations as the following may appear: (a) there may be excessive "tightness" in the leadership, as represented by "holding the reins tight," by "heavy-handedness," by constant domination on the part of the leader; (b) there may, on the other hand, be excessive "looseness," as represented by "no sense of direction or leadership" on the part of the person in charge; (c) there may be a lack of objectivity or impartiality on the part of the leader, as represented by "taking sides" too noticeably, by passing judgment upon all contributions rather than submitting these to the scrutiny of the group itself, by "steering" the deliberations of the group along the road which the leader believes to be the proper one; (d) there may be lack of imagination on the part of the leader; (e) there may be lack of analytical and of synthesizing abilities on the part of the leader, with the result that the subject is not properly "taken apart" or "put together."

The participation. The participation of the members of the discussion group may also be at fault, perhaps because of personality and similar problems, and perhaps because of ignorance of the proper method of participating in such a situation. Some of the more common problems are these: (a) there is a lack of preparation: too little general background information and/or too little specific information concerning the matter at hand; (b) there is a lack of enthusiasm or a desire to advance the work of the group; (c) there may be dogmatism and belligerency on the part of some members, especially when differences of opinion become acute or frequent; (d) there may be "unevenness" in participation: too much participation by some members and too little by others, whether conscious or unconscious; (e) there may be poor listening: participants may be preoccupied with their own views or even inattentive so that they do not understand fully or clearly the contributions of others.

The physical situation. While it may be emphasized that the mere arrangement of chairs will not necessarily distinguish a good discussion or conference from a poor one, it can properly be said that the physical situation is, indeed, an important element. (Experiments with groups of different sizes have shown that, other things being equal, the product of a conference and the human satisfactions attendant upon a conference are often related to the physical situation.) Among the considerations to be noted are the following four: (a) there is a poor arrangement of chairs and table (perhaps too formal, perhaps unsuited to the size of the group, perhaps inadequate for the audience in the case of the panel discussion); (b) there is a lack of *comfortable* arrangements (chairs uncomfortable, no provision for notetaking, and so forth); (c) the heating, lighting, and ventilation are poor or not as good as they might well be; (d) there are no facilities or provisions for such visual aids as a blackboard, charts, and similar means of implementing the discussion process. (Lest it be thought that we are emphasizing costly or special arrangements, it should be noted that virtually all of the facilities needed in this connection are in the typical conference or meeting room, or are readily available in the church. As will be noted later, it is normally a matter of recognition of the problem and of doing some advance, not costly, planning.)

With these introductory considerations in mind, we now proceed to an analysis of the principles and methods pertaining to the discussion process as a whole, to the leadership of discussion, to participation in discussion, and to special matters related to each type of discussion. It is our conviction, based upon years of experience, that a knowledge of these principles and methods will be a real help in improving one's skills of leadership, participation, and coaching.

chapter 11

Subjects
and Problems
for Discussion

The Personnel Committee of the church is in session. The Parish Executive (Business Manager) has reported that the wage and salary scales of the Civil Service employees in the community and those of the employees of the adjoining university have been raised by 5 per cent. Realizing that competition, if not other considerations, will force him to take some action, he says to the committee, "What should we do?" With this problem before it, the committee proceeds to find a solution (an answer) from among a variety of possibilities—possibilities which arise as they are suggested by the committee members during the discussion. (Note that no one possibility is suggested by the question itself.)

However, let us imagine that the question put to the committee was, "Should we raise our salaries and wages by 5 per cent?" Here, many aspects of the problem and of the discussion would be the same as those in the first illustration; and perhaps the solution would be the same. However, there would be one important element of difference. In this instance, *one* possible solution is named; and it must inevitably serve as the focal point in the discussion.

The Executive Board of the Men's Club is meeting to discuss the Christmas Party which for years it has provided for some fifty underprivileged boys in one section of the community. At the suggestion of the chairman of last year's committee, the Board has decided to devote two meetings to this subject, the first to evaluate what has been done for the past few years, and the second to consider possible alternatives. By common consent, the subject for this meeting is solely, "How good is what we have been doing?" (or "What judgment should we make regarding what we have been doing?"). It has been similarly agreed that not until the next meeting should the question of "What to do?" be asked.

Let us look into one more meeting in the church. It is a meeting of the Official Board (or its equivalent); and as a part of the program, the officers of the Senior High Fellowship are conducting a panel discussion for the purpose of informing the members of the Board about the work of the Fellowship: objectives, organization, and program. Here the starting point is the question, "What is the Senior High Fellowship?;" and the concluding point will consist of "factual" answers to this question. (The same elements would also be present if a symposium were to be the form of the discussion.) [1]

From these brief glimpses of church groups in action, we can readily observe several relevant facts: (1) some quite different matters are being discussed—those matters which inevitably arise in connection with the work of the respective groups; (2) the outcome of the respective discussions will necessarily be different (determination of a policy decision, increase in the amount of information and understanding, and so forth); (3) the outward forms of the discussions—small groups *vs.* large groups, "no audience" *vs.* "audience," and other variables—are different. It is with the first two of these circumstances that we are concerned in this chapter. (The third will be considered in Chapter 16.)

Here we may ask five questions: (1) What subjects are considered in what we are calling "discussion or conference situations"? (2) What *kinds* of problems are presented for discussion? (3) What are

---

[1] See Chapter 16 for a discussion of the *panel* and the *symposium*.

the relationships between these kinds of problems and the kinds of discussion groups? (4) What are some values in identifying the kinds of problems for discussion—of what value is this analysis? (5) What are some rules or suggestions regarding the phrasing of discussion problems?

Subjects for Discussion or Conference

As we have noted, the subjects for discussion or conference are determined by the *purposes, interests, concerns, and needs of a given group.* They are in no way restricted by the existence of the process called "discussion." For instance, if the Personnel Committee is concerned with salaries and wages, then salaries and wages are subjects for discussion in meetings of such a committee. Similarly, the Church School Board will consider program, teaching staff, literature, and similar maters. Likewise, the Women's Society will be concerned with program, meetings, membership policies, and related topics.

Our point is that discussion or conference is a methodology for the consideration of those subjects which normally are, or should be, the business of a group. We are concerned, in this chapter, with the principles and methods which will help to make the discussion of these inevitable subjects as satisfactory as possible.

The Kinds of Problems Presented for Discussion

Perhaps the glimpses which we have had of groups in action have suggested the three basic kinds of problems which people encounter in life and which, therefore, are those associated with discussion or conference—that is, with either decision-making or learning groups. In the interests of convenience, we can classify them as problems of *fact,* as problems of *value,* and as problems of *policy.* Also, as we noticed in the case of the Personnel Committee, in particular, some problems are *general* in character in that they do not suggest any one kind of answer. On the other hand, others are *specific* in that they name a particular answer, then inquire whether it is *the* answer or solution. With these considerations in mind, we shall systematically consider the kinds of problems which are amenable to discussion.

Problems of Fact

A problem or question of *fact* is one which is concerned with the existence or occurrence of things, with the nature of phenomena, or with the nature of concepts or ideas. It is not concerned with policies, programs, or courses of action; and it is not concerned with appraisals, evaluations, or judgments concerning the goodness or badness, adequacy or inadequacy, of a person, policy, program, or course of action.

While it may appear, at first thought, that problems or questions of *fact* are not usually the basis for profitable discussion or conference, it will be discovered, upon further thought, that many workshops, study groups, and other bodies start with this type of problem. To think only of the church, for example, let us note such questions as: "What is the Christian Way of Life?" "What are the Implications of the Christian Way of Life for the Layman in His Business or Profession?" "What is the World Council of Churches?" "What are the Implications of the World Council of Churches for Us?" "What is the Senior High Fellowship?" "What is Our Missionary Program?" "Is Our Missionary Program Undergoing a Change?" "Did World War II Change Our Missionary Program?"

It is clear that such questions or problems as these arise from persons' desires to secure answers in the realm of "fact"—meanings, happenings, nature of institutions, and so forth, as well as interpretations of these phenomena. While, of course, many committees and commissions would not be concerned with this kind of problem, there is a vital need for discussions of this "factual type," especially in study groups. (It is clear, of course, that such questions of *fact* as, "How Many Persons Were Enrolled in the Church School Last Year?" or "What Church School Study Materials Are in Use at X Church?" are hardly suitable for discussion. The best way to get purely factual answers to such questions as these is by counting or by directly observing and investigating. However, any analysis, interpretation, or evaluation of these data *would* be the basis of profitable discussion.)

General Problem of Fact. A general problem of fact may be defined as one in which the problem is that of "finding the facts." ("What is the Christian Way of Life?") In essence, we may say that the question is "wide open" in that no answer is indicated and no suggestion of an *alleged fact* is made. This type of problem is usually phrased in the form of a question beginning with the word "who" or "what" or "how" or "when."

Specific Problem of Fact. A specific problem of fact may be defined as one in which the problem is that of finding whether an *alleged fact* or a hypothesis is "true" or tenable—in other words, is the proper answer. ("Is the Christian Way of Life That Which is Set Forth in the Sermon on the Mount?") In contrast to the *general* problem of fact, this type of problem *does* suggest an answer or a hypothesis (an alleged fact); and the discussion group seeks to test the validity of this hypothetical answer. (While it might appear that this type of problem would be less desirable than the *general,* it should be noted that many problems of this *specific* type *do* arise— many hypotheses *are* proposed for consideration, and many hypotheses *should be* formulated for study. Furthermore, in many instances it is the existence of *specific* types of problems which raises the very questions for discussion.)

Problems of Value

A problem, or question, of *value* is one which is concerned with the goodness or badness, adequacy or inadequacy, strength or weakness, of something—an idea, a program, an institution, or a person. Like the problem of *fact,* it is not concerned with policies, programs, or courses of action to be adopted or recommended by the discussion group; rather, it is concerned with "value judgments" regarding something which is placed under scrutiny.

Within the life of the church, discussion or conference groups might consider such problems of *value* as: "How Worthwhile is the World Council of Churches?" "Is the National Council of Churches an Improvement Over the Old Federal Council of Churches?" "Is This Church School Program Satisfactory?" "Is a Midweek Service Worthwhile?" "Is a Parish Executive (Business Manager) Worth the Expense Involved?" "Is a Lay Parish Visitor as Good as a Clergy Parish Visitor?" "Is an Every-Member Canvass a Good Idea?" "Are the Church School Materials of Our Denomination Adequate?"

It is clear that such questions or problems as these arise from persons' desires to secure answers in the realm of appraisals or "value judgments"—how good, how adequate, how satisfactory in the light of certain criteria or "yard-sticks." It is clear, too, that not only study groups but also many committees, boards, and related groups will have occasion to raise questions of this type as they investigate and discuss programs, plans, institutions, and persons that may be of concern to them.

General Problems of Value. A question of *value,* like a question of *fact,* may raise a *general* problem or question. ("How Worthwhile is the World Council of Churches?" "What About This Type of Church School Program?" "How Should We Regard This Type of Church Organization?") No indication of a possible answer or of a possible basis for an answer is given; rather, this is, again, a wide-open question in that it merely raises a broad question in the area of appraisal.

Specific Problems of Value. Similarly, a question of *value* may pertain to a *specific* hypothesis, alleged value judgment, or answer. ("Is This Type of Church School Program Adequate in Terms of Pupil Interests and Needs?" "Is This Type of Church Organization Functional?") Here a possible *kind* of answer, or the basis of determining an answer, is indicated in terms of either the *area* of a "yes-or-no" answer or the *yard-stick* which is the basis of the question.

Problems of Policy

A problem, or question, of *policy* is one which is concerned with a course of action, a policy, or a decision which is to be adopted or rejected. (Needless to say, questions of *fact* and of *value* may be included in the consideration of policies; but in this case the end-product is a decision regarding a policy or a course of action.)

Within the life of the church, discussion or conference groups might consider such *policy* problems as: "What Should We Do to Alleviate the Overcrowding at the Morning Service?" "Should We Inaugurate a Second Morning Service?" "What Changes, if any, Should We make in Our Church Staff?" "Should We Add a Parish Minister?" "Should We Adopt the X Series of Church School Materials?" "Should We Have a Series of Family Night Suppers and

Meetings?" "How Can We Solve the Problem of Inadequate Church School Space?" "Should We Repair the Organ Rather Than Purchase a New One?"

General Problem of Policy. Like general problems of fact and of value, *general* problems of *policy* open up a topic for consideration without indicating any possible answers or any limits for answers. Furthermore, the answers will not be "yes or no" answers; rather, they will be in the form of statements of policy. ("What Should We Do to Alleviate the Overcrowding at the Morning Service?") As a general rule, this type of problem is phrased in the form of a question which begins with the word "what" or "how," whereas the *specific* problem of *policy* (to which we shall refer in the next paragraph) begins with the word "should."

Specific Problem of Policy. As may be surmised from the preceding analysis, *specific* problems of *policy* are concerned with possible courses of action, with suggested hypotheses, and with "yes-or-no" answers to alternatives named in the question itself. ("Should We Adopt the X Series of Church School Materials?") As in the other types of *specific* problems, a discussion will arise in response to a hypothetical or alleged answer which is suggested in the question itself. While it may be said that this type of problem may be too restrictive in that it is likely to result in a consideration of only the course of action which is named, it should be noted that this type of query *does* arise. More important, however, is the fact that the discussion does not necessarily need to be limited to the hypothesis named—in fact, a yes-or-no answer will be valid only to the extent that *all* alternatives to the solution named in the question are carefully considered.

Relationships Between Kinds of Problems and Kinds of Groups

It may be said that there is no necessary or inherent relationship between a *kind* of problem and a *kind* of discussion or conference group. This is true because any kind of question may be raised by any person or group in the normal course of thinking about persons, places, programs, policies, and institutions.

However, it should be said that normally the groups concerned with problems of *fact* are study groups, workshops, and the like: groups, whether large or small, seeking to increase their knowledge or understanding of a subject which is presented as a problem or question. Whether they use the round-table method or the panel discussion method or the symposium method, they are interested in increasing their level of information or of understanding about a subject.

Similarly, problems of *value* may be generally identified with study groups that are seeking to learn about a subject concerning which value judgments are being made. On the other hand, what we have called "decision-making" or "action" groups may also be concerned with problems of *value,* inasmuch as they are often called upon to make statements concerning the goodness or badness of something.

With respect to problems of *policy,* the identification may be accidental, in that both study groups and action groups are concerned with such matters. However, it is clear that this is a type of problem which is directly associated with committees, commissions, and boards which have "policy business" as their principal concern.

(Let us emphasize one matter here. No one group is automatically an action group or a study group; its type depends upon its function or its business at a given time. For example, the Official Board may be an action group with respect to a certain subject, or it may be a study group as it listens to a panel discussion on "The Youth Fellowship." However, committees, commissions, and boards are likely to be action groups in most cases, the very reason for their existence being the presence of one or more *policy* problems which they are asked to solve. On the other hand, a Bible Study group or a Church School class will normally use discussion procedures for the purpose of *learning* about a problem or topic.)

One further point should be emphasized. In the course of deliberating upon one type of problem, a group may find itself faced with one or more subsidiary problems of the same or a different type; and it must be prepared to handle them carefully and systematically as such. For instance, a committee faced with a problem of *policy* will inevitably be faced with one or more problems of *fact* regarding the existing situation or *status quo* (its nature, the factors causing it, the effects resulting from it, and so forth). In addition, as it evaluates one or more possible solutions or remedies, it will be faced with problems of *value*.

In essence, then, it may be said that a discussion group will have before it at any one time, one major problem of *fact* or *value* or *policy*. Also, it should be noted that in the course of the study of this problem, this group will encounter one or more related problems of different types, even though the underlying substance of the discussion remains the same.

Some Values in Identifying the Kinds of Problems for Discussion

As will be noted more fully in the next chapter, good discussion, in terms of content and also in terms of participant satisfactions, does not "just happen." Rather, it depends largely upon the application of specific principles and methods pertaining to preparation, leadership, participation, and related factors.

Among these factors are principles and methods associated with *approaches to the analysis of problems,* and it is here that a recognition and understanding of the items and steps in the analysis of the three types of problems will be of service. To put the matter briefly at this point, the *necessary* steps in the discussion of a problem of *policy* are different in number and kind from those in a problem of *fact*—with somewhat similar differences observable between other pairs of types of problems.

As we shall observe in Chapter 12, each type of problem has its inherent scheme of analysis and development. Hence an important aspect of proper procedure in discussion or conference is the recognition of the kind of problem which lies before the group. Let us take only one example for illustration at this point.

Suppose that a group is confronted with a question of *value*. What are the necessary items in analysis, and to what extent are they different from those in a question of *policy?* With the question of *value,* the group must: (1) define and delimit the problem; (2) analyze the situation and gain a clear understanding of the *status quo;* (3) organize a set of criteria by which to make value judgments regarding the subject to be evaluated; (4) gain a clear understanding of the subject to be evaluated; (5) make an evaluation in terms of these criteria. On the other hand, with the question of *policy*, the group must take steps (1), (2), and (3) and then do considerably more. It must set forth solutions or courses of action, then evaluate each course of action in terms of the *status quo* and the criteria, and finally determine the ideal course of action.

A further value, associated with the careful identification of the type of problem before the group, pertains to its mission or task. If, for example, the problem is one of *fact*, the outcome, and report of outcome, will be in the nature of a factual statement. If, on the other hand, the problem is one of *value*, the outcome will be in the nature of a value judgment; while the outcome of a discussion of a problem of *policy* will be in the nature of a proposal concerning a course of thought or action.

Some Rules or Suggestions Regarding the Phrasing of Problems

While it is true that a group *can* discuss a topic or a proposition with some measure of profit, it should be emphasized that the best *form* for a discussion problem is a question (an interrogative sentence). Let us briefly examine this observation.

The principal objection to a mere *topic* is that it does not focus upon a problem, does not raise a question, does not delimit the subject. For instance, "The Morning Service," "The Church School," "Church School Lesson Materials"—to name only a few topics—do not invite specific, purposeful discussion. Only after issues have been raised and questions have been asked, does a problem evolve. It is better to begin with a question which has precise meaning and definite limits.

The principal objection to a *proposition* is that it represents a judgment, an answer, a settled opinion regarding the subject at hand. While a proposition *is* the proper form in which a motion is phrased or a statement for debate is presented, it is less likely to invite *inquiry* than is a question. Similarly, it is less likely to foster objectivity, open-mindedness, and careful diagnosis, or to arouse attention and interest than is a question.

Our advice, then, is essentially this: Whenever possible, phrase the problem for discussion in the form of a *question with wording which is as specific and definite as possible.* If the problem does not reach the discussion group as a question, note the three kinds of questions or problems which we have considered in this chapter, and cast the subject into one of these three types and into one of the subsidiary *general* or *specific* forms.

chapter 12

Patterns of Thought and Organization

The Importance of Coherent Sequence of Thought

In every walk of life a high premium is placed upon clear and coherent analysis of subjects and upon systematic development of the details which are suggested by this analysis. In the realm of oral communication, this is taken for granted, and is demanded in what we call *speechmaking*. In fact, one of the principal points stressed in Part One of this book is just this; and we have provided several pages of suggestions concerning the orderly analysis and organization of speeches of exposition and of advocacy.

Precisely the same principle applies in discussion or conference, even though it might appear, at first glance that "thought in process," "reflective thinking," or "problem solving" would, by their nature, be less orderly and coherent than would "products of thought" (speeches, sermons, and reports, for instance). However, while there may be an occasional difference in *degree,* there need be absolutely no difference in *kind.*

Our thesis is (and it has been proved in experience) that discussion or conference *can* be orderly, clear, and coherent, with a logical progression even though it be spontaneous "thought-in-process." Furthermore, our thesis is that in the interest of good discussion, as represented by valid outcomes in terms of content and by member satisfactions, there *must* be as much orderliness as is humanly possible. (Recall, for instance, the unhappiness and discontent that frequently result from scattered, hit-or-miss, wandering committee meetings, and also the failure of such meetings to achieve their full potentialities in terms of content or substance.)

It is because discussion or conference *can* be clear and orderly, and because it *must* be clear and orderly if it is to be satisfying, that we are considering the subject of "Patterns of Thought and Organization" at some length in this chapter. We shall raise three questions: (1) What relationship exists between the *purposes* of discussion groups and patterns of thought? (2) What relationship exists between *types of problems* and patterns of thought? (3) What are some specific patterns of thought for the respective types of problems?

Relationships Between Groups and Patterns of Thought

We noted in Chapter 10 that discussion groups or conferences have basically two purposes: *policy-determining* and *learning*. In the first instance, the outcome of the group's deliberations consists of a decision, a solution to a problem or an answer to a question, which becomes the basis of a recommendation or action. (For example, the decision of the Personnel Committee to raise wages and salaries by 5 per cent.) On the other hand, the outcome of the learning group's deliberations consists of a body of information which the members did not possess before the discussion began and which constitutes the answer to the question that expressed the nature of the problem before this group. (For example, the body of information which the Official Board or a similar study group possesses after a discussion of such a question as, "What is the High School Fellowship?")

As for the relationship of the group's purpose to its "pattern of thought," we suggest that there is no *necessary* connection except as the purpose of the group may dictate the type of problem to be discussed. For example, both an action group and a learning group may study a problem of *policy;* and as we shall soon see, the basic pattern of thought in each case would be the same. Similarly, both groups might be studying a problem of *value* (evaluation of a person, program, institution, and so forth), with the basic analysis and train of thought the same in each case.

We should realize, however, that this absence of any inherent relationship does not detract from the significance of our previous statement concerning the importance of "patterns of thought." All that it does mean is that other considerations dictate the kind of pattern which will be relevant in a given case. It is to these other considerations that we shall now turn.

Relationships Between Types of Problems and Patterns of Thought

When we investigate the nature of patterns of thought in terms of the nature of problems, we *do* find a clear relationship—a significant one with respect to the closeness of association and also with respect to the specific patterns that are useful in the respective cases. (In our investigation we shall first consider problems of *policy* inasmuch as this type of problem is most frequently encountered by discussion groups other than those which have "learning" as their sole purpose. We shall then consider problems of *value,* then those of *fact.*)

Problems of *policy* are perhaps most satisfactorily studied by means of what we shall call the "problem-solving pattern of thought," which will be analyzed in the next section of this chapter. Second, problems of *value* are most satisfactorily studied by a variation of the problem-solving pattern of thought, which lends itself particularly to the task of setting up a set of criteria for the purpose of evaluating the person, program, institution, and so forth under scrutiny. (This, too, will be analyzed in some detail.) Third, problems of *fact* (which, as we have seen, are frequently the bases of discussion by "learning groups") are most profitably studied by means of certain patterns of thought which can be readily adapted to the needs of specific groups and to the demands of the specific subjects under investigation. We shall call these patterns: *time order, space order, cause-effect order, journalistic order,* and *special topical order*—all of which will be analyzed in the next section of this chapter.

Specific Patterns of Thought

For Problems of Policy

The theory of "scientific method" and experiences in problem-solving procedures suggest that a thorough analysis of a problem of *policy* should include the consideration of such questions as:

1. What is the precise problem before us (its meaning and limitations)?
2. What are existing circumstances, what causes them, and what are some consequences of these circumstances?
3. What is our "yard-stick" for the measurement of possible solutions (what criteria, what goals, are to be kept in mind)?
4. What are the possible solutions (what alternatives are available)?
5. What are the relative merits of these possible solutions?
6. What, therefore, is *the* solution to the problem?
7. What steps should be taken to implement this solution?

In the light of these experiences and these questions, we are suggesting that, other things being equal, the ideal discussion of a problem of *policy* should have a "pattern of thought" embracing seven topics, or units, as follows.[1]

Definition and Delimitation of the Problem. Because all problem-solving (not only that pertaining to matters of *policy*) has its root in some kind of difficulty, need, or perplexing situation, the first task for the problem solver or the discussion group is to *locate* the problem as clearly as possible. This involves at least two mat-

---

[1] Some features of this analysis were set forth by John Dewey in *How We Think,* published in 1908. This "pattern of thought," or variations of it, has become essentially the standard in this connection; and nearly every work on problem solving or discussion methods has incorporated this concept in its analysis of "solitary thought" and of "group thought."

ters: (1) setting forth the precise meaning with as much freedom from ambiguity and vagueness as possible; (2) determining the limits or the boundaries of the problem (what is, and what is not, included).

The development of this step may be aided and achieved by the use of such questions as:

1. What is the problem?
2. What is the meaning of the terms used to state the problem?
3. What are the limits of the problem?

Perhaps an example would be helpful here. If a committee, for instance, were discussing the question "What Should Be Done to Solve the Problem of Church Office Space?" it would need to know precisely what is meant by "office space" (all offices, business offices, certain business offices, pastors' offices, or church school offices). Also, the committee should know what limitations, if any, are to be noted (time limitations, short-range plans, long-range plans, relationship to other plans of the church, and so forth). Clearly, not until such considerations as these are systematically handled, can problem solving progress with meaning and efficiency.

A somewhat similar responsibility would be faced by a group considering the question: "Should We Raise the Wages and Salaries of Our Lay Staff by 5 per cent?" Does this mean "overtime" as well as "regular time"? Does the "5 per cent" mean before or after such deductions as taxes and Social Security, for instance? Does this include the Business Manager as well as others? Does this include the part-time persons who are paid by the hour? When does this take effect? Is this to be a permanent adjustment? Needless to say, careful consideration of such matters as these is necessary to provide a "common denominator" for the ensuing discussion and to avoid misunderstandings regarding the context or setting for the analysis of conditions and of possible solutions. (While it is true that answers to some of these questions may appear to constitute features of a *solution* to the problem—and undoubtedly they may be—it is imperative, we believe, that the discussion group at least make itself aware of the presence and importance of these questions.)

Analysis of the Present Situation (Status Quo). When the exact nature of the problem has been determined (terms made clear and limits noted), it is then necessary to make a careful analysis of the "present situation"—of circumstances as they exist. This analysis must necessarily include the clearly observable phenomena within the limits of the problem (those items which would appear in a "picture" of the *status quo*). Ordinarily, too, it should include the inferred *causes* of these phenomena (those factors which make the "present situation" what it is). Perhaps, as well, it should include the actual or the possible *effects* of the existence of the immediately discernible factors in the *status quo* or the continued existence of this *status quo*. (It might be well to recall at this point what we regard as a "good diagnosis" by a physician. This good diagnosis would certainly include a careful survey of "what is going on" and also a canvass of the forces causing these conditions. Perhaps, too, this physician would take into consideration the *effects* of the conditions which he finds in his basic diagnosis so that he can get the most thorough and clear picture of "what is going on.")

The development of this step may be aided by the use of such questions as:

1. What are the manifestations of the problem?
2. What are the "effects" which can be observed?
3. What is the *status quo* with respect to this problem?
4. What are the causes of the problem?
5. What are some consequences of the conditions observed in (1–3) above?

Let us continue the example of the problem of Church Office Space. In developing this step, the committee will necessarily make a survey of all relevant features of the *status quo,* noting all items which serve to create a problem (noise, lighting, crowded conditions, and so forth). In addition, it will need to consider any relevant reasons for, or causes of, these conditions; and it also will need to consider the relevant and important results or consequences of these conditions. Not until it has done all three of these things will it have a complete diagnosis of *conditions, causes of these conditions,* and *consequences of these conditions.*

Analysis of Criteria, Goals, or Standards of Value. The third step in the complete process of problem-solving is the determination of what is to be expected of any given solution (the goals of the group or the yard-stick by which the solutions are to be measured). This step has two important uses and values; one in terms of the *content* of the discussion and one in terms of the *attitudes of the participants.*

In terms of *content,* this step is important. Obviously, no value judgment of any worth can be made until the evaluator knows what he wants the subject being appraised to be and to do (although some persons do attempt to make judgments upon the basis of not only superficial diagnosis but also inexact or uncertain criteria). In terms of *attitudes of participants,* this step is also important. The establishment of criteria will help the group to proceed on an objective basis and will allow it to accept or reject certain suggested solutions without seeming to favor or to attack persons or groups.

This aspect of the problem-solving process consists of doing at least two important things: (1) determining the exact criterion or criteria—separately and distinctly, and (2) determining the priority or relative weight of these criteria (which is most important, which is next in importance, and so forth).

The development of this step may be achieved by the use of such questions as:

1. What are the desires of the person, or persons, trying to solve this problem?
2. What criteria or values are operating?
3. By what set of principles should the solutions be evaluated?
4. What is the priority of these criteria or values?
5. What is the relative weight attached to these criteria or values?

In our problem of Church Office Space, the committee will want to determine what it desires in this connection; what the ideal solution should accomplish, what the attributes or "marks" of this solution should be. For instance, one committee which discussed this problem agreed upon the following criteria:

1. There should be at least 1,500 square feet of space available for the office staff.
2. The office staff, except for the secretary of the Department of Education and possibly except for the senior minister's secretary, should be in one location in the church.
3. The office should be on the first floor.
4. There should be the absolute minimum of interference with the use of the Chapel. (In other words, there should be no

interference from office noises, and there should be adequate space for the reception of wedding and funeral groups and of other persons waiting to enter the Chapel.)

5. There should be the absolute minimum of interference with the present use of space by church organizations and functions.

6. There should be no interference with the basic architectural design or the quality of construction of the church structure.

7. There should be no interference with possible long-range plans for expansion of the church property. (In other words, both long-range and short-range needs should be kept in mind.)

8. The working conditions should be comfortable, well-lighted, and well-ventilated.

9. While the factor of *expense* is not the primary consideration, it should be kept in mind, and should be used as a final determinant if necessary.

Suggestion of Possible Solutions. The fourth step is the suggestion of possible solutions to the problem or answers to the question. Here a discussion group will set forth, as clearly as possible, the essential features of as many possible solutions as it can determine.

While it is true that some possible solutions or hypotheses may have occurred to some members of the discussion group during the preceding three steps, it is believed by most students of the problem-solving process—and this belief has been corroborated by experimental evidence—that this stage of *suggesting solutions* should await formal and careful *diagnosis* and the *setting up of criteria.* Also, while it may be said that perhaps this step and the next step (Evaluation of Solutions) should be merged (a solution suggested, then immediately evaluated), it is the conviction of many persons that evaluations are best carried out after as many solutions as possible have been "laid out" before the discussion group. This procedure is especially desirable in the interest of thoroughness, inasmuch as an early initiation of the evaluation process may actually prevent the suggesting of some solutions. Further, some persons believe that this plan of "separate steps" has a further advantage of causing the problem solver to concentrate upon *expository* material first (the details or features of a possible solution), then upon *critical* materials later (the relationships among the nature of the problem, the set of criteria, and the details of one or more possible solutions).

Our position concerning this step is this; problem-solving requires the two steps of Suggestion of Solutions and Evaluation of Solutions; some attempts at problem-solving break down in one degree or another through failure to understand clearly the precise nature of solutions or to make a systematic appraisal of the solutions; therefore, we advise careful attention to *both steps,* although we would prefer that the two steps of Suggestion of Solutions and Evaluation of Solutions be separate insofar as possible.

The following are typical questions which may assist in the development of this step of Suggestion of Solutions:

1. What are the possible solutions?
2. What are the possible answers to the basic question?
3. What is the exact nature of each solution, at least as tentatively conceived?
4. How are the possible solutions related to each other (in terms of details, not in terms of relative merits)?

In our problem on Church Office Space, the committee will want to consider the possible alternatives to the present office arrangements. For instance, the committee which we previously mentioned gave careful consideration to seven possible solutions, as follows:

1. Retain most of the present office space and convert the area under the Great Hall balcony, cutting a new door from the corridor into Great Hall, cutting two doors in the present east wall of Great Hall, and constructing a sound-proof partition between this new area and Great Hall.
2. Retain most of the present office space and convert some of the space at the rear of the Great Hall balcony.
3. Convert the present check room and store room in the basement.
4. Convert the large room to the west of the check room in the basement.
5. Convert the area now occupied by Dr. A's office and the space to the north of this office.
6. Convert Room 4.
7. Convert Room 3 and one "bay" of Room 4, at the same time retaining some of the present office facilities.

Evaluation of Possible Solutions. The fifth step in problem-solving is the systematic evaluation of possible solutions. Here the problem solver brings together the three factors of *present situation, criteria,* and *solutions,* in order to determine to what extent each proposed solution measures up to the standards in the light of existing circumstances.

As in other aspects of problem-solving, there are, at this point, variations in procedure within the framework of the necessary elements. Specifically, should each proposed solution be evaluated in terms of all factors in the *status quo* and in terms of each criterion *before* the next solution is considered (we shall call this "Plan A"), or should every proposed solution be evaluated in terms of one factor in the *status quo* or one of the criteria, then in terms of a second factor or criterion (we shall call this "Plan B")? To put it another way: should the "vertical" approach (one proposed solution at a time) be used, or should the "horizontal" approach be used?

Realizing the several arguments in favor of each alternative, we say that there is probably no *inherent* advantage of one approach over the other. Our concern is with *completeness* and *consistency;* we insist that the problem solver include all necessary elements in appraisal and that he be consistent. (If he embarks upon "Plan A," he should continue with it throughout this step in problem-solving.)

The following questions suggest the nature of this step:

1. What will be the consequences of the adoption of each proposed solution?
2. To what extent will each proposed solution answer the basic question or solve the problem?
3. What is the relation of each proposed solution to the relevant elements in the *status quo?*
4. What is the relation of each proposed solution to the criteria or values?
5. What are the advantages and disadvantages of each solution or combination of solutions?

To return to our example of Church Office Space, we find that the committee, using "Plan A" (the vertical method), made the following appraisal of the seven proposed solutions:

Proposal No. 1: Convert the area under the Great Hall balcony:

(a) Would meet criterion (1).

(b) Would meet criterion (2).

(c) Would meet criterion (3).

(d) Would meet criterion (4) only to a low degree, in that many office noises would be adjacent to the Chapel and in that the reception problem would remain in part.

(e) Would not meet criterion (5), in that the capacity of Great Hall would be reduced by some 100 seats for dinners and meetings; also, unless an expensive sound-proof wall were erected, there would be interference with day-time meetings in Great Hall.

(f) Would possibly not meet criterion (6), in that it would substantially alter the appearance of Great Hall.

(g) While it would not directly interfere with long-range plans which might envision a new location for the office, it would represent such a commitment in expense that it might not meet criterion (7).

(h) Would meet criterion (8).

(i) Would be the most expensive of the proposals.

Proposal No. 2: Convert some of the space at the rear of the Great Hall balcony:

(a) Would meet criterion (1) . . . and so forth.

Had this committee chosen to use "Plan B" (the horizontal method), a report of its findings would have included the same materials. However, as previously noted, the *starting point* in the outline or report would be a factor in the *status quo* or a criterion; and the proposed solutions would be evaluated in terms of each of these elements.

Determination of the Best Solution. The sixth step in problem-solving is, necessarily, that of bringing together the several appraisals or value judgments arrived at in the fifth step in order to answer the question: where do these several, separate evaluations lead us?

In its simplest form, this step may consist of a mere mathematical computation of the "plus" and "minus" judgments noted in the fifth step, with the proposed solution having the largest

number of "plus" judgments declared "the winner." Through varying degrees of complexity, this sixth step may include highly qualitative judgments regarding each proposed solution, may include
judgments made upon combinations of individual solutions, or may
include judgments made upon modifications of previously suggested solutions. In any event, the purpose is to arrive at a judgment concerning *the* best answer to the question or *the* best solution to the problem. The following are the typical questions
designed to assist in a careful synthesis of appraisals:

1. What are the relative merits of each proposed solution in
   terms of purely quantitative considerations?
2. What are the relative merits of each proposed solution in
   terms of quantitative considerations, but taking into further
   consideration the relative weight given to the several criteria
   and/or the significance of the several elements in the *status
   quo* (the relative seriousness of these several elements)?
3. What are the relative merits of each proposed solution in
   terms of both quantitative and qualitative considerations?
4. What are the relative merits of possible combinations or
   modifications of the proposed solutions?
5. What, therefore, appears to be the best solution, and why?

The Committee on Office Space carried forward its problem-
solution efforts in terms of this step. The following statements from
its report may be helpful here:

> In the light of these evaluations, the committee concluded that the
> 2nd, 3rd, 4th, 5th, and 7th possibilities failed to meet a sufficient
> number of the criteria to be considered further. In a further study
> of the 1st possibility, it was felt that the problems pertaining to the
> 4th, 5th, and 7th criteria were so important as to make it unwise to
> recommend this proposal.
> The committee, therefore, made a further study of the 6th pos-
> sibility (Room 4). Finally, it voted to create a subcommittee to study
> the present use of Room 4 and to determine whether the program
> activities could be moved to other parts of the building into existing
> space or to space which can be prepared at little expense. Subse-
> quently, this subcommittee reported that by the use of some second
> and third floor rooms and that by the preparation for the Church
> School Toddlers group of the space available under Room 3 and
> under a part of Room 4, all present activities of Room 4, except
> meetings of the Official Board (which should be held on the first

floor), could be adequately cared for. Furthermore, this subcommittee recommended that the Official Board be asked to authorize the use of the Chapel for its own business meetings as occasion arises.

The committee then accepted this report of the subcommittee. At the same time it considered the wisdom of enlarging the sacristy adjacent to the Chapel in order to provide a more adequate waiting room space and of having the office of the senior minister's secretary adjacent to this sacristy and, of course, near to his office. (Her office would not interfere with the operations of the Chapel because she could be provided with a noiseless typewriter or she could carry on other activities as necessary.)

Finally, the committee adopted the following motion: That a recommendation be made to the Official Board that it authorize the Board of Trustees to convert Room 4 into the church office and that it authorize the use of the Chapel for its own business meetings as occasion arises, it being understood that the senior minister's secretary would probably be near to the Chapel and that the enlarged sacristy would be provided.

This recommendation (which was adopted) constituted, then, the committee's answer to the basic question, or its solution to the problem, presented to it.

For Problems of Value

As previously defined, a problem of *value* is concerned with the evaluation or appraisal of a person, program, institution, and so forth, which is already in existence. ("How Good is the X Set of Church School Lesson Materials?") Necessarily, a thorough development of such a problem involves a consideration of the following questions: (1) What is our problem? (2) What is the *status quo* (what are the circumstances under which we are making the appraisal *or* what is the setting for our appraisal?)? (3) What are the criteria by which we shall make our appraisal? (4) What is the nature of the subject to be evaluated? (5) What is the evaluation or final judgment based upon the relationships between the criteria and the subject to be evaluated?

In a sense, this process is like that used in the consideration of a problem of *policy*, except that in the problem of *value* we evaluate only the subject named. The locating and defining of the problem is exactly the same process as is the careful analysis of the *status quo* (including reasons for its nature). Likewise, the handling of criteria and the process of measuring or evaluating are the same as in *policy* questions.

Let us briefly review this process in terms of the question named above—the evaluation of the X Set of Church School Lesson Materials. First, of course, we must determine precisely what our problem is: what we are concerned about and what not, what the terms mean (what, in general at least, is meant by the X Set of Church School Lesson Materials). Next, we must know what the present situation is (the nature of the setting within which the materials are to be evaluated—the students, the teachers, the physical plant, and the instructional situation). Then we must determine our criteria, our wants, objectives, or goals. Next, it is imperative that we know in detail what we are evaluating (the precise nature of the X Materials, the philosophy underlying them, their objectives, and their features). Finally, we make our evaluation by bringing together the three basic elements: the X Materials, the criteria, and the circumstances under which they are to be used.

For Problems of Fact

It will be recalled that a problem of *fact* is one which pertains to the "nature of things," to classifications, to attributes of things. ("What is the High School Fellowship?" "What is the Christian Message?" "What are the Points of Similarity or of Difference Between X Denomination and Y Denomination?")

Here, of course, we are not concerned with evaluation or with the determination of policies. Rather, our purpose is to "get at the facts" and to give meaning to these facts. Hence, the plans of organization previously discussed are, in the main, hardly relevant here. On the other hand, there are several systems of organization or "plans of attack" which may be suggested. (No one of these is the best; each has values under certain conditions.) In each instance, of course, the particular plan of development is preceded by the step of defining and delimiting the subject or problem.

Time Order. In this circumstance, after the problem has been located and defined, the discussion will begin at a certain time or date, or at a certain step in a process, and move forward or backward from that starting point. For instance, in a discussion of "The History of X Denomination," this plan of organization might be particularly useful. Similarly, in a discussion of the question "What Have Been the Major Steps in the Efforts Toward Achieving Church Unity?" the *time order* might be used to advantage.

Space Order. Here the discussion will consider the material in terms of spatial relationships: east to west, north to south, outside to inside, inside to outside, bottom to top, top to bottom, center outward in concentric circles, and so forth. While it might appear that this plan of organization would have little relevance to the discussion of problems or questions, it will be found to be useful in the consideration of such questions as "What Is the Program of the Board of Missions?" or "What Has Been the Deputation Team Program of the Student Foundation During the Past Year?" (Of course, other plans may be useful, as will be seen in a moment; however, *space order* may be a desirable approach.)

Cause-Effect Order. Here the discussion will consider the material in terms of factors which may be designated as "causes" and sub-sequently in terms of "effects," or vice versa. For instance, a church study group found this plan helpful in discussing the question "What Next in Church Unity?." Here it analyzed such factors as recent church unions, inter-church conferences, the National Council of Churches, the World Council of Churches, and so forth, in an attempt to determine likely *effects* or *results* of their work and influence. Whereas this group used the cause-to-effect plan of organization, another group used the effect-to-cause approach in its study of "What Were the Causes of the Reformation?" First, it analyzed the essential features of the Reformation; then it proceeded to investigate the factors which caused it.

Journalistic Order. Here the discussion will consider the material in terms of such questions or factors as: Who? What? When? Where? Why? How? (or some selected combination of these typical questions). For instance, a panel discussion on the subject of "What Is the High School Fellowship and What is its Program?" (by officers of the Fellowship, with the Church Official Board as the audience) used essentially this pattern in its attempt to develop the material systematically. Again, a group discussing "What Is the World Council of Churches and What Is Its Program?" used this plan of organization to advantage.

Special Topical Order. In this case the discussion will consider the material in terms of (1) topical divisions with which the discussants are familiar *or* (2) in terms of divisions which are peculiar to the subject *or* (3) in terms of questions which are suggested by the subject. (Actually, the possibilities in this category are almost limitless. However, it is imperative that some logical or natural sequence be selected and maintained in order that the discussion not become incoherent or aimless.)

It may be possible, for instance, that the major topics will be those like (1) Economic, Political, Social *or* (2) Objectives, Underlying Principles, General Features, Specific Details *or* (3) the major topics of Education, Theology, and Church History, for instance. Again, these topics may be ones which inevitably grow out of a specific subject. For example, a group at a church conference-workshop discussing the question "What is the Place of Communications in the Church?" used the following plan of organization:

1. What do we mean by Communications?
2. What are the several forms in which it appears?
3. In terms of internal relationships in the church, what are some of the *needs* for communication?
4. What are some of the forms of communication related to No. 3?
5. What are some breakdowns in the forms of communication noted in No. 4?
6. What can be done to avoid these breakdowns?
7. In terms of external relationships, what are some of the *needs* for communication?
8. What are some of the forms of communication related to No. 7?
9. What are some breakdowns in the forms of communication noted in No. 8?
10. What can be done to avoid these breakdowns?
11. What is the layman's place "in this picture"?
12. What is the clergy's place "in this picture"?

Conclusion

As we bring this discussion of patterns of organization to a close, we reiterate the theme of this chapter—*discussion or conference need not be incoherent or aimless even though it is "thought-in-process" and, as a rule, spontaneous and unrehearsed* (in the sense that speeches and sermons are, ideally at least, carefully prepared in advance). There *are* specific approaches to the analysis of questions and problems of *policy, value,* and *fact.* To the extent that we recognize this fact and use these resources, discussions and conferences will be that much better in terms of content and also of personal satisfactions.

With this thought in mind, we are providing, in summary, an outline of the principal items in the pattern for each type of problem.

Problem of Policy

1. Define and Delimit the Problem.
2. Analyze the Present Situation *(Status Quo).*
3. Analyze the Criteria, Goals, or Standards of Value.
4. Suggest Possible Solutions.
5. Evaluate the Possible Solutions.
6. Determine the Best Solution.

Problem of Value

1. Define and Delimit the Problem.
2. Analyze the Present Situation *(Status Quo).*
3. Analyze the Criteria, Goals, or Standards of Value.
4. Determine the Nature of the Subject to be Evaluated.
5. Evaluate the Subject under Consideration.

Problem of Fact

1. Define and Delimit the Problem or Subject.
2. Develop the Subject via One of the Following:
   (a) Time Order.
   (b) Space Order.
   (c) Cause-Effect Order.
   (d) Journalistic Order.
   (e) Special Topical Order.

chapter 13

The
Substance
of Discussion

The charge is frequently leveled against group discussions, conferences, and committee meetings that they are lacking in real
substance; that they are "thin," are merely "talk sessions" based
upon hearsay and impromptu personal opinion. No doubt there is
some truth to these observations, even though they may be somewhat exaggerated. However, at least two important points need to
be noted here: (1) not all discussions, conferences, or committee
meetings *need* to be unprepared, because advance notice and
preparation *can* often be achieved; (2) of necessity, many discussions (in board meetings, for instance) do arise spontaneously and in
impromptu fashion, although they do not *necessarily* have to be
"thin" or uninformed if certain safeguards are observed.

What we are saying is this: discussion or conference *can* have
substance; and frequently the leader or chairman, as well as the
other persons involved, may be in a position to provide means of
guaranteeing this substance. Furthermore, good substance, based
upon as much preparation as possible and associated with careful
handling of available materials, will do much to influence the

worth of solutions and also the amount of time saved in discussions and conferences. In other words, discussion or conference *must* have substance lest it be merely a process of exchanging superficial, off-hand remarks.

Part A: Finding the Substance

Sources of Materials

The sources of materials for discussion or conference (as for any type of oral or written communication) are several: general observation, conversation, general experience, comparable experience, general reading, specific investigation, and so forth. It will be noted that some of these sources are inherent in, and arise out of, one's everyday activities and experiences. In fact, perhaps these are the principal sources of materials used in the majority of committee meetings and conferences, wherein no advance notice has been given of specific problems to consider and wherein problems arise out of the very meeting itself. (As we shall observe later, however, even here some controls can be exercised with respect to the nature and validity of the materials.) It will be noted, also, that one of these sources (specific investigation) implies both guided or controlled experience and reading, investigation, or inquiring. Let us briefly consider these sources.

As will be noted later, the "raw materials" of discussion—and of reasoning or thinking—are basically two: (1) facts and (2) the opinions of persons other than the discussant or reasoner. Hence, it follows that the sources of materials are those which yield facts and opinions. Clearly, even random or general observation can yield an almost infinite number of "facts" about the world in which we live—people, institutions, practices, events, and so forth—as well as evidences of what people are saying about these phenomena. Similarly, conversation, general experience, controlled experience, and general reading will yield countless facts as well as judgments about facts made by others. In like manner, specific investigations, involving observation, conversation, inquiry, and reading, are designed to secure "facts" and opinions expressed by others.

In the case of specific investigations, use may be made of such common sources of information as: (1) reference books and bibliographies; (2) books; (3) periodicals; (4) newspapers; (5) pamphlets and documents; and (6) guides, digests, and compendia of information prepared for use in the study of certain subjects.

In this discussion of sources of materials, mention should be made of an important and valuable source of information available during the course of the discussion itself: the "resource person" or the "subject-matter expert." As the name implies, this person is one who is especially well informed on the subject being considered; and his role in a discussion, conference or committee meeting is to supply that information when it is needed. He is not the leader, nor is he a regular participant or member of the group. His function is to supply information and perhaps to make such comments upon that information as he is requested to make—*but that is all.*

Nor is this the only resource available during the course of the discussion or conference. As the discussion proceeds, records can be consulted, experts summoned, or information obtained by telephone. The point is that even though the discussion be impromptu or spontaneous, it can be carried forward without resorting to mere hearsay.

Actually, we need to do little more at this point than to remind ourselves of these readily available resources and to use them in order to provide the maximum of "substance" in discussion.

Guides to Preparation

While, of course, many discussions and committee meetings develop spontaneously and without the opportunity for *specific* preparation, others *do* occur under conditions that permit at least some preparation by the leader or chairman and by the other members of the group. In fact, it may be said that frequently there are more opportunities for *specific* preparation than might appear at first thought. It is with these thoughts in mind that we suggest two guides to preparation: (1) the Exploration Sheet or Study Guide, and (2) the Discussion Outline.

The Exploration Sheet or Study Guide

The Exploration Sheet or Study Guide, which is designed to systematize and direct the preparation for discussion, consists of a set of questions organized according to the pattern of thought or the plan of organization relevant to the problem or question being considered (recall the subject of "patterns" in Chapter 12).

Ordinarily, this instrument will be prepared by the leader or chairman as a means of assisting the group in its preparation. Upon some occasions, it may profitably be constructed by the participant himself as the first step in his own preparation. In either case, the Study Guide provides the means of systematizing one's investigation of a problem, and it serves to *reduce random investigations to a minimum*. Specifically, it provides means of discovering what kinds of questions need to be answered in connection with the thorough analysis of a subject, in what areas of the subject one possesses at least some information, and in what areas specific investigations must be undertaken. It also provides means of structuring investigations—major points, minor points, types of evidence, and so forth.

Aside from suggesting possible sequences of ideas and "trains of thought," the Study Guide serves as a means of bringing together the necessary materials for discussion mentioned in the preceding section (facts and opinions derived from observation, experience, and reading, for instance). In fact, the use of this instrument may well assure, other things being equal, a higher level of discussion as represented not only by a systematic approach but also by an abundance of relevant "substance."

Perhaps a specimen Study Guide (in this instance pertaining to a problem of *policy*) will help to suggest the nature of this instrument and its possible applications to a variety of subjects for discussion.

What Set of Church School Lesson Materials Should We Select?

Definition and Delimitation
1. What do we mean by Church School lesson materials?
2. Are we concerned with anything more than these materials?
3. Are any time limits to be considered (one year; more than one year; and so forth)?

Status Quo
   4. What is our present situation?
   5. What kind (kinds) of teaching methods are in use?
   6. What physical equipment is in use, or available, in the Church School?
   7. What kinds of backgrounds and preparation are evident in the Church School students?
   8. What kinds of backgrounds and preparation are evident in the Church School teaching staff?

Criteria
   9. What do we want to accomplish?
   10. Do we want "graded materials"?
   11. Do we want different materials for each grade?
   12. Do we want Bible-centered materials?
   13. Do we want "application-type" materials?
   14. Do we want work-book type materials?
   15. Do we have considerations of cost?
   16. Are there other considerations?

Possible Solutions
   17. What is the nature of Set A?
   18. What is the nature of Set B?
   19. What is the nature of Set C?
   20. Are there any other possibilities?

Evaluation of Solutions
   21. Would Set A meet the criteria?
   22. Would Set B meet the criteria?
   23. Would Set C meet the criteria?
   24. Would any other possibilities meet the criteria?

Determination of "the" Solution
   25. Which set most fully "measures up" to the criteria?

The Discussion Outline

The Discussion Outline is designed to systematize and direct one's preparation for discussion and to serve as a record of the preparation that has been made. Ordinarily, both the leader and the members of the discussion group or committee can profitably prepare such an outline.

If properly conceived and constructed, this instrument can

stimulate investigation, clarify thinking, and prepare one to express himself in discussion more adequately than would be the case if his contributions were to be completely impromptu in terms of both ideas and language. This outline should not be thought of as a speaker's outline; and a person should certainly not attempt to speak from it or be bound by it during the discussion. It has served its purpose if it has stimulated and systematized *preparation* and has provided a means for a person to express himself at least tentatively upon the subject before him. In essence, it may be said to represent one's best thinking at the time when it was made.

With respect to the *form* of the Discussion Outline, it may suffice to say that the customary principles and rules of *outlining* should be kept in mind (symbols for divisions, indentation, relationships between major and minor points, and citation of sources).

The following portion of a specimen Discussion Outline will suggest the nature of this instrument and its possible applications to various subjects and types of problems.

What Set of Church School Lesson Materials Should We Select?

Definition and Delimitation
   1. By "Church School Lesson Materials" we mean those books, pamphlets, visual aids, and teachers' guides which are prepared by, and made available through, some central agency as a church denomination headquarters.
   2. We are concerned only with materials of this type and in this sense. We are not concerned with "home-made" materials or with supplementary materials, except as these may suggest the adequacy or inadequacy of the materials which we would purchase.
   3. We are thinking primarily of a permanent adoption, although we may well keep a one-year trial period in mind.

Status Quo
   4. Our present situation consists essentially of:
      a. A complete, traditional organization (Superintendent, Principals, and so forth).
      b. A graded Church School.
      c. A corps of regular teachers and a somewhat similar corps of substitutes.
         . . . and so forth.
   5. Several kinds of teaching methods are in use:
      a. Classroom discussion with homework.
      b. Classroom discussion without homework.
      c. Project methods.

    d. Case methods.
    e. Extensive use of visual aids.
    f. Little use of visual aids.
      . . . and so forth.
  6. The physical equipment is quite varied and adequate:
    a. Generally acceptable classroom furniture.
    b. Blackboards.
    c. Special equipment for various grades.
    d. Projection equipment for some rooms.
      . . . and so forth.
  7.   . . . and so forth.
  8.   . . . and so forth.

(The outline might be completed in terms of the units suggested by the Study Guide on pages 197-198, with, perhaps, fuller development of each point than that indicated here. Also, there might be documentation of each point, as desired.)

As we leave the subject of Study Guides and Discussion Outlines, we wish to emphasize two matters of importance to leaders and participants alike:

1. These instruments are not to be confused with typical agenda or lists of *topics* to be considered in a meeting. These provide means of analyzing and developing problems, whereas agenda (which *do* have important values) merely list topics or matters to be considered.

2. Study Guides and Discussion Outlines are subject to wide variations in terms of completeness of development, as desired by the persons who prepare them. For example, some persons may wish only a set of major headings, whereas others may want complete documentation. Also, a *leader* may wish only a general guide, whereas a *participant* may want a detailed analysis of the subject.

Part B: Using the Substance

It may be said that the substance of discussion or conference consists of (1) the raw materials of facts and opinions which a person *finds* and (2) the reasoning or thinking which he does with these raw materials. (This is not to say that the materials are always adequate, or that the reasoning process is always valid; this merely says that the *process* involves *reasoning* about *materials* possessed by the thinker.) Let us consider the nature and uses of raw materials (evidence) and of "reasonings" from these materials.

The Nature, Sources, and Uses of Evidence

"Evidence" may be defined as *matters of fact and of opinion used as the basis of reasoning.* "Matters of fact" may, in turn, be thought of as statistics, cases, and similar materials—phenomena which are observed, described, classified, and reported. "Opinions" are points of view held by a person, or persons, other than the one who is doing the reasoning or thinking, and who has interpreted or evaluated phenomena.

The sources of these types of *evidence* may be the reasoner (the discussant) himself or another person, depending upon the nature of the material. Specifically, the sources of *facts* are observations made by the reasoner himself *and also* the testimony of another person or persons. For example, if I wish to know how many grades are represented in the Church School of X Church, I can go to that church on a Sunday and actually observe and count the number of grade-classes in session. On the other hand, I can ask the Superintendent of that Church School; and his statement, or testimony, will give me the information.

The source of *opinion evidence,* on the other hand, is, by definition, another person. For example, opinions or judgments regarding the X Set of Church School Lesson Materials which I might use in my thinking would be those of some person whose statement I would hear or read.

These matters of *fact* and *opinion,* as we have previously said, constitute the raw materials of reasoning. Hence, in a very real sense, they are a part of the raw materials of discussion or conference. If they are good, they necessarily provide good raw materials for the reasoning process; if not, they can seriously affect the validity or truth of the reasoning process which is based upon them. Hence it is important to determine the tests of good *evidence*—the evidence itself and the source of this evidence—in terms of "logical adequacy" and of "psychological adequacy." (By the former, we mean those tests which are based as exclusively as possible upon "logical" or quite impersonal factors; by the latter, those tests which take into consideration feelings, attitudes, or prejudices which people hold toward the person, or persons, who are associated with the matter at hand.)

While the tests of *evidence* may be as many as twenty in number, perhaps the following *nine* may be most useful to us here:

Tests of Logical Adequacy

1. Is the evidence clear?
2. Is the evidence consistent internally?
3. Is the evidence consistent with known facts and with other units of evidence?
4. Is the evidence consistent with logical argument?
5. Is the *source* of the evidence competent?
6. Is the *source* of the evidence free from prejudice?
7. Is the *source* of the evidence reliable?

Tests of Psychological Adequacy

8. Is the evidence in harmony with the beliefs of the other participants in the group situation?
9. Is the *source* of the evidence a person whom the other participants in the group situation are willing to accept?

The Nature and Tests of Reasoning

Perhaps the most satisfactory way to define "reasoning" is to designate it as *the process of inferring conclusions from evidence or from other conclusions.* In the first instance, it consists of using facts or opinions (of another person) to arrive at a thought or conclusion different from that specifically embodied in the evidence itself. For example, I can start with the *fact* that *A* Church has been satisfied with the *X* Church School Lesson Series and the *fact* that *B* Church has been similarly satisfied and the *fact* that *C* Church has had a similar experience, then reason that the *X* Series satisfies churches. In the second instance, it consists of joining two or more "ideas" or propositions and forming a new conclusion or idea. Here is an example: If I believe (have an idea) that a certain church denomination includes certain practices in its services of worship, I then reason that the services of a given church of that denomination will quite probably include these practices.

As for the *types* of reasoning, it is convenient and accurate to think in terms of the following four: *Example, Analogy, Cause,* and *Sign.* Let us consider the nature of each and the respective tests which will enable us to detect good reasoning from bad.

Example. Reasoning from example may be defined as the *process of inferring conclusions from specific instances, cases, or examples.* This is exemplified by the illustration of churches *A, B,* and *C* in connection with satisfactions derived from the *X* Set of Lesson Materials referred to previously.

The tests of reasoning from example are essentially as follows:

1. Are the examples adequate in number?
2. Are the examples typical?
3. Are negative examples adequately accounted for?

Let us review these tests in the light of the illustration just mentioned. Our first test raises the question of *whether three cases are enough.* (Do we need *five* examples, or *ten,* or *more?*) The second test inquires whether Churches *A, B,* and *C* are typical, or representative; or whether they are unique or exceptional. The third test inquires whether any negative (dissatisfied) churches have been named and "explained away" as nontypical or insignificant in number. (Parenthetically, it should be noted that if the answer to each question is "yes," the reasoning is good in terms of that factor; otherwise, there is what we commonly term a "fallacy" in reasoning.)

Analogy. Reasoning by analogy may be defined as the *process of making a comparison between two cases, in one of which a certain factor is known to exist, while in the other case this same factor is under question and is to be inferred through the reasoning process.* Let us illustrate: Knowing that Church *A* has found the *X* Series of Church School Lesson Materials to be satisfactory, we reason that Church *B* (presumed to be at least quite similar) has found (or would find) this series to be satisfactory.

Needless to say, this type of reasoning is good only if certain conditions are present. Hence, we should note the following three tests:

1. Are there any points of similarity?
2. Do the points of similarity outweigh the points of difference?
3. Are the points of difference adequately explained?

Let us review these tests in the light of our illustration. Test (1) raises the question of whether Church *A* and Church *B* are similar in any respects (size, location, organization of the Church School, objectives of the School, denomination, and so forth). If not, the reasoning, of course, can hardly be valid. Test (2) raises the question of the extent to which differences between the two churches (at least *some* differences almost inevitably exist between any two things or persons) are significant. For instance, how significant are differences in *location* (if there are such differences), or in the *organization of the Church School,* and so forth (if differences do exist)? In essence, this is a qualitative matter—assessing the relative importance of similarities and differences. Test (3) raises the question of the extent to which elements of difference are considered and "explained away." In essence, this test complements the second test by focusing attention upon possible points of difference and by providing a means of handling them in terms of importance or of impact upon the reasoning process. For instance, have we made adequately clear the differences in size or in location (if they do exist) and also "explained them away" to our own satisfaction and, ideally, to the satisfaction of others?

Cause. Reasoning from cause may be defined as the *process of proceeding from a phenomenon (idea, concept, and so forth) called a "cause" to an inferred effect or result,* or of *proceeding from a phenomenon called an "effect" to an inferred cause.* The former process is commonly called cause-to-effect reasoning; the latter, effect-to-cause.

Let us illustrate. If we reason that the adoption of the *X* Series will increase interest on the part of our Church School students, we are inferring that the lesson series will be a *cause* producing the *effect* of increased interest. Effect-to-cause reasoning would appear if we were to reason that the increased interest during this past year on the part of the Church School students at Church *A* was caused by the adoption of the *X* Series. (Increased interest is the *effect;* adoption of the *X* Series is the *cause.*)

As in the other types of reasoning just described, there are openings for error based upon certain obvious, but important, tests. Let us review some of these tests.

Some Tests of Cause-to-Effect Reasoning
1. Is there *any* cause and effect connection?
2. Is the cause adequate to produce the effect?
3. Is there a probability that no other effect may result from the particular cause?

In terms of our illustration of the X Series, the first test means, in essence: Is there any valid, logical reason to assume a causal relationship between "interest" and the adoption of these materials? If there is such a reason . . . "so far, so good." If not, our inference is no more valid than to infer that "breaking a mirror will produce X years of bad luck." The second test raises the question whether there is enough "strength" in the X Series to produce "interest," even though there is, admittedly, a connection between lesson materials and "interest." The third test inquires whether some other effect than "increased interest" will probably be created by these materials—"less interest" or interest of a different kind than that which is desired or inferred.

Clearly, if the answer to each of these test questions is "yes," the reasoning is good; if not, what we call a "fallacy" is present.

Some Tests of Effect-to-Cause Reasoning
1. Is there *any* cause and effect connection?
2. Is the assigned cause adequate to have produced the effect being considered?
3. Is there a probability that no other cause operated to produce the effect being considered?

In terms of our illustration of the X Series, the first test, like that in cause-to-effect reasoning, asks: Is there any valid, logical reason to assume a causal relationship between "interest" and the adoption of these materials? The second test raises the question: Was the evident increase in "interest" caused by the adoption of the X Series? The third test raises the question: Could the evident increase in "interest" have been caused by some factor other than the adoption of the X Series? As in the other cases, a "yes" answer to each question implies good reasoning, a "no" answer, implies a fallacy.

Sign. Reasoning from sign may be defined as the *process of infer-*

*ring associations or correlations which are not truly causal in nature
—proceeding from substance to attribute or from attribute to substance.*

This form of reasoning is observed when we say, for instance, that
a certain building must contain an altar because it is a church, or
that a certain building must be a church because it contains an
altar. (Substance to attribute and attribute to substance reasoning,
respectively.)

Let us look at the basic tests of this type of reasoning.

Some Tests of Substance to Attribute Reasoning
  1. Is the substance identified accurately?
  2. Is the attribute inherent in the substance?

In terms of our example, the first test asks whether we are sure
that the building (substance) actually is a church; and the second
test asks whether an altar is an inherent feature or attribute of a
church. If the answer to either question is "no," the reasoning is not
valid—a fallacy is present.

Some Tests of Attribute to Substance Reasoning
  1. Is the attribute identified accurately?
  2. Is the attribute a certain or probable sign of the substance?

In terms of our example, the first test inquires whether we are
sure that the object named is definitely an altar; and the second
test asks whether a church inevitably or probably "follows" from the
presence of an altar. If the object is not actually an altar; or if some
"substance" other than a church might be indicated by the presence
of an altar, the reasoning is, of course, fallacious.

We know that there is no one easy means of giving "solid substance" to a discussion, conference, or committee meeting. Factors
of subject, time, and the desires and capacities of the participants
determine, of course, the amount of "content" and the level of
reasoning. To the extent, however, that preparation is carried on
systematically and thoroughly whenever possible, and that attention is given to the principles of evidence and reasoning, there is a
reasonable expectation that the "substance" of a meeting will be
satisfying and profitable, and the solutions to problems will be
more adequate than those based upon "hearsay" discussion.

For purposes of review and of indicating how these types of evidence and modes of reasoning might be introduced into a discussion, let us consider an example. In the course of a discussion on "Should We Introduce a Choir Processional into Our Morning Worship Service?" the following contributions might be made:

> MEMBER A.   I am in favor of a processional. For one thing, the fact that the other three churches in this city use and like the processional [factual evidence] makes me believe that the processional is generally liked by churches that use it (reasoning from example). Also, I am impressed by the comment made by our organist that this would greatly improve our service [opinion evidence].

> MEMBER B.   Yes, but I know of a church just like ours which doesn't like it. I believe, therefore, that we wouldn't like it [analogy]. Furthermore, I am afraid that our introduction of it would cause unhappiness among some of the choir members [cause-to-effect reasoning].

> MEMBER C.   Regarding B's last point, I know of a church where increased enthusiasm among choir members stemmed from the introduction of the processional into the service [effect-to-cause reasoning].

> MEMBER A.   Yes, I agree with C. I believe that increased enthusiasm usually has followed the introduction of the processional. Another point—a processional is always associated with a dignified church service [attribute-to-substance reasoning]. If we want a dignified church service, we really need a processional [substance-to-attribute reasoning].

Note that the two types of evidence (expressed or implied) and the several forms of reasoning appear spontaneously and naturally as thoughts and contributions evolve. Clearly, they comprise the "substance" of discussion.

chapter 14

Leadership
of Discussion
or Conference

L et us look in upon a committee meeting. The leader is a pleasant, dynamic, alert person who is doing his best to make the meeting a success in terms of the substance of the discussion and also in terms of personal satisfactions. However, something is wrong—some persons seem to get irritated and give up; decisions seem to be influenced in large measure by the judgment of the leader. It appears to be increasingly "his" discussion and less and less the members' meeting. Why? Not because of anything in the leader's manner or personality, nor in his basic interpersonal relationships. Rather, because he is acting as "the expert," the person with "the answers," the person whose knowledge and judgment are made to seem the best in the group. He is the arbiter in the discussion, and the decisions are based largely upon his recommendations.

Let us look in upon another meeting. This leader, too, is pleasant and friendly; but something seems to be wrong. The members are restless and somewhat irritated; the discussion seems to be floundering. In this case we observe that the leader, or chairman, is saying almost nothing; that he is letting things go pretty much their own way. Yes, the discussion "belongs to the members"; but there is no *real* leadership; nobody sees the discussion as a whole; nobody synthesizes the materials; nobody clarifies contributions; and nobody has the responsibility of helping each person to contribute his best.

While we might look at other meetings to note the kinds and methods of leadership in evidence, perhaps these two examples will suggest some of the problems pertaining to leadership of discussion groups or conferences. First, we find the leader who conceives of his role as being that of the "expert"; second, the leader who believes that he should exercise no specific role other than, perhaps, that of convening the group and introducing the subject; we might call this "leaderless discussion."

Conceptions of Leadership

At the outset, therefore, we should inquire as to the conceptions of leadership that are before us and the conceptions that, ordinarily, will be most useful.

As may readily be inferred from the preceding illustrations and from our many experiences in discussion or conference, leadership involves at least two important relationships: (1) to *procedure,* and (2) to *substance.*

Regarding the former (procedure), a leader may, in a sense, exert no leadership at all. He may merely start the meeting and then retire to let the discussion proceed as the other members so desire. At the other extreme, a leader may maintain a "heavy hand," guiding the group through the several stages of its thinking, clarifying, summarizing, providing transitions, calling attention to matters to be considered in the deliberations, and so forth. (It might be said that he considers it his function to "call the plays" in terms of procedure, or method, and to direct the group to follow the procedure which he believes to be most satisfactory.) Needless to say, other leaders may be at stages along the continuum from "no leadership" to "maximum leadership," varying in terms of both *kind* and *degree*—doing or not doing certain things and/or doing certain things to a greater or lesser degree.

Regarding the relationship to the *substance* of the discussion, a leader may refrain from any participation as far as the content it-self is concerned (one extreme), or he may regard himself as the authority and pass the more or less final judgment on all aspects of the subject (the other extreme). Other stages on this continuum might consist, for instance, of a leader's making the same kind of comments which any other member of the group might make (just "another participant"), or of his making final decisions upon certain factors, such as a piece of evidence, for example. As noted above, the differences may vary in both kind and degree—doing or not doing certain things or doing certain things more at some times than at others.

While much may be said for each of these and related concepts or positions regarding both *procedure* and *substance,* it is our belief that the ideal leader should be at about the midpoint on the "procedure continuum" and at the nearly extreme nonparticipation point on the "substance continuum." *In other words, the ideal leader will attempt to give direction and guidance and to provide clarification; but at the same time, he will not be, in any sense of the term, an authority on the substance or a participant in the same way as are the other members of the group.* (In this latter sense, he is like the chairman described by Robert in his *Rules of Order,* who does not participate in debate while he is in the chair.)

With these considerations in mind, we shall now consider some of the qualities of the ideal leader, some of the things which a leader should and should not do, some methods which the leader may well use in handling the normal, routine situations in discussion or conference, and some methods useful in certain difficult situations.

Some Qualities of the Ideal Leader

Experience has shown that while there *are* various types of leaders —and that perhaps similar results *are* achieved by diverse approaches and methods—there *are* certain qualities which lead to success in this activity. We shall present nine qualities which we believe to be important and to be significant means to the end of good leadership.

1. He should be objective—not prejudiced or opinionated. (As

suggested previously, the leader should keep himself in a position to be on equal terms with all discussants, not "for" some and "against" others.)

2. He should be alert and sensitive to individual and group reactions. (In essence, this means that he should, in a sense, be constantly asking himself, "What is going on? What is meant by cues and signs emanating from facial expressions, tones of voice, types of verbal responses, and language?")

3. He should know and understand people. (This means that he should know motives and "what makes people tick"; that he should be able to diagnose behavior and provide himself with reasons, if possible, for the things that he hears and sees.)

4. He should be patient and self-restrained, yet firm. (The good leader avoids both impatience and curtness, on the one hand, and inertness and indifference, on the other. He strives to be kindly and genial, trying to smooth ruffled feathers; yet he makes his presence felt at all times.)

5. He should have, or try to develop, a warm personality. (Ideally, the discussion leader should be in the role of "friend" to all participants, and should radiate the warmth so necessary to create a favorable atmosphere for an understanding discussion of problems.)

6. He should try to exercise a good sense of humor when a light touch may be needed to ease the group over difficult situations. (This does not mean that levity is a desirable circumstance; rather, it means that a change of pace and a degree of informality may assist in the development of even a serious and profound subject in discussion or conference.)

7. He should know the process of problem-solving and related patterns of thought which may arise in discussion. (This means, simply, that he has trained and disciplined himself to think logically and cogently about problems and other subjects which people consider in discussion and conferences.)

8. He should be able to analyze and synthesize. (Here we are speaking of processes of "taking thing things apart" and "putting things together," of seeing relationships among ideas and phenomena. Needless to say, the kind of leadership to which we have referred in this chapter places a high premium upon these attributes, in that one of the most important functions of the leader

—as we see him and his functions—is that of helping the group to take problems apart, to correlate their individual contributions, and to point up the perhaps diverse ideas that inevitably arise in a group situation.)

9. He should have, or try to develop, skill in oral communication, skill in phrasing thoughts, and also skill in voice and manner. (Needless to say, much of the success of a discussion will depend upon the leader's ability to "say the right thing at the right time"— to capture and phrase ideas and combinations of ideas in order to move the group along as expeditiously as possible. In addition, he needs to have all of the good attributes of the effective oral communicator in terms of the audible and the visible means of expression. Perhaps it is not too much to say that he, even more than the other discussants, needs these qualities to a high degree.)

What the Leader Should and Should Not Do

Within the context of the principles which we have set forth thus far, some specific *do's* and *don't's* may be suggested. In general, it may be said that the leader *should:*

1. Try to secure the process of problem-solving or the development of a similar pattern of thought; without being dogmatic, he should encourage the group to begin at a well-defined point and to proceed with as few digressions as possible.
2. Attempt to secure the most co-operative type of participation.
3. Assist the group in providing for the introduction of information when it is needed.
4. Try to keep the discussion clear.
5. Try to handle conflict constructively—to help in the resolution of differences of opinion or in the elimination of clashes resulting from personality or other factors.

In like vein, it may be said that the leader *should not:*

1. Dominate the group's work.
2. Make the "machinery of discussion" superior to spontaneous responses from the participants.
3. Talk every time that some member contributes.

4. Assume the role of an authority in the subject being discussed unless he has special qualifications; even then, he should remember his basic role as a leader.
5. Summarize the progress of the discussion to the point of intruding or of slowing down the group process.
6. Present a point of view on the subject under discussion, but should be an objective interpreter of contributions from all members of the group.

Some Methods Useful in the Normal Processes of Discussion

During the course of any discussion or conference, there are at least five situations or conditions in which the skillful leader can do much to assist the participants to do their best. It is our purpose here to indicate these situations and to outline some methods which may be useful for the leader.

Getting the Group Acquainted

Clearly, one of the first responsibilities of the leader is to make it possible for the members of the group to become acquainted (or better acquainted)—to be sure of names and to feel a sense of belonging. While the alert and ingenious leader will, of course, think of a number of means of achieving this goal, we might suggest (1) the use of informal introductions, by the leader or by the members themselves; (2) the use of name cards or name tags; (3) the use of informal conversation for a few minutes prior to the start of the actual discussion, conference, or committee meeting. Needless to say, these methods may be used singly or in any desired combination.

Getting the Discussion Started

The second clear responsibility of the leader is to get the discussion or conference started in some definite and satisfying way. Again, a good leader will think of several methods, among which will perhaps be the following: (1) Make a brief statement pertaining to the purpose of the group and the nature of the problem or subject before the group; (2) present a case, illustration, or incident setting forth the problem or the subject under consideration; (3) ask for incidents and experiences of a kind which most of the group have had and about which they may talk freely; (4) state the issues in the problem or the subdivisions of the subject; (5) ask specified questions of the group; (6) in the case of a "value" or "policy" problem, in particular, present one or two points of view concerning solutions to the problem; (7) in a similar situation, ask some member to present his view concerning the problem and, if possible, the solution.

As noted above, certain of these methods may, if desired, be used in combination, although each may well serve as a satisfactory "opener" for the discussion. With respect to (6) and (7), one word of warning should be noted. While these methods *may* be desirable in terms of stimulating attention and interest, as well as in terms of getting specific proposals before the group, they have one weakness —that of skipping the important steps in the problem-solving process which lead to the "suggestion of solutions." Perhaps the best advice which we can give upon this point is: Realize what the advantages *and* the disadvantages are, and make your decision in terms of what you wish to accomplish.

Helping All Members to Contribute Their Best

As the discussion proceeds, the skillful leader will constantly be on the alert to use methods of keeping *all* members "in the picture" and of making all members feel the desire to contribute as fully as possible. Among the several methods available are the following three: (1) Recognize and compliment contributions presented in a helpful manner (For example: "Thanks, Mrs. White; here is certainly a good point for us to consider." "An illustration— just what we need here—thanks, John." "Certainly we must see both the positive and the negative points; you are helping us, Mary, by bringing up that objection."); (2) encourage contributions from all parts of the group; (3) try to recognize, even call upon, different persons from time to time. (In the next section of this chapter we shall suggest some methods useful in handling the reticent, non-responsive member.)

Keeping the Discussion Moving and Clear

As previously noted, one of the most important functions of the leader is to keep the discussion moving on a coherent and logical basis and to keep it clear and meaningful. It has been our observation that several methods may be useful at this point: (1) Maintain a happy medium between tedious movement and too-rapid progress —between staying too long upon one point and fostering shallow and superficial treatment of ideas; (2) be careful to recognize the time for movement to another step in the thinking process; (3) try to avoid deadlocks by securing tentative conclusions or an agreement to suspend judgment until further information is available; (4) encourage every person to speak to the point at hand; (5) supplement oral contributions with blackboard notations if possible (visual aids are always effective in clarifying situations).

Again, it should be emphasized that these methods often may be used in combination; in fact, the skillful leader will actually use each a number of times during the course of a committee meeting or discussion.

Bringing the Discussion to a Satisfying Conclusion

It is frequently said by participants in a committee meeting or conference that "we aren't quite sure of what we have accomplished" or "we haven't arrived at anything clear or specific." While such a situation may seem almost inevitable in view of the spontaneous character of discussions and of the fact that many persons are contributing ideas, the skillful leader can surely bring the discussion to a clear and satisfying conclusion.

As in the other situations, he has several methods before him, among them: (1) The use of a brief summary based upon the steps in problem-solving; (2) the use of a summary based upon the issues or upon questions raised in the discussion; (3) the use of a summary based upon the conclusions arrived at by the group; (4) the use of a summary based upon the recommendations which a policy-determining or "action" group is prepared to present to another group.

For the purposes of illustration, let us suggest a summary pertaining to the committee on the Church Office, to which we have previously referred. A leader might well say:

> As I understand our discussion—and please correct me if I am wrong—we did the following:
>
> 1. *Regarding the precise problem before us,* we agreed that we are thinking primarily of the main office, although other offices may be considered if they are logically related. Also, we agreed that we are concerned with an immediate solution, although we must, necessarily, keep in mind long-range plans pertaining to the church.
>
> 2. *Regarding the several aspects of the problem,* we agreed that noise, crowded conditions, poor lighting, interference with the use of the Chapel, and other factors make this a serious situation. We further agreed, I believe, that the physical circumstances—rather than poor use of these physical circumstances by our office personnel—really cause this problem to exist.
>
> 3. *Regarding our criteria or basis for judgment,* we agreed that the following nine factors must be taken into consideration: (a) There should be at least 1,500 square feet of space available for the office staff; (b) the office staff, except for the secretary of the Department of Education and possibly except for the senior minister's secretary, should be in one location in the church; and so forth.
>
> 3. *Regarding possible solutions to our problem,* we agreed that the following seven locations might well be taken into consideration: (a) Retain most of the present office space and convert the area under the Great Hall balcony, cutting a new door from the corridor into Great Hall, cutting two doors in the present east wall of Great Hall, and constructing a sound-proof partition between this new area and Great Hall; (b) retain most of the present office space and convert some of the space at the rear of the Great Hall balcony; (c) and so forth.
>
> 5. *Regarding the relative merits of these seven possibilities,* we agreed that . . .
>
> 6. *Regarding our ultimate decision and the essence of our policy resolution,* we agreed that . . .

Some Methods Useful in Handling Difficult Situations in Discussion

During the course of any discussion or conference, certain situations which stem from human frailties and related factors are likely to confront the participants and to disrupt, in some degree, the smooth, satisfying, and productive course of the deliberations. It is our purpose here to indicate five of these situations, and to suggest methods which the leader may use to cope with them.

Handling the Ready-Talking, Interrupting Member

In this situation we find the person who may be quite pleasant and friendly, but "a problem" because of his tendency to "move in" at almost any moment. The skillful leader may try to cope with him by (1) interrupting him pleasantly and asking him to state his point briefly; (2) interrupting him pleasantly, summing up his contribution; and turning to others in the group; (3) asking him to yield to others; (4) requesting (as a last resort) recognition by the leader before speaking. It is important that the leader not show resentment or belligerence in his own manner, but that he be pleasant and cordial as he interrupts this type of participant.

Handling the Nonresponsive Member

Here we find the person who "just won't talk," the person who *may* be informed and seemingly interested, but who makes no verbal contribution to the work of the group. The leader may find one or more of the following methods to be helpful: (1) If this person is reticent, do not force him; but eventually ask a question of him, and finally bring him into the discussion; (2) if he seems to be a deliberate, careful thinker, give him time, ultimately directing a question at him (ideally, this question should be one that is easy to answer—a simple question of *fact*, for instance—lest the difficulty of formulating an answer or of expressing himself should actually aggravate the situation); (3) suggest that those who have made contributions turn to the others for comments; (4) during a "break" or a recess, converse with this person, trying to "warm him up" (this procedure has proved to be unusually effective in "bringing into the discussion" persons who have been nonresponsive for a number of reasons).

Handling the Too-Assertive Member—the Person Prone to Make Unsupported, Sweeping Statements

Here we find the participant who, whether well-informed or poorly informed, has a tendency to make broad generalizations or sweeping statements without explicit regard to supporting or illustrating materials. While his outward manner of contributing may be pleasant enough, this assertive tendency may be as disruptive as would be an antagonistic or belligerent manner.

The leader may find one or more of the following methods to be useful in handling this situation: (1) Ask the person making the statement to repeat the assertion and to explain it (frequently, he will make important qualifications or will include supporting material which was not previously presented); (2) encourage the group to present supporting material for all points of view that are introduced; (3) provide, if necessary, for the introduction of evidence via a reference source, a resource person, a consultant, or another means.

Handling the Person Who Is Over-Anxious to Settle the Problem

In this situation we discover the person who is inclined to "short-circuit" the typical processes of analysis—of methodical deliberation upon a problem or a subject. As in some of the preceding instances, this participant may be completely friendly and quite co-operative, his fault being that he wishes to jump to the final stages of the reflective thinking process almost at the outset. For instance, in a problem of policy, he may think at once of "solutions" instead of the ramifications of the problem; or he may not take the trouble to think of "criteria" before proposing and evaluating "solutions."

The leader may find some of the following methods helpful in meeting this type of circumstance: (1) Encourage the person to use the problem-solving, or other relevant, pattern of thought, indicating, if necessary, the nature of the steps in the appropriate pattern; (2) ask this person a question or two concerning steps in the thinking pattern which he wishes to omit; (3) point out wherein this group avoided trouble at earlier stages by using a systematic procedure, or wherein another discussion group found this methodical procedure to be beneficial; (4) as a last resort, handle this person as you would a ready-talking, interrupting member; for instance, interrupt him, sum up his contribution, and turn to others in the group.

Handling the Antagonistic, Belligerent Person

Here we find the person with clearly disruptive behavior in terms of voice and manner. He uses the "downward inflection," the domineering tone, and other *audible* indications of antagonism. Again, he manifests through facial expression, haughtiness of manner or "expressions of indifference," an attitude which is almost certain to introduce reactions which are quite foreign to any honest differences of opinion which are related to the subject itself.

While this type of participant is extremely difficult to handle, methods such as the following may be of value to the leader: (1) Divert any caustic or belligerent remarks from the other members of the group to yourself, making yourself the butt of the attack; (2) sum up in a quiet voice and in less "charged" words the antagonistic remarks made by this type of person; (3) in a conciliatory and co-operative manner, comment upon the apparent reasons for anger or antagonism; (4) remind the group that frank discussion requires self-control, and that while honest differences of opinion are not only inevitable but actually desirable, these differences are far different from manifestations of antagonism.

If, at first thought, we appear to have set almost impossible demands upon the discussion leader, it should be recalled that discussions can literally be "made or broken" by the leader. The wrong conception of one's task, ineptitude in handling the normal situations, and bungling attempts to meet the difficult situations can cause irreparable damage, even to a group composed of the best-intentioned participants. Hence, it is imperative that attention be given to means of making oneself as competent as possible in this important task.

Moreover, it will be found that with attention to the proper conception of one's task and to some of the fundamental principles and methods which we have just considered, the task of leading a discussion group will become increasingly rewarding in terms of personal satisfactions and improved development of the content of the conference.

chapter 15

Participating
in Conference
or Discussion

As in the preceding chapter, let us look in on a discussion or conference in action. In this case we find a number of features which are good and some which interfere with the work of the group in terms of *substance* and of *member satisfactions.*

It is clear that most of the participants are well informed, are desirous of finding a solution to the problem at hand, and are free from any overt traits of personality behavior which would suggest dogmatism, belligerency, or antagonism. However, some appear to be quite "closed-minded" (to have preconceived ideas to which they tenaciously hold) and vigorously to be attempting to persuade others to agree with them. In addition, they appear to want to speak as often, and for as long a time, as possible, even frequently interrupting others. On occasion, also, they are somewhat impatient with those members who are trying to analyze the problem according to a pattern of thought which provides for orderliness and thoroughness.

Needless to say, these persons are likely to interfere with the most satisfactory development of the discussion and to cause personal resentments among the other members of the group. In short, they lack some of the attributes of a good participant.

Perhaps it would be helpful to analyze the subject of "Participating in Discussion" by setting out some of the desirable characteristics of a participant in a discussion or conference, and then by indicating some desirable methods of contributing in a group situation.

Desirable Characteristics of a Participant in Discussion

As we think of a discussion or a conference, especially in terms of the part played by the individual participant, certain well-defined attributes come to mind—attributes which distinguish the helpful, co-operative member of the group from the person who either makes no worthwhile contributions or creates disruptive situations as the discussion proceeds.

Let us consider these characteristics under two headings: (1) Content and (2) Attitudes and Procedures.

Content

Needless to say, the desirable traits of a participant, in terms of the substance or content of the discussion, may be numerous or few, depending upon the thinking of the person presenting the list. For our purposes, the following three may be most significant: (1) Possession and use of adequate information, (2) ability to think logically, (3) ability to analyze and synthesize—to develop the subject in terms of a systematic pattern of thought. In our judgment, the possession of these attributes by the participants in a discussion or conference will do much to insure the making of a good evaluation or the adopting of a good policy-solution to a problem.

Information. As emphasized in Chapter 13 ("The Substance of Discussion"), one of the essentials of good discussion is *substance*—adequate content or evidence—without which any committee meeting, discussion, or conference would necessarily be superficial or "mere talk." It follows, therefore, that the participant who will pull his own weight must have as much information as possible in order that his contributions may have real substance. In short, he must have prepared himself as fully as possible in terms of the suggestions made in Chapter 13; and he must bring the results of this careful preparation to bear throughout the discussion.

Logical Reasoning. The mere possession of information, no matter how good or voluminous, is not enough. Again, as suggested in Chapter 13, it is the ability to *use* this information logically and systematically that characterizes the good thinker, the good participant in discussion. What this means, in essence, is that the good participant will be able to reason cogently from specific cases (reasoning from *example*), from similarities (reasoning by *analogy*), from cause to effect or from effect to cause (reasoning from *causation*), or from associations of attribute and substance (reasoning from *sign*). He will be able to put together the information which he possesses and to give it new meanings in terms of relationships which stem from the reasoning process. In this connection he will know the tests of good reasoning and will, thereby, be in a position to avoid *fallacies* in his thinking.

Systematic Analysis. As emphasized in Chapter 12 ("Patterns of Thought and Organization"), clear and coherent sequence of thought constitutes one of the essentials of good discussion or conference. In other words, the good discussion does not ramble aimlessly just because it is spontaneous "thought-in-process." In consequence, it follows that the good discussant will place a high premium upon systematic analysis of a subject and upon careful development of this subject in terms of a clear and coherent pattern of thought. What this means is that he will know the patterns described in Chapter 12 (those pertaining to *decision-making* or problem-solving and those pertaining to *learning*), will school himself in the development of ideas in terms of these patterns, and will conscientiously strive to participate at all times in terms of these patterns. For example, he will keep in mind the fact that a *problem of policy* will most satisfactorily be studied in terms of the "pattern of reflective thinking," which includes such steps as *Definition and Delimitation of the Problem, Analysis of the Existing Situation, Determination of Criteria, Suggestion of Solutions, Evaluation of Solutions,* and *Determination of the Best Solution.* He will know that good participation means careful adherence to this pattern insofar as possible, whether or not the leader of the group appears to be directing the discussion in this way. In short, the good participant possesses a disciplined mind, which analyzes and synthesizes materials in terms of a systematic sequence of thought and which values orderliness and thoroughness in discussion.

Attitudes and Procedures

Experiences in committee meetings and similar discussion groups emphasize the fact that *content* alone is not the essence of such gatherings of people. These experiences show clearly that the *people* in the discussion are important factors; that their attitudes, behavior, and methods of contributing will often make or break a meeting. For our purposes here, the following three attributes are of particular importance: (1) a spirit of co-operation and of awareness of others, (2) an attitude of open-mindedness, and (3) adequacy in communication.

Spirit of Co-operation and of Awareness of Others. Repeatedly, we have stressed the fact that discussion or conference represents co-operative activity—working together in an attempt to solve a problem or to explore the ramifications of a subject. To the extent that each participant thinks of his primary duty as that of working with others and of relating his information and judgments to those of others, the discussion will meet this goal. Of course, this does not mean "loss of self" or subordination of one's ideas to those of another; rather, it means co-operation and a realization that other persons and ideas are present in the discussion and should be constantly kept in mind. It means that while there will, of course, be honest differences in terms of evidence, of objectives, and of reasoning, there will also be honest attempts to reconcile these differences in terms of the common good.

Attitude of Open-Mindedness. Growing naturally out of the preceding paragraph is the *attitude of open-mindedness*—a kind of objectivity which recognizes and accepts the worth of another person's ideas without necessarily overlooking the intrinsic worth of one's own ideas. A willingness to learn, a willingness to receive new information and new ideas, a willingness to change one's original viewpoint—all are evidences of this desirable attitude in discussion.

Lest it be thought that this requirement makes of the discussant a person with no judgments, no set of values, no convictions, we should emphasize an important fact: there is no reason why judgments cannot be held and why ideas cannot be introduced into discussion. In fact, discussion would be fruitless without judgments and ideas. We should, therefore, make a careful distinction between judgments and ideas that are vigorously held and defended convictions, on the one hand, and equally clear and carefully conceived *tentative* judgments and ideas, on the other. What we are asking for is the latter—what we choose to call *hypotheses* or tentative judgments which are subject to modification as new ideas are brought into the discussion. In fact, as said repeatedly in this and other chapters, here is the essence of discussion—the building of idea upon idea, of evidence upon evidence to the point where decisions which represent "thought-in-process" and collective endeavor are finally formulated. Lacking this collecting and synthesizing of ideas, discussion becomes but a series of monologues and an unhappy experience for all of the participants.

In our judgment, the good participant should actively value the group achievement as one which is built upon a wider base of evidence and experience—and is the product of a fuller and more complete probing or study of the problem—than could possibly be the case with solitary thought. Consequently, he should come to the discussion anticipating that he will be made aware of new information and will be led into new lines of thought by the group, and that this experience will do much to improve his understanding of the problem and his plan for dealing with it.

Adequacy in Communication. Even though most discussion or conference is informal and of the "sit down" type of speaking, the standards which we normally associate with oral communication are certainly applicable. In short, a clear, enthusiastic, well-modulated voice and a friendly, lively, direct visible manner are much to be desired.

Such a method of communication is needed in terms of the *content* of the discussion as well as of *member satisfactions*. Effective communication on the part of each participant is an important protection against the overlooking or misunderstanding of a contribution which may represent a significant point or a crucial item of analysis.

Nor are these characteristics of voice and manner the only factors to be kept in mind. In addition, there are factors of *language*—the "semantics" of contributing. How frequently are conversations and discussions rendered ineffective or distressing by misunderstandings and confusions resulting from language that is ambiguous, vague, and distracting, or that gives rise to extraneous or irrelevant reactions! As is the case with voice and manner, the suggestions are simple. We should try to contribute in language that is simple and clear, that meets the tests of good grammar and syntax, that "tells our story" in as straightforward a manner as possible.

Some Suggestions Regarding Methods in Contributing

As noted in several preceding chapters, discussions, conferences, and committee meetings are usually informal; and the participants' contributions are normally spontaneous and are presented in a give-and-take manner. Hence, little should be said here about the kinds of specific preparation and about organization of contributions which were discussed in chapters on Public Speaking, for instance.

However, in the interest of effective group work, as represented by good content and by member satisfactions, some suggestions regarding attitudes and procedures in *contributing* may be helpful. We shall briefly consider seven such suggestions.

Contribute in Terms of the "Pattern"

The first suggestion to be made regarding participation in discussion is to be aware of, and heed, the underlying pattern of thought that is being developed. (Hopefully, it is a meaningful pattern somewhat like one of those which we have previously described for learning groups or for policy-determining groups.) The good participant is aware of "where the group is" at any moment—what ground has been covered, what principal ideas are in focus, and where the group is likely to move next. He makes it his business to be ready to participate at any moment in terms of this pattern of thought—to make *relevant,* as well as meaningful, contributions.

Contribute in Context

It is important and helpful not only to know where the group is but also to contribute, via a "bridge," to what has just been said by another participant. This reference to a "bridge" has both a figurative and a literal implication, both of which are important to the orderly and clear progression of thought on the part of all members of the group.

In the figurative sense, contributing in context means *joining* one's thoughts to what has just been said, or building on to the preceding remarks, either by supplementing ideas or by presenting contrasting materials. Perhaps the best test of this practice of contributing in context is to see whether an outline of the flow of thought would disclose an orderly progression in terms of topical or of argumentative relationships. In the parlance of the athletic encounter, our advice is to "follow the ball."

In the literal sense, this means so phrasing one's contributions that there is a verbal bridge to your remarks, as "Extending this idea a bit farther, I suggest. . . ." Or, "While I agree in general with what has just been said, I. . . ." Or, "In line with this, I. . . ." Or, "Let's look at this in another light." Here the attempt is to join one contribution to another by stating either a supplementary or a contrasting line of thought.

What we are saying is that one's contributions should implement the natural flow of ideas, and that, fully as important, the phraseology should reflect this natural flow and should build verbal bridges to succeeding ideas.

Contribute in the "Explanatory Manner"

In discussion, perhaps more than in other communication situations, it is important to make completely clear the basis for one's contributions toward the development of an idea or the solution of a problem. This is particularly true because of the "thought-in-process" nature of discussion, wherein thoughts build upon one another, and because of the co-operative nature of discussion, which substitutes group thought for solitary thought.

Here, above all, there is need for the use of means of fostering group understanding; and one of the best means of accomplishing this is by presenting the *rationale or basis for an idea* advanced by a participant.

In consequence, the ideal discussant will so contribute as to make clear the *background* of his remarks, the *rationale of thought* for them, the *assumptions* underlying these remarks, and the *chain of reasoning* which led to them. In other words, he will say, in effect, "Let me tell you what went into my thinking on this matter," or "Here is why I have this to say," or "The trestlework of my ideas is this." By this means, the participant will enable each of his associates not only to know the nature of his propositions but also to understand and appreciate what lies behind them. In other words, the participant will thus make it possible for the other members of the group to see precisely the claim to truth that underlies his contribution. While this manner of contributing may take more time than the mode which says, in effect, "Here are my ideas; take them or leave them," it has the clear advantage of exposing helpfully the reasoning process which is behind the conclusions that are presented.

Contribute with Tact

This aspect of participation is of great importance in view of the seeming paradox of discussion or conference—*co-operation* in the face of inevitable *differences* in evidence, in reasoning from evidence, in criteria or values, as well as in many personal characteristics of the participants. We have repeatedly noted that only through *co-operation* can "thought-in-process" achieve worthwhile results, and we have also noted that a multitude of differences may enter to disrupt any spirit of co-operation that might exist. What, then, is a possible means of reconciling these seemingly irreconcilable factors?

One answer is "tact" in contributing—being courteous, not interrupting rudely, and showing consideration. In terms of discussion or conference, tact also means evaluating another person's ideas without referring to him personally; in other words, keeping the discussion (especially adverse criticism) on the level of *ideas* rather than on that of *personalities*. In terms of discussion, it also means trying to find points of agreement or of common ground—of which there will surely be many, even among significant differences.

In summary, then, this method of contributing involves thought-fulness, consideration, polite disagreement, and difference of opinion tempered with avoidance of personalities and with exploitation of elements of agreement and of grounds for co-operation.

Contribute Clearly and Efficiently

Because *communication* is the essence of discussion or conference, it is imperative that we contribute in a manner that is clear and efficient. In the area of the *content of the discussion,* this means that our language meets the most rigorous tests of clear, unambiguous, and unequivocal word choice and of grammatically correct and easy-to-follow sentence structure. Furthermore, this means that there will be as much fluency as possible, as represented by concise and accurate presentation of one's thoughts. In the area of *voice and action,* this means that we will speak clearly and with meaningful inflection, and that we will accompany this good speaking with an enthusiastic manner and with meaningful physical responses.

Listen Carefully

While at first thought this admonition may seem unrelated to contributing in discussion, it is, in reality, a major factor in good participation. Unfortunately, many participants do not "hear all that is said" because they have not trained themselves to hear all that is said and to interpret this meaningfully. Others do not "hear" because they consciously or unconsciously hear only what they want to hear or because they are too busy formulating rejoinders to listen with any degree of care to what is being said beyond the point of first disagreement.

The remedy includes at least three important attitudes and practices: (1) try to "get all that is said"—listen to *all* that is being said, and avoid private thinking or day-dreaming; (2) derive meaning from what is said by carefully making associations, implications, and inferences; (3) resist the temptation to present a rejoinder as soon as a controversial matter is introduced. In other words, the good participant listens intently, tries to get "the whole story," avoids listening only for purposes of rebuttal, and carefully notes

attitudes and feelings of the other discussants, together with responses which they make to the contributions of others.

Participate in the Spirit of Desiring to Understand
Another Person's Point of View

This concept of participation in discussion or conference has
been reserved to the last because, in a sense, it represents the climax,
and the epitome, of effective membership and activity in this co-
operative endeavor. Here is the essence of co-operation; the means
by which real "thought-in-process" can be achieved, perhaps the
best means by which member satisfactions can be realized.

A person who wishes to participate in this spirit will be more
interested in *understanding* than in merely *reacting*. In consequence,
he will honestly desire to receive new information and ideas, will
respect other persons and their ideas, and will try to see things as
other persons see them. With regard to methods and procedures, he
will ask other persons to state their ideas, will ask questions about
points not understood, will earnestly seek to discover reasons for
disagreement (if any), and will be prepared to state other persons'
ideas as clearly and forthrightly as they attempted to do.

Here is a rather large and demanding order indeed, but there
can be no denying that this epitomizes all that is desirable in terms
of *attitude* and *procedure*. Without it, discussion or conference can
hardly be a co-operative enterprise in group thought; with it, there
can be co-operation, understanding, meaningful interaction, synthesis of materials, creation of new ideas out of this synthesis, and
member satisfactions of a high order. Like some other suggestions
which we have made, it may seem to be time-consuming; but the
end result, we believe, makes the method desirable.

We have set forth in this chapter a list of the desirable characteristics of a participant in a discussion or a conference, and also
a number of desirable methods of contributing in a group situation.
It is evident that we have not attempted to answer such questions
as: Should a person seek recognition from the leader before speaking? For how long should a person speak (short contributions or
long contributions)? Is it proper to interrupt another participant?

We have purposely refrained from dealing with such questions because the answers depend almost entirely upon the many variables of: size of the group, nature of the persons who are participating, degree of involvement of the participants, amount of "give and take" among members that exists or is desirable, degree of formality desired, and other factors peculiar to any one discussion situation. Suffice it to say that participation should be of the type that makes possible, and encourages, all of the qualities of good discussion which we have repeatedly set forth in this and other chapters.

As a means of indicating some of the more important considerations regarding Participation and of providing a ready-reference guide by which to measure a member's contribution to the group process, we are including here a checklist of seven items:

1. How satisfactory is my *knowledge of the problem*—my *level of information?*
2. How satisfactory is my *reasoning from this information?*
3. How satisfactory is my *skill in following the pattern of thought?*
4. How satisfactory is my participation in terms of *willingness to promote discussion?*
5. How satisfactory is my participation in terms of *co-operation in thinking and in contributing?*
6. How satisfactory is my participation in terms of *speaking skills (voice, manner, and so forth)?*
7. How satisfactory is my expectation that I shall receive new information and further understanding of the problem from this group?

chapter 16

Types of
Discussion
Groups

D iscussions or conferences, as perhaps experience has shown (and as suggested in preceding chapters), are carried on under a variety of circumstances and in groups which have different formats and procedures. These formats vary from those in which a few persons "discuss" around a table or in a somewhat similar informal situation (perhaps chairs in a circle, for instance) to those in which two, three, four, or perhaps six or eight persons carry on a quite informal discussion in the presence of another group of persons (the audience), on to those in which a similar number of persons discuss a subject via separate speeches also in the presence of an audience. These may be termed, respectively, *the round-table, the panel discussion,* and *the symposium.*

Each of these principal types of discussion groups has its peculiar values and purposes in terms of (1) the number of persons to participate, and (2) the purpose of the discussion.

With respect to the former consideration, it is clear that if only some ten to fifteen persons are participating, there will be no problem with the round-table. Each person can easily be seen and heard by each other person, and each person can participate freely without fear of keeping others from having a similar opportunity. If, however, more than fifteen or twenty persons are participating, it may be desirable to devise some means by which a few persons can participate quite intensively for a part of the time, with the remainder participating in an open-forum period. In this situation, it may be well to consider the use of the panel discussion or the symposium.

With respect to the *purpose* of the discussion, it is quite clear that the round-table will be used for the "policy-determining" committee and may be used for the small "learning" group (see Chapters 10 and 11). Normally, the panel discussion and the symposium will be used by the "learning" group, especially when "experts" are used to discuss a problem for the benefit of the remainder of the group, who constitute the audience.

Perhaps it will be most helpful if we develop this subject by (1) exploring the nature of each of the three types of groups; (2) commenting upon the relative values of each type; and (3) presenting some suggestions for each type.

The Nature of Each Type

The Round-Table

This type of discussion group may be defined as one in which each person may contribute at any moment, in which the thread of the discussion is taken up by the members as they have something to say, and in which, as a result, the stimulus-response pattern is constantly changing as attention is directed from one person to another. This is the typical committee or conference group—seated around a table or informally in chairs arranged in a circle.

The Panel Discussion

This type of discussion group may be defined as one in which a few persons (the panel) carry on a discussion in front of an audience, which usually participates later in a question-and-answer period.

The members of the panel may be members of the total group, or they may be "experts" brought to the discussion as speakers.

The Symposium

The symposium may be defined as a type of discussion group in which two or more persons, under the direction of a chairman, present, in separate speeches, the various phases of a problem, with the audience participating vocally in a subsequent question-and-answer period. As in the case of the panel discussion, the speakers may be members of the total group, or they may be experts brought to the discussion by the group itself.

The Relative Values of Each Type

At the outset it should be emphasized that no one of these types of discussion groups is "the best." In fact, each has some marked values and also marked limitations in terms of certain goals and considerations which may differ from group to group and situation to situation. For this reason, we shall systematically analyze each of the three types, indicating its inherent values and limitations. In this way, a person who may be responsible for selecting the type of group in a given case will be able to correlate his wishes and the corresponding characteristics of each type, thereby making a decision upon the basis of more than guess-work.

The Round-Table

Inherent in this type of discussion group are the following characteristics or outcomes:

1. *Breadth.* The contributions will be as broad as the number of participants—perhaps six, eight, or ten.
2. *Variety.* The contributions will be as varied as the ideas represented by the number of participants, together with the interplay of ideas among the participants as the discussion progresses.
3. *Spontaneity.* The discussion will be a constant give-and-take of

contributions, with each person reacting spontaneously to the impromptu contributions of the other members of the group.

4. *Freedom.* There will be no restrictions in terms of previously prepared material or "speeches." Except for such restrictions as those imposed by a logical pattern of thought, the discussion will proceed as the members of the group desire.

5. *Participation by All Members.* By definition, the round-table includes all members as potential contributors at any moment; there is no "audience," there are no designated "speakers."

6. *Less Order and Economy of Time Than With Prepared Speeches.* By the nature of spontaneous, give-and-take discussion, there is less organization of ideas and less economy of phrasing than would be true if the speaking were the product of such preparation as that usually associated with assigned speeches, such as those found in the symposium.

It should be emphasized that these six characteristics are not the result of good or poor preparation, participation, or leadership. These attributes are inherent in the very nature of the round-table, with its informal speaking on the basis of the give-and-take of ideas; and while the quality of preparation, participation, and leadership *may* modify these characteristics to some degree, the basic qualities are always present in this type of discussion group.

Hence it follows that if one desires the first five of the attributes listed above and does not object to the presence of the sixth, he will choose the round-table as the format or type of discussion situation for a group of not more than, perhaps, twelve to fifteen persons.

The Panel Discussion

Inherent in this type of discussion group are the following characteristics or outcomes:

1. *Considerable Breadth.* The contributions will be as broad as the number of panelists—usually three to five.

2. *Variety.* The contributions will be as varied as the ideas represented by the number of participants, plus the inevitable interplay of ideas among the participants as the give-and-take discussion progresses.

3. *Spontaneity.* The discussion will be a constant give-and-take

of contributions, with each person reacting spontaneously to the impromptu contributions of the other panelists.

4. *Freedom.* There will be no restrictions in terms of previously prepared material or speeches. Except for such restrictions as those imposed by a logical pattern of thought, the discussion will proceed as the panelists desire.

5. *Provision for a Large Group.* By definition, the panel discussion consists of a panel of discussants and of an audience of almost any number of persons, provided facilities are present that will make it possible for each member of the audience to hear the discussion itself and also the contributions made in the open-forum period.

6. *Some Participation by All Persons.* Even though only the panelists participate vocally in the major portion of the discussion, members of the audience may ask questions, and perhaps make comments, in the open-forum period.

7. *Less Order and Economy of Time Than With Prepared Speeches.* Here the same situation obtains as in the round-table.

Again, it should be emphasized that these are inherent characteristics, not the result of types of preparation, participation, or leadership.

Hence, it follows that if one desires the first five of the attributes listed above and does not object to limited participation by all members and less order and economy of time than with prepared speeches, he will choose the panel discussion for a group which is too large for the round-table format.

The Symposium

Inherent in this type of discussion group are the following characteristics or outcomes:

1. *Some Breadth.* The contributions will be as broad as the number of speakers—perhaps two, three, or four.

2. *Some Variety.* The contributions will be as varied as the ideas represented by the number of participants, plus whatever interplay may result from impromptu adaptations made by the speakers as they develop their prepared speeches.

3. *Order, Compactness, and Economy of Time.* On the assumption that the speakers have made careful preparation, it may be said that the contributions will be well-organized, well-phrased, and well-developed in terms of relevant materials.

4. *Provision for a Large Group.* By definition, the symposium consists of a group of speakers and of an audience of almost any number of persons, provided facilities are present that will make it possible for each member of the audience to hear the speeches and also the contributions in the open-forum period.

5. *Less Spontaneity and Creativeness Than in the Round-Table and Panel Discussion.* On the assumption that the speeches have been prepared in advance and that on-the-spot adaptations are comparatively few, it may be said that there will be little give-and-take and little development of *new* ideas beyond those included in the advance preparation; in other words, the discussion will represent largely the "product of thought" rather than the "process of thought."

In the light of these circumstances, it follows that if one desires a well-organized and carefully phrased analysis of a problem or subject in a format suitable for a large group, and does not object to the absence of as much spontaneity and creativity as are likely to be present in the panel discussion, he will choose the symposium.

At this point we should note that some persons find a combination of the panel discussion *or* the symposium *and* the round-table to be a means of securing *all* of the outcomes which may be desired, even with a large group. Specifically, they select the panel discussion or the symposium as the means of developing the subject for the large group; then they "break up" the large group into a number of round-tables for further discussion of the subject, with a possible return to the large-group format for the "pooling" of ideas and the formulation of conclusions. (This technique is sometimes referred to as the "buzz-group" method of discussion.) Needless to say, this plan creates some problems of organization and of management; but it does make possible the achievement of breadth, variety, spontaneity, freedom, and maximum participation by all persons.

Perhaps we should emphasize, at this point, the fact that teachers in the Church School can well consider the values of all three of these types of discussion groups. Not only is the discussion method itself of great value as a teaching method (studies have shown that comparable students have learned from 17 per cent to 25 per cent more factual content from the discussion method than from the lecture method), but the several types of groups have important uses and values.

Specifically, the symposium and the panel may be useful in setting forth units of material by "experts" for groups of more than, perhaps, twelve to fifteen persons. Teachers or others (including especially well-qualified students) may present a body of material in much the same way that a lecturer or instructor might do in a single speech. The round-table, or small discussion group, may be useful in analyzing and evaluating the implications of the symposium or panel. Also, it may be useful in carrying forward and applying these implications. (In some instances, several of these smaller groups may meet simultaneously.) Again, the round-table may be used in exploring and analyzing the content of a given lesson-unit, such as a chapter in a book, a topic, or an issue concerning which a reading list or set of references has been provided. In any event, the alert Church School administrator or teacher will find a number of helpful uses for each of the three principal types of discussion groups.

Some Suggestions for Each Type

In preceding chapters we have presented suggestions concerning preparation, leadership, and participation in discussion or conference; and much of what has been said there has relevance here. However, certain specific matters of preparation and of conduct of discussions under the respective circumstances will be mentioned at this point.

The Round-Table

In order to provide the best conditions for discussion, the person in charge, probably the leader, should arrange the chairs in a circle or around a table, if possible. By this means, each person will be able to see and hear each other discussant most easily; and the conditions which make most conversations effective and satisfying can be secured. In addition, he should provide, if possible, for such aids to discussion as a blackboard, other types of visual aids, and means of recording the progress of the discussion. All in all, he should do everything he can to secure the maximum of friendliness, co-operation, and ease of carrying on and recording the discussion.

The Panel Discussion

In order to provide the best conditions for the panel discussion, the person in charge, usually the leader, should make careful advance preparations and also should observe a number of special problems which inevitably arise in this format. The following suggestions may be helpful in this regard:

1. Select, as panel members, persons who have special competence in the subject under discussion.
2. Arrange to seat the panelists so that they can easily be seen and heard by all members of the audience. (If necessary, try to secure a public address system with a microphone for each panelist.)
3. Arrange to seat the panelists so that the maximum amount of informality and of give-and-take can be secured. (Ideally, this would include seating in a semicircle or around three sides of a table.)
4. Seat the panelists, if possible, on the basis of personal traits, points of view, and speaking ability—placing in the "end positions" those persons most likely to participate most extensively and enthusiastically.
5. Observe all features of the round-table that can be adapted to an audience situation.
6. Maintain constant adaptation to the audience in terms of content and of speaking. (This means that both the panelists and the leader, certainly the latter, will use illustrative material and language that are meaningful to the audience, and will observe all of the features of good speech delivery, especially in terms of eye-contact, clarity of speaking, and projection of voice.)
7. Arrange for a question-and-answer (open-forum) period, and respect the time limits so that this period will not be crowded out.

The Symposium

As in the case of the panel discussion, the person in charge should make careful advance preparations and also observe a number of problems which inevitably arise in this format. The following are some of the more important steps which should be taken in order to secure the best conditions for discussion:

1. Select speakers who are competent in both subject matter and delivery. (Many symposium discussions have failed because speakers have not been adequate in terms of the "visible" and the "audible" aspects of oral communication.)
2. Select speakers and assign their topics in terms of a specific plan of development of the subject under discussion. (Ordinarily, this plan would be one of the following: (a) the "pattern of reflective thinking;" (b) topical subdivisions of the problem or subject; or (c) interests of, or points of view held by, the speakers.)
3. Arrange for a chairman to introduce the speakers, make necessary transitions between speeches, and conduct the open-forum period.
4. Make the necessary physical arrangements, including a rostrum or other vantage point at which the speakers may stand (or sit) and a public address system if necessary.
5. Arrange for a question-and-answer (open-forum) period, and respect the time limits so that this period will not be crowded out.

Again it should be noted that no one of these types of discussion groups is necessarily better than any other. Each has its peculiar uses and values, depending upon the number of persons to participate and the purpose of the discussion, as well as upon certain values or objectives which the sponsor or group may have in mind. Perhaps a rapid listing of some specific cases may be helpful as we conclude this analysis of types of groups.

1. The Board of Elders of the church of which one of the authors is a member conducts its monthly meetings as a round-table. (This is quite natural for a group of some 15 persons and a group which is essentially policy-determining.)

2. At a recent meeting of the Joint Boards of this same church (a group totalling 35 persons), the panel discussion format was used in a "learning situation," in which the subject for discussion pertained to past, present, and future activities of these and related boards.

3. At the latest Annual Meeting of this church (attended by some 500 persons), the symposium format was used for the concluding 45 minutes of the program, when the subject "What Lies Ahead in the New Year?" was being discussed.

In each of these cases, the particular format, or type of discussion group, had certain advantages which no other might have had. In the first case, the size and purpose of the group made the round-table logical and inevitable. In the second case, the size of the group made either the panel discussion or the symposium quite necessary; and this was also true of the third group. In the second case, it was believed that the panel discussion might provide for a spontaneous give-and-take which the symposium could not, and this was deemed desirable by the sponsors. In the third case, the sponsors wished to have "neat," well-organized, specific contributions from representatives of four areas of the life and work of the church—hence, the symposium with four speakers.

It is important to note, we believe, that in each instance a decision as to type, or format, was made by the persons in charge; no one type necessarily had to be used without any consideration of relative merits in terms of specific needs and wishes of the participating group.

As we said earlier, the round-table is probably the ideal format or type of group if no more than twelve to fifteen persons participate. If, however, the group is larger, and if special participation by some persons is desired, the panel or symposium may well be selected. Again, if variety, spontaneity, and constant give-and-take are desired, the panel may be one's choice as against the symposium, which features more *organized* preparation, more *formal* contributions, and perhaps more order, compactness, and economy of time.

Clearly, no one type is the best; the ultimate decision depends upon the criteria regarded as important by the person who is making the plans.

chapter 17

Presiding
at
Meetings

The person who is a leader in the church will face at least three major situations in which he will be required to serve as chairman, moderator, or leader: (1) the group discussion, conference, or committee situation; (2) the business meeting of such an organization as the women's society, men's club, or board of elders, for instance; (3) the program meeting of one of the organizations of the church—perhaps a separate meeting or perhaps an after-dinner meeting. The first of these situations was discussed at some length in Chapter 14. It is the purpose of this chapter to present some suggestions regarding the second and third situations.

Business Meetings

In general, the chairman of a business meeting has the responsibilities of planning the agenda (or order of business) and of conducting the meeting in a fair, orderly, and dignified manner.

He should not be a partisan or a proponent of any item of business; neither should he favor any person beyond the rules of established procedure. (If this means that the president of an organization is "muzzled" or placed in the position of being unable to exert what he regards as the proper leadership of an item of business, ordinarily he should ask somebody else to serve as chairman, or he should step out of the chair when a certain issue is before the group.)

Specifically, the duties of the chairman of a business meeting may be itemized as follows:

1. He prepares the agenda, or order of business.
2. He calls the meeting to order.
3. He calls for the items of business in the order indicated in the agenda.
4. He provides for the introduction of business according to the custom of Parliamentary Procedure.
5. He conducts debate and other features of the orderly disposition of business according to established rules.
6. He conducts voting in a fair and orderly manner.
7. He courteously expedites the transaction of business, helping the members of the assembly to participate happily and efficiently.
8. He closes the meeting according to established rules.

While there is no pat formula for the successful functioning as a chairman, it may properly be said that a good understanding of the principles and methods of Parliamentary Procedure is of great value and should serve as a guide. For this reason we shall review some of its more important features and indicate their applicability here. (It may be said with certainty that a good grasp of these principles of Parliamentary Procedure is virtually imperative if one is to do a satisfactory job of conducting a business meeting.)

Perhaps it will be helpful to consider such topics as: (1) The Object of Parliamentary Procedure; (2) The Basic Principles of Parliamentary Procedure; (3) Some Duties and Rights of Members of an Assembly; (4) The Usual Order of Business; (5) The Steps in a Motion; (6) Motions for Specific Purposes; (7) Amendments; (8) Committees; and (9) Voting.

The Object of Parliamentary Procedure

The object of Parliamentary Procedure is to provide a guide for conducting business meetings. It provides a set of rules and principles for an orderly method of conducting these meetings, and it is the means by which the will of the majority can be determined in an orderly manner. Parliamentary Procedure is not the technical body of principles which some persons believe it to be. Neither is it a means by which the "tricky" person can advance his own ends; actually it is a defense against such persons. It provides for free debate, which should assure a fair hearing for all members of the group; and finally, its basic principles are flexible enough to serve the needs of every type of meeting, formal or informal.

The Basic Principles of Parliamentary Procedure

For all practical purposes, there are four basic principles underlying the system of rules commonly referred to as Parliamentary Procedure:

1. *The Principle of Equality.* This principle holds that every member is the equal of every other member in the right to introduce, debate, and vote upon business.

2. *The Principle of Free and Full Debate.* This principle holds that unlimited discussion, *if relevant,* is a basic right, which should be curtailed only when the group decides that its welfare will be furthered by such action.

3. *The Principle of Rule by the Majority Without Tyranny to the Minority.* This principle says that in return for the privilege of participation, the member agrees to abide by the decision of the majority.

4. *The Principle of One Question or Proposal at a Time.* This principle holds that although several proposals may be pending, only one should be "immediately pending" or in the immediate focus of attention and subject to vote.

Some Duties and Rights of Members of an Assembly

Within the framework of the object and principles of Parliamentary Procedure, five basic duties and a similar number of basic rights quite naturally emerge:

The Basic Duties
1. A member must properly obtain the floor before speaking.
2. A member should not speak upon a matter until it has been properly brought before the assembly.
3. A member should not interrupt another member unless the motion which he is about to make permits it.
4. A member should refrain from personalities in debate.
5. A member should abide by the spirit, as well as by the letter, of Parliamentary Procedure.

The Basic Rights
1. A member has the right to offer in the proper manner any motion which he may consider to be wise.
2. A member has the right to explain or to debate a motion unless the Parliamentary rules specifically prohibit.
3. A member has the right to call for a "point of order."
4. A member has the right to hold the floor, when legally obtained, until he has finished speaking (unless time limits prevail).

The Usual Order of Business

The following items, or steps, are those commonly included in the agenda of a business meeting. While the number may be varied in terms of the nature of the organization and in terms of the wishes of the persons concerned, the basic order should be followed if possible, inasmuch as it is based upon the principle of "past, present, and future"—with the exception of items (1) and (2).

1. Call to Order.
2. Roll Call (if necessary).
3. Reading, Correction (if necessary), and Approval of the Minutes.

4. Reading and Acceptance of the Treasurer's Report.
5. Reports of the Other Officers.
6. Reports of Standing Committees.
7. Reports of Special Committees.
8. Unfinished (Old) Business.
9. New Business.
10. Adjournment.

The Steps in a Motion

With very few exceptions (those cases in which a motion does not require a "second" or is not debatable, for instance) the following are the necessary steps in "the life history of a motion." We shall list the steps, then briefly indicate the nature of each step, especially in the light of the chairman's responsibilities. (We are merely *listing* the steps at this point so that the chairman can see them in brief, outline form.)

1. The Motion is *made.*
2. The Motion is *seconded.*
3. The Motion is *stated.*
4. The Motion is *debated.*
5. *Debate is stopped.*
6. The Motion is *put.*
7. The *Vote* is *taken.*
8. The *Vote* is *announced.*
   (Between Steps (4) and (5), several other steps *may* be introduced—for instance, "to amend," and so forth.)

Let us now briefly note the nature of each step and the implications of these steps for the chairman, in particular.

1. According to the rules of Parliamentary Procedure (and also to "good sense"), some member of the assembly must state his wishes or point of view in the form of a declaration—a motion. The chairman may "call for a motion," or a member may merely ask for recognition and introduce the motion, saying, "I move . . .".

2. Because it is assumed that a motion should be considered only if at least two persons support it (or are desirous of having it considered by the assembly), Parliamentary Procedure provides for the step of "seconding." If the chairman so desires, he may ask "Is there

a second?"; or he may merely listen for a "second." In any event, if somebody other than the "maker" of the motion wishes to do so, he says "I second the motion" or "Second."

3. When the motion has been seconded, the chairman then proceeds to the third, and very important step, that of "stating the motion." Consisting of a word-for-word statement of the motion, this step is imperative for at least three reasons: (a) the maker of the motion must be able to know whether the chairman has accurately heard the wording; (b) all members of the assembly must be able to hear the motion (something that might be impossible were the person in front of them and facing them not to repeat it); and (c) the secretary must be given time in which to record the exact wording of the motion. As previously indicated, this step consists of a careful, word-for-word restatement of the motion.

4. In this step, the members of the assembly speak for and against the motion. While some authorities on Parliamentary Procedure prescribe rules for the conduct of debate (a speech *for* the motion, a speech *against,* a speech *for,* and so forth), we shall not introduce such considerations in this brief review.

5. As suggested by the name of this step, its purpose is to stop debate (or discussion) preparatory to the taking of a vote. Actually, there are three means by which debate may be stopped, the differences among them being essentially in terms of formality. (a) By *silence*—wherein the chairman assumes the absence of further debate to be a sign that the members are ready to vote. In this case, the chairman says, "Are you ready to vote?;" and if there is no dissent, he proceeds to the next step. (b) By a *call for the question*—wherein some member informally says "question," indicating that he, at least, wishes a vote to be taken. In this case, the chairman says, "The question has been called for. Are you ready to vote?" and if there is no dissent, he proceeds to the next step. (If any member should wish to continue the debate, he has the right to do so.) (c) By the *introduction of the motion called "the previous question"*—in which a member "moves the previous question," a motion which requires a second and also a two-thirds favorable vote for passage. In this case, the chairman calls for a second (if one is not immediately forthcoming), states the motion, and takes the vote. If the required two-thirds vote is registered, debate is stopped even though some members may wish to continue discussion of the motion.

6. In order that all members of the assembly can know exactly the details of the motion upon which the vote is about to be taken, Parliamentary Procedure requires the chairman to *put* the motion at this point. Here he restates the motion exactly as he understands it to be worded—as originally stated or as modified if any amendments have been made.

7. This step consists of the taking of the vote upon the motion. As will be indicated in a few moments, there are *five* methods of voting, each of which has certain purposes and reasons for being used.

8. This step consists of the announcement by the chairman of the outcome of the voting as he understands it. Perhaps the most common statement is this: "The motion is carried" (or, "The motion is lost"). In the case of a recorded division through "the show of hands," "a rising vote," roll call, or balloting, the chairman may announce the exact vote, as "The motion is carried by a vote of ten to six."

Motions for Specific Purposes

While Parliamentary Procedure is not, as previously stated, a highly technical body of rules, it does helpfully and specifically provide for means of doing exactly what a member may wish to have done at almost any point in a business meeting. The following nine purposes or wishes, for instance, may properly be associated with specific motions, as indicated below.

1. *To Introduce a Matter of Business*
   Use a Main Motion
2. *To Alter a Motion*
   Amend   (or)
   Refer to a Committee
3. *To Defer Action*
   Postpone Indefinitely   (or)
   Refer to a Committee   (or)
   Postpone to a Certain Time   (or)
   Lay on the Table   (or)
   Make a Special Order

4. *To Suppress a Question*
    Object to Its Consideration   (or)
    Postpone Indefinitely   (or)
    Lay on the Table   (or)
    Move the Previous Question, and
      Reject the Motion

5. *To Suppress or Limit Debate*
    Limit Debate by Motion   (or)
    Move the Previous Question

6. *To Consider a Matter a Second Time*
    Take from the Table   (or)
    Consider at the Time to which it
      was Postponed   (or)
    Consider at the Time of the Com-
      mittee Report   (or)
    Consider as "New Business" if Pre-
      viously Postponed Indefinitely   (or)
    Reconsider   (or)
    Rescind   (or)
    Discharge the Committee if it fails
      to Make a Report

7. *To Reverse a Previous Decision*
    Reconsider and Defeat the Original
      Motion   (or)
    Rescind

8. *To Set Aside a Rule*
    Suspend the Rule

9. *To Protect a Member from Discomfort, and so forth*
    Use the Question (Motion) of
      Rights and Privileges

Amendments

The motion "to amend" is a subsidiary motion which can be applied to all motions except those listed as being not subject to amendment. It must be relevant, and it must not have the effect of merely changing the original motion from affirmative to negative. An amendment may be amended, but this amendment of an amendment may not be amended. When a motion is under consideration, only one amendment of the first degree is permitted at one time, although any number may be offered in succession.

Amendments are of four types, representing four purposes for which motions may be modified: (1) To *add;* (2) To *insert;* (3) To *strike out;* (4) To *substitute.*

Committees

The subject of "committees" may, perhaps, best be discussed here under the following three headings: (1) Types of Committees; (2) Specific Purposes of Committees; (3) Means of Appointing Special Committees.

1. *Types of Committees.* Committees may be classified as: (a) *Special*—those appointed at a special time for a specific purpose; (b) *Standing*—those appointed at a regular time to perform regularly designated functions; (c) *Committee of the Whole*—the entire assembly acting informally, and usually under special circumstances.

2. *Specific Purposes of Committees.* Committees are constituted: (a) To investigate a matter and to *report facts;* (b) to consider and *report on a resolution;* (c) to consider a matter and *report recommendations;* (d) to *perform a specific duty* for the assembly (committee "with power to act").

3. *Means of Appointing Special Committees.* Special committees may be appointed: (a) By a statement in the motion which proposes the committee action; (b) by ballot; (c) by nominations from the floor, with vote following; (d) by designation from the chairman, at once, before adjournment, or later.

Voting

The subject of voting may be considered at this point under two headings: (1) Forms of Voting, and (2) The Place of the Chairman in Voting.

1. *Forms of Voting.* There are five quite distinct and frequently used forms: (a) *Aye's and No's*—comparison of volumes of sound; (b) *Raising of Hands*—"division" of the assembly by the "show of hands"; (c) *Rising*—"division" of the assembly by asking each mem-

ber to "stand and be counted;" (d) *Yeas and Nays*—a roll call, with each member responding by saying either "yea" or "nay"; (e) *Balloting*—the casting of secret ballots.

2. *The Place of the Chairman in Voting.* If the chairman is a member of the organization which is conducting the business, he has the *right* to vote upon any matters before the assembly. In the case of the first three methods of voting, it is customary for the chairman to vote only when his vote will affect the result, although he *may* vote under any circumstances if he wishes. In the case of roll-call voting, his name is called last; in the case of voting by ballot, he must vote before the polls are closed.

In concluding this section on the chairmanship of a business meeting, we are appending a Table of Selected Parliamentary Motions, based upon *Robert's Rules of Order, Revised.*[1] While there are more than fifty motions which may properly be used in the conduct of business, those included in the Table are the ones more commonly encountered in the typical situations. It will be noted that in each case, five questions are asked and answered: (1) Does the motion require a second? (2) Is it amendable? (3) Is it debatable? (4) What vote is required? (5) May one interrupt a speaker (a person who "has the floor") in order to make the motion?

Program Meetings

As stated previously, a leader in the church may be called upon to serve as chairman or presiding officer of a "program meeting": a dinner meeting, a meeting with one or more speakers, or a meeting at which business is rarely, if ever, transacted. Here his responsibilities are, necessarily, different from those in a business meeting; but they are fully as important. In fact, many such meetings are "made or broken" in terms of the competence or incompetence of the chairman. Specifically, some such meetings are poorly planned; in some, the usual amenities and courtesies are quite overlooked; some have no time schedule; and in some of them, the different portions of the program (including the speakers) are poorly introduced.

---

[1] Henry M. Robert, *Robert's Rules of Order, Revised* (Chicago: Scott, Foresman and Company, 1943).

SELECTED PARLIAMENTARY MOTIONS
(Based upon *Robert's Rules of Order, Revised*)

Motions	Second?	Amendable?	Debatable?	Vote?	Interrupt Speaker?
Main or Principal					
1. Original Main	Yes	Yes	Yes	Maj.	No
2. Reconsider	Yes	No	Yes (1)	Maj.	Yes (2)
3. Rescind	Yes	Yes	Yes (1)	Maj. (3)	No
4. Take from Table	Yes	No	No	Maj.	No
Subsidiary					
1. Postpone Indefinitely	Yes	No	Yes	Maj.	No
2. Amend	Yes	Yes	Yes (1)	Maj.	No
3. Refer to Committee	Yes	Yes	Yes	Maj.	No
4. Postpone Definitely	Yes	Yes	Yes	Maj.	No
5. Limit Debate	Yes	Yes	No	2/3	No
6. Previous Question	Yes	No	No	2/3	No
7. Lay on Table	Yes	No	No	Maj.	No
Incidental					
1. Suspend a Rule	Yes	No	No	2/3	No
2. Leave to Withdraw a Motion	No	No	No	Maj.	No
3. Objection to Consideration	No	No	No	(4)	Yes
4. Point of Order	No	No	No	Chair	Yes
5. Appeal from Chair	Yes	No	(5)	Maj.	Yes
6. Division of Question (6)	Yes	Yes	No	Maj.	No
Privileged					
1. Make a Special Order	Yes	Yes	Yes	2/3	No
2. Question of Privilege	No	No	No	(7)	Yes
3. Take a Recess (8)	Yes	Yes	No (9)	Maj.	No
4. Adjourn (8)	Yes	No	No	Maj.	No
5. Fix Time for Next Meeting	Yes	Yes	No	Maj.	No

(1) Undebatable, however, when the motion to be reconsidered, rescinded, or amended is undebatable.

(2) Interrruption permitted only to make motion. Consideration has the rank of the motion to be reconsidered.

(3) Certain exceptions; see pages 169, 170 [in *Robert's Rules of Order*].

(4) A 2/3 vote in the negative is necessary to defeat this motion.

(5) Undebatable when it relates simply to indecorum, to transgression of the rules of speaking, or to priority of business; or if made during a division of the assembly or while the immediately pending motion is undebatable.

(6) Motion refers to resolutions or propositions relating to the same subject although each part can stand alone.

(7) Chairman decides whether the question is one of privilege. If it is, the motion is then made and handled as a main motion.

(8) Not always privileged; see pages 59, 60, 65.

(9) Undebatable if made when another question is before the assembly.

In general, the chairman of a program meeting has the responsibility of planning the program, planning the physical set-up
(chairs, tables, and seating, for instance), considering what amenities
and courtesies should be attended to (announcements made, persons welcomed, and so forth), and introducing the several features
of the program.

Let us take up these four responsibilities in order.

Planning the Program

While there is no typical "agenda" for program meetings, certain
features naturally fit into certain places in the program. For instance, a dinner meeting with a program consisting of a single
speech might properly have the following items in its "agenda":

1. Invocation.
2. Dinner.
3. Brief remarks by the chairman (to introduce the program and
   to set the "tone" for the occasion).
4. Words of welcome by the chairman (or person appointed by
   him) together with introductions of special guests or other
   persons.
5. Announcements.
6. Introduction of the speaker by the chairman (or person appointed by him).
7. Open-forum period conducted by the chairman (if such a
   period is indicated).
8. Benediction by person appointed by the chairman.
9. Adjournment.

Planning the Physical Set-Up

While certain features of the physical set-up may be determined
by the nature of the place of meeting, it is usually the responsibility
of the chairman to make decisions concerning such items as: (1)
Whether or not there shall be a speaker's table; (2) how the tables
(at a dinner meeting) shall be arranged; (3) what persons shall sit
at the speaker's table, and in what order; (4) whether there shall be
a public-address system (if available); and (5) how the lighting shall
be arranged behind the speakers or the speakers' table.

Needless to say, there is no one formula for each of these items, although such considerations as comfort, convenience, and the role of persons present should be kept in mind. With respect to Item (5), the chairman should be conscious of the fact that lights behind a speaker or a speakers' table are likely to cause considerable discomfort to the persons in the audience; and he should take steps to have these lights dimmed or turned out during the program portion of the meeting.

Considering the Amenities and Courtesies

A good chairman will always think of the customs, courtesies, and words of welcome which will do much to make the occasion a happy and comfortable one for all persons present. While, of course, there is no formula to be applied here, the chairman may well recall what was done in this connection at a meeting which he remembers with particular pleasure. In addition, he may well make a mental inventory of the anticipated situation, and ask himself what special words and actions should be included in order to make everybody feel welcome, "at home," and comfortable.

Introducing the Several Features of the Program

Of course, one of the important functions of the chairman is to introduce the different parts of the program and to provide transitions from one part to another. Again, there is no formula which can be cited here; the special circumstances and the good judgment of the speaker will determine the nature of his handling of these functions. Perhaps one admonition should be stressed, however: *Make the introductions brief and to the point;* and similarly, make the transitions brief and relevant. Frequently, chairmen slow down the progress of the meeting and introduce irrelevancies by making long introductions and telling unnecessary (and often boring) anecdotes. The best principle is: *Keep the program moving with brief introductions and transitions presented in a spirit of friendliness, warmth, and enthusiasm.*

At the close of this chapter we wish to emphasize one important point in particular: *Any person who is to preside at any type of*

meeting should provide adequate time for reviewing his respon-
sibilities and for developing his plans to fulfill these responsibilities.
Last-minute review and preparation are almost certain to result in
less than satisfactory leadership (if not failure). Conversely, the
rewards of careful preparation are significant.

(At this point it might be well to review the suggestions regarding
The Speech of Introduction and *The Speech of Welcome* found
in Chapter 9 in Part One of this book.)

INDEX

Index